"Convergences and divergences on major theological themes of both Lutheran and Reformed traditions are brought to light. Irenic in spirit and lucid in writing, this book is a welcome theological *ressourcement*; it will also fructify true ecumenical dialogue. Edification and illumination are the gifts of Kolb and Trueman, for whom readers can be grateful."

—**Dennis Ngien**, Tyndale University College and Seminary, Toronto, and Wycliffe College, University of Toronto

"Robert Kolb and Carl Trueman are not only experts in their respective traditions, but they are both marvelous writers. This is a needed book. Too many who adhere either to the Lutheran confession or the Reformed have not taken time to read their opposites. Further, as Trueman notes in the preface, most Evangelicals ignore issues that are vital to the two great confessional Reformation traditions. Well-informed readers may quibble here and there, but all must admit that this volume is a great contribution to genuine ecumenicity, which requires honest exposition, inquiry, and dialogue rather than the papering over of genuine differences. This volume is much to be commended."

—**R. Scott Clark**, Westminster Seminary California

Between
WITTENBERG
and GENEVA

Between
WITTENBERG
and GENEVA

Lutheran
and Reformed Theology
in Conversation

Robert Kolb
and Carl R. Trueman

B
Baker Academic
a division of Baker Publishing Group
Grand Rapids, Michigan

© 2017 by Robert Kolb and Carl R. Trueman

Published by Baker Academic
a division of Baker Publishing Group
PO Box 6287, Grand Rapids, MI 49516-6287
www.bakeracademic.com

Printed in the United States of America

Library of Congress Cataloging-in-Publication Data
Names: Kolb, Robert, 1941– author.
Title: Between Wittenberg and Geneva : Lutheran and reformed theology in conversation / Robert Kolb and Carl R. Trueman.
Description: Grand Rapids : Baker Academic, 2017. | Includes index.
Identifiers: LCCN 2017017488 | ISBN 9780801049811 (pbk. : alk. paper)
Subjects: LCSH: Luther, Martin, 1483–1546. | Lutheran Church—Doctrines. | Reformed Church—Doctrines.
Classification: LCC BR333.3 .K645 2017 | DDC 230/.4—dc23
LC record available at https://lccn.loc.gov/2017017488

17   18   19   20   21   22   23   7   6   5   4   3   2   1

Contents

Preface

CARL R. TRUEMAN

This book owes its origin to two independent conversations that Bob Kolb and I had with Dave Nelson at Baker Publishing Group some years ago. Each of us was concerned about a couple of related phenomena that we had noticed among seminary students. The first was the failure of many of them to understand the differences between being confessional and being Evangelical.[1] The second was a similar failure to understand the differences between Lutherans and Reformed. Indeed, I have lost count of the number of times over the years that I have heard students refer to Luther as "Reformed" and had to correct them by indicating that he was a Lutheran reformer, not Reformed. What both Bob and I wanted to do was to write a book that would explain the differences between our two communions.

Both of the problems we noted above with regard to our students derive from their not really understanding the Lutheran and Reformed confessional traditions. Neither tradition is really part of the broader movement of Evangelicalism, which has its roots in the revivals—and revivalism—of the eighteenth century. Evangelicalism tends to regard as matters of little importance those things that are vital to the confessional traditions of the Lutheran and Reformed churches. However, even many students from within Lutheran and Reformed churches have not been well catechized in their own tradition

---

1. Bob and I regard ourselves as "evangelical" in the small *e* Reformation sense: Protestants who hold to the gospel of justification by grace through faith. Here I am using Evangelical/Evangelicalism with a capital *E* to refer to the modern movement, rooted in the revivals of the eighteenth century, that draws much of its strength from Baptist and parachurch circles.

and have therefore been left vulnerable to more Evangelical streams of Protestant life. This weakens their confessional identity.

For example, Evangelicals tend to focus on soteriology and fail to grasp why sacraments—the major point of dispute between the two magisterial Reformation traditions—are of any great moment. Indeed, when they do take a strong stand on such, it is typically in the form of an odd antisacramentalism that rejects infant baptism, a point that decisively separates them from the confessional Lutherans and Reformed. Yet, perhaps attracted by the heroic stature of Luther or Calvin, many Evangelicals try to appropriate these figures for their own cause, selecting those doctrines they appreciate and unwittingly domesticating the Reformers and the Reformation in the process.

This problem is typically most evident in classes dealing with the Marburg Colloquy (1529), the famous face-to-face confrontation between Luther and Zwingli. When students hear that Luther was prepared to refuse to reach full agreement with the Reformed because of his insistence on the real presence of Christ in the Lord's Supper, they are—to put it mildly—confused and sometimes distressed. That the sacrament would be a sufficient basis for such drastic action seems to them absurd or an act of willful pride or a vestige of medieval Roman Catholicism that Luther somehow failed to reject. In sum, instincts shaped by the antisacramental culture of modern Evangelicalism render Luther's stand incomprehensible.

It was this problem that led Bob and me to talk separately to Dave, with the idea that it might be helpful to produce a book outlining Lutheran and Reformed positions on various doctrines in a manner that would help students to see what is at stake both in the confessional disagreements between our two traditions and in the differences between the confessional Protestantism that finds its origin in the Reformation and the Evangelicalism that originates in the revivalism of the eighteenth century. But we also wanted to do so in a manner that, while not minimizing or relativizing those differences, avoided the bitterness that has often characterized such engagement in the past. The years since 1529 have seen more than their fair share of recrimination, bitterness, and mutual misrepresentation by both sides. We wanted to produce a book reflecting our commitment to the catholic faith of the Christian church and our respect and affection for each other as Christian brothers who serve the same Lord and Savior.

To accomplish this task, we chose a set of eight topics on which there is both considerable overlap and at times significant disagreement between our two traditions. Readers will see the latter most obviously in those chapters dealing with the person of Christ, baptism, and the Lord's Supper. Christ and the Lord's Supper are, of course, interconnected topics and were the primary historic points of conflict between Lutheran and Reformed. Indeed, they remain so today. But the reader will also see that, along with the sharp points of disagreement, there is significant commonality on many elements of the faith. For example, justification by grace through faith is crucial to both traditions. In fact, it is hard to imagine what the Reformed faith would look like if it had not borrowed this basic insight from Luther. On that point, all Reformation Protestants are the sons and daughters of Dr. Martin, and all should gratefully acknowledge that fact.

Bob and I wrote all the essays in order to present our confessional traditions in a consistent manner. Our contributions are paired in each chapter, with Bob's portion coming first, but they have not been written so as to be in direct, point-by-point dialogue with each other. Our hope is that they thus represent the starting point for future dialogue—in the classroom, in the local church context, perhaps even at the denominational level. Both Lutheran and Reformed traditions are churchly. While we appreciate some aspects of Evangelicalism, we believe that the only real way of engaging in true ecumenical discussion with a view to greater unity among Christians is to do so within the church itself and between denominational bodies.

The reader will also note certain methodological differences between Bob's essays and those I have written. The differences reflect not simply our own personalities as writers but also differences between our traditions. Lutherans have defined what it means to be "Lutheran" in several ways. Some claim the name on the basis of adherence to certain basic tenets represented by Luther and/or Lutherans over the centuries, such as "justification by faith alone" or "freedom." Some have done so with more recourse to confessional documents, such as the Augsburg Confession or Luther's catechisms, some with a nominal pledge to take those documents seriously. Another approach defines "Lutheran" as adherence to the confessions contained in the Book of Concord of 1580, or at least to the Augsburg Confession and Luther's Small Catechism—some preferring to accept these documents *quatenus* (insofar as) they agree with Scripture, others *quia* (because) they agree with Scripture. Some have included not only a strict adherence to Scripture and the Lutheran confessions but also a general agreement with selected portions of the teachings of the great dogmaticians of the seventeenth century. Among those who wish to represent the historic Lutheran confession of the faith seriously are some who emphasize Luther's own writings, while others limit their definition of what is Lutheran to the teachings of the Book of Concord. Bob is committed to upholding the Book of Concord in a strict manner, but in this volume he reflects his belief that the writings of Luther present the best "Lutheran" offer for conversation in the whole household of faith; therefore to a large degree his presentations focus on Luther's expression of the biblical message and ways it can function today.

The Reformed faith has also been defined in various ways. In recent years at a popular level, "Reformed" has come to mean little more than "broadly Calvinistic on the issue of divine grace" and thus functions as a virtual synonym for an Evangelicalism with anti-Pelagian tendencies. This bears little relationship to what has historically been known as the Reformed faith, because the latter was inextricably connected to particular forms of church life and worship as they were forged in the conflicts of the Reformation. In the academy, the term is often used to refer to theologians who operate within a specific denominational context, regardless of the specific content of their work. In this sense "Reformed" has a very broad reference, which on the surface is of little help in defining theological content.

I am a confessional Reformed Christian, a theological identity with a more specific and definite content. The term means that (like Bob) I take very seriously the formal confessions of the sixteenth and seventeenth centuries. As a Presbyterian, this commitment is specifically to the Westminster Confession and Catechisms. Other Reformed believers, particularly those from Dutch or German traditions, look to the so-called Three Forms of Unity: the Belgic Confession, the Heidelberg Catechism, and the Canons of Dort. The differences between Presbyterian and continental Reformed traditions are negligible, focused on technical details relative to church polity. On the essentials of the Reformed faith, there are both common origins and confessional consensus. Like confessional Lutheran believers, the confessional Reformed also look to the great ecumenical creeds of the ancient church. On that point of ecclesiastical outlook, we are both agreed.

Yet there is a fundamental difference between the ways in which Lutheranism and Reformed theology are defined. As noted above, Lutheranism always has to wrestle with the central and dominant figure of Luther. Not only did Luther write some of the fundamental parts of the Book of Concord; his personal theological commitments also exerted a decisive influence on the shape of Lutheran theology. Reformed theology by contrast was eclectic in origin, with no dominant figure fulfilling the same role within the tradition as Luther with his. The unfortunate prominence of the term "Calvinism" obscures this fact by implying that Calvin is the dominant influence. In fact, Calvin did not write any of the confessional standards adhered to by modern Reformed Christians, nor did he so dominate the tradition that his personal theological predilections stand out as unique. Numerous theologians shaped the Reformed tradition, and while Calvin was undoubtedly of great importance, the best we can say of him is that he was first among equals.

For this reason, the sections in this volume on the Reformed tradition are shaped less by Calvin and his biography than by the actual confessional documents of the Reformed tradition and the light shed by many great Reformed thinkers on the issues addressed in those documents. Certainly Calvin features heavily in the theological narrative. But others—for example, John Knox, Heinrich Bullinger, Zacharias Ursinus, Robert Bruce, John Owen, and Herman Bavinck—also play their part. Above all, it is the confessional material that dominates discussion of Reformed theology and church life. Thus, in contrast to Bob, who sees Luther as the best guide to Lutheran theology, I am convinced that the consensus underlying the confessional documents of the Reformed faith rather than any one figure offers the best Reformed contribution to these discussions in the household of faith.

It is in this spirit of friendship, catholicity, ecumenism, and love for our distinct traditions and for the great communion of saints transcending any denominational division that we offer this book to students of the Lutheran and the Reformed faiths in the hope that it will foster better understanding both of their own traditions and of their Christian brothers and sisters with whom they have principled differences on important issues and yet with whom they share a mighty Savior.

Abbreviations

BC	*The Book of Concord*, ed. Robert Kolb and Timothy J. Wengert (Minneapolis: Fortress, 2000)
BSELK	*Die Bekenntnisschriften der evangelisch-lutherischen Kirche*, ed. Irene Dingel (Göttingen: Vandenhoeck & Ruprecht, 2014)
Calvin, *Institutes*	John Calvin, *The Institutes of the Christian Religion*, trans. Henry Beveridge (1845; repr., Grand Rapids: Christian Classics Ethereal Library, n.d.)
CP	*The Sermons of Martin Luther* [the Church Postil], ed. and trans. John Nicholas Lenker (1905; repr., Grand Rapids: Baker, 1983)
CR	*Corpus Reformatorum: Opera quae supersunt omnia*, ed. C. G. Bretschneider and H. E. Bindseil (Halle and Braunschweig: Schwetschke, 1834–60)
Dennison	James T. Dennison, *Reformed Confessions of the 16th and 17th Centuries in English Translation, 1523–1693*, 4 vols. (Grand Rapids: Reformation Heritage Books, 2008–14)
DLGTT	Richard A. Muller, *Dictionary of Latin and Greek Theological Terms: Drawn Principally from Protestant Scholastic Theology* (Grand Rapids: Baker, 1985)
EA^2	*Dr. Martin Luther's sämmtliche Werke*, Erlangen Ausgabe [Erlangen ed.], 2nd ed. (Frankfurt am Main and Erlangen: Heyder & Zimmer, 1862–85)
LW	*Luther's Works*, ed. Jaroslav Pelikan and Helmut T. Lehmann (St. Louis: Concordia; Philadelphia: Fortress, 1958–86)
MSA	*Melanchthons Werke in Auswahl* [*Studien-Ausgabe*], ed. Robert Stupperich, 6 vols. (Gütersloh: Bertelsmann, 1955)
PRRD	Richard A. Muller, *Post-Reformation Reformed Dogmatics*, 4 vols. (Grand Rapids: Baker Academic, 2003)
RD	Herman Bavinck, *Reformed Dogmatics*, ed. John Bolt, trans. John Vriend, 4 vols. (Grand Rapids: Baker Academic, 2003–8)

Turretin,   *Institutes of Elenctic Theology*, ed. James T. Dennison Jr., trans. George
Institutes   Musgrave Giger, 3 vols. (Phillipsburg, NJ: P&R, 1992)

WA   *D. Martin Luthers Werke*, Weimarer Ausgabe, 65 vols. (Weimar: Böhlau,
              1883–1993)

WA BR   *Briefwechsel* [*Correspondence*], 18 vols. in *D. Martin Luthers Werke*, Wei-
              marer Ausgabe (Weimar: Böhlau, 1930–85)

WA DB   *Die Deutsche Bibel, 1522–46*, 12 vols. in 15 in *D. Martin Luthers Werke*,
              Weimarer Ausgabe (Weimar: Böhlau, 1906–61)

WA TR   *Tischreden* [*Table Talk*], 6 vols. in *D. Martin Luthers Werke*, Weimarer
              Ausgabe (Weimar: Böhlau, 1912–21)

1

Scripture and Its Interpretation

Protestants are people of the book. Both Lutherans and Reformed place the reading and preaching of Scripture at the very heart of the public ministry of the church. The medieval church saw the Mass as the point where God made himself savingly present with his people, but the Reformers saw that role fulfilled above all in the public proclamation of the Word. For them, it was the pulpit, not the altar, that became key to church life. Indeed, there could be no sacrament without the proclamation of the Word. And when the Word was read and preached, it was not merely for the sake of conveying information. In the proclamation of the Word, God really confronted people with his presence. Whether this was for judgment or salvation depended on whether the Word was received in faith or rejected in unbelief.

Since the Word preached is central to both Lutherans and Reformed, then a number of other questions must be addressed. First, there is the issue of what exactly Scripture is. Preaching as an act must be shaped by what the Bible is understood to be. Second, there is the issue of interpretation. A sermon is not simply a recitation of the biblical text. The movement from text to sermon is governed by rules of textual interpretation. Both what those rules are understood to be and also how they are to be applied are crucial to the action of preachers as they proclaim the Word to their congregations.

Both Lutheran and Reformed traditions have produced many great and faithful theologians and preachers, all of whom are marked by their high view of the Bible as the written Word of God, by the care with which they expound and apply the text, and of course by their love for the gospel of the Lord Jesus Christ.

Holy Scripture in the Lutheran Tradition

Martin Luther encountered God's presence, power, and promise in the words
of Holy Scripture. At first against his own desires but in obedience to his monastic superiors' direction, Luther took his assignment to prepare himself to
teach Bible at the university level as a call from God and devoted himself to
his studies with the energy and zeal of a young Augustinian friar who sought
salvation in the performance of his vows of chastity, poverty, and obedience.
These studies contributed to the transformation of a man whose personality
prepared him for taking what God has to say with utmost seriousness and
for throwing himself totally into searching the Scriptures to find eternal life.[1]

Luther's Encounter with Scripture

Increasingly, Luther recognized all his efforts to save himself from his sinfulness as insufficient. His personality easily sensed the lows and highs of
life. This trait blended with his depiction of God as the almighty Lord and
Creator of all that exists. His teachers, schooled in large part in the Ockhamist
tradition delivered to them by Gabriel Biel, the foremost German theologian
of the late fifteenth century, had bequeathed to him this image of the Author
and Designer of all things, who had determined what the laws governing his
universe were to be. Luther never abandoned this conviction, although he
certainly refined it through his biblical study. His instructors also cultivated
belief in the covenant or pact that this almighty God had created according to their schema of salvation. This covenant promised grace sufficient to
perform the works that would prove the sinner's righteousness before God
to all who did "what was in them," who performed their best "out of purely
natural powers." Luther stumbled over this impossible requirement. Slowly, as
he gave his first formal university lectures on the Psalms (1513–15) and then
on Romans (1515–16) and Galatians (1516), he found a path to a different
depiction of both God and what it means to be human. He redefined what it
means to be a Christian: one who places absolute trust in this almighty God
who longs to renew his conversation with his rebellious human creatures. It
was through Luther's engagement with the biblical text that the structure
bequeathed him by medieval scholastic thought, focused through Aristotelian
lenses on human performance, began to crumble.

1. This essay stems in large part from Robert Kolb, *Martin Luther and the Enduring Word
of God: The Wittenberg School and Its Scripture-Centered Proclamation* (Grand Rapids: Baker
Academic, 2016); and Kolb, *Luther and the Stories of God: Biblical Narratives as a Foundation
for Christian Living* (Grand Rapids: Baker Academic, 2012).

The Bible was anything but absent from the world of medieval Christians. Indeed, the church discouraged the few literate laypeople of the late Middle Ages from reading Scripture without ecclesiastical guidance. Nevertheless, liturgical Scripture readings, other portions of the liturgy, visual images in altars and other pious art, and other media conveyed portions of Scripture to the faithful. Two problems, however, plagued this absorption of Bible stories. First, they were incorporated into the individual's worldview alongside and not always distinguished from the stories of the saints, handed down particularly in the *Legenda aurea*—literally, "golden things to be read"—of Jacob of Voragine, a thirteenth-century Dominican and archbishop of Genoa. Second, the biblical narratives or maxims were placed into a set of presuppositions forged in the era of the conversion of the pagan tribes to Christianity, which vitiated the message of the prophets and apostles. Insufficient personnel for delivering fundamental instruction in the faith resulted in a version of Christianity that used biblical language and narrative but presumed that divine power was available from many intermediaries capable of providing help for time and eternity. Christian saints assumed functions earlier performed by pagan gods and goddesses. Furthermore, the relationship between God and his human creatures was anchored in the performance of God-pleasing activities, particularly the performance of sacred or religious rituals—above all, the Mass. Its divine effects were mediated through a priestly hierarchy, made concrete for most Christians in the person of the local priest but with ultimate authority in the bishop of Rome, the pope. This framework for experiencing Scripture and constructing a worldview became increasingly unsatisfactory in the minds of many in the late Middle Ages. New forms of piety were invented, new reform movements launched. But all failed to develop, in Christopher Ocker's words, "a literary method for handling the narrative construction of the Bible as a whole."[2] Precisely such a method Luther found in his redefinition of what it means to be Christian and in his distinguishing God's plan for human action and performance from God's gift of salvation through the pronouncement on believers of the forgiveness of sins and new life won by Christ.[3]

As he plunged into the Psalms and then Romans and Galatians for his first university lectures in the 1510s, Luther found that God takes the initiative in restoring the relationship lost when Adam and Eve doubted God's Word

---

2. Christopher Ocker, *Biblical Poetics before Humanism and Reformation* (Cambridge: Cambridge University Press, 2002), 21–22, 211.

3. Erik Herrmann, "'Why Then the Law?': Salvation History and the Law in Martin Luther's Interpretation of Galatians, 1513–1522" (PhD diss., Concordia Seminary, St. Louis, 2005), esp. 236–47.

in Eden. He comes to human beings, in the flesh, to bestow forgiveness, life, and salvation. God does this as a person. Luther's apprehension of God was intensely personal; he was extremely sensitive to God's personality as a loving Father whose wrath burns against all that disturbs and destroys life as he designed it for his human children. As this person with deep emotions, God is a God of conversation and community. He speaks, and when he speaks, things still happen—come into being anew—just as in the beginning (Gen. 1). God created human beings to be his conversation partners. He immediately sought renewal of the conversation in Genesis 3:9, when Adam and Eve stopped listening to him. Luther believed that God has never stopped talking and calling rebellious human creatures back to himself, so that he may speak a re-creating Word of absolution, of the restoration of righteousness in his sight, through words that arise from Scripture. These words of God are delivered in a variety of oral, written, and sacramental forms.

Scripture and Tradition

Indeed, Luther did not believe that Scripture is the only source from which God's people hear his voice. Like Martin Chemnitz in his *Examination of the Council of Trent* (1565–73), Luther believed that the content of Scripture, not some magical use of its precise words, carries out God's will. Chemnitz saw the Holy Spirit at work as the church handed down God's Word in seven ways. This "tradition"—defined by Luther and Melanchthon as not only the content but also the act of sharing the message with the next generation[4]—began with words from Jesus and his disciples recorded by their contemporaries. The second mode of tradition is the entire Scripture itself. The third expresses itself in the "rule of faith," summaries of the biblical message that believers prepare for purposes of evangelization or instruction. Fourth, the message of Scripture is passed down through those who interpret and teach its texts. The development of dogmatic terminology based on Scripture, such as "Trinity," constituted Chemnitz's fifth form of the handing down. "The catholic consensus of the fathers" could, sixth, repeat what was being handed down from former times in the faithful interpretation of the biblical message. Likewise, the ancient "rites and customs" of the church could convey that message. Chemnitz did not allow as valid or biblical an eighth use of the term "tradition," those teachings claiming to be true although they "cannot be proved with any testimony of Scripture but which the Synod of Trent nevertheless commands to be received and venerated with the same

4. Peter Franekel, "Revelation and Tradition: Notes on Some Aspects of Doctrinal Continuity in the Theology of Philip Melanchthon," *Studia Theologica* 13 (1959): 97–133.

reverence and devotion as Scripture itself."[5] Such "human commandments" Chemnitz rejected sharply.

All acceptable traditions, for Chemnitz as for Luther, rested on and were in full agreement with God's Word in Scripture, which alone had ultimate authority.[6] Chemnitz and his fellow authors of the Formula of Concord (1577) affirmed that "the prophetic and apostolic writings of the Old and New Testaments [are] the pure, clear fountain of Israel, which alone is the one true guiding principle, according to which all teachers and teachings are to be judged and evaluated."[7]

God Speaks from Scripture

God's use of his Word as the instrument of his power and the expression of his promise becomes concrete through human use of Scripture alone. No other foundation exists for the proclamation of the church and for the life of every believer. The authority of Scripture rests on God's very presence in its words. He had chosen written human language as the rendezvous point for continuing into later ages the conversation he had been conducting through the Old Testament prophets, through Jesus's teaching, and through the apostles as they corresponded with the early congregations of believers. Though some scholars argue that Luther did not hold to *sola Scriptura*, "Scripture alone," because he used the writings of ancient fathers and contemporaries to present his message, he found in Scripture the authority to judge all other presentations of God's message. "Whatever does not have its origin in the Scriptures is surely from the devil himself. All God's works, especially those having to do with salvation, are thoroughly set forth and attested in the Scriptures."[8] Failure to grasp this concept of the Almighty's ability to take created human words as a place where he is present and through which he exercises his power makes Luther's interaction with the Bible difficult to understand. William Graham points out that modern understanding is constrained by the gap between "our own modern, Western, post-Enlightenment world of the printed page and *all* past cultures." Luther's understanding that Scripture is "a manuscript with a voice—or still better, a manuscript that was the medium of God's voice"—confounds most

---

5. *Examen Concilii Tridentini von Martinum Chemnicium*, ed. Eduard Preus (Berlin: Schlawitz, 1861), 86; *Examination of the Council of Trent by Martin Chemnitz (1522–1586)*, trans. Fred Kramer (St. Louis: Concordia, 1971–86), 1:272–73, cf. 223–307.

6. *Examen*, 8–13; *Examination*, 1:49–63.

7. BSELK 1310/1311; BC 527.

8. WA 8:491.14–17; LW 36:144.

modern readers of the reformer's works. For Luther, in Graham's words, "it was the most natural thing in the world for him to talk . . . of God *speaking* in what he had *written*."[9]

Luther did not use the terminology of "inspiration" frequently, as subsequent generations of Lutheran theologians would.[10] He translated the θεόπνευστος (God-breathed) of 2 Timothy 3:16 with *eingegeben* (literally, given into, poured into). For Luther, the words of Scripture are the Holy Spirit's gift to the writers and the readers. Scripture is "the Holy Spirit's own special book, writing, and word."[11] "Nowhere can the Spirit be found more present and more active than in the very holy letters which he wrote."[12] "God is everywhere, but he is really to be found in the Holy Scriptures, in his Word, more than anywhere else."[13] Genesis comes from "the Holy Spirit himself," according to Luther.[14]

Luther was certain that "the Word is flawless, so that not an iota in the law or the divine promises is defective. Thus, we dare not yield to any sect, not in a single stroke of the pen in Scripture, no matter how much they may shout and slander us for destroying love by adhering strictly to the Word."[15] This led him to insist: "It is necessary for us to preserve the phrasing of Holy Scripture and to remain with the words of the Holy Spirit."[16] The authority of Scripture not only determined what the church confessed and proclaimed; it also prevented wandering off into vain speculation, for instance about details of daily life at the time of the patriarchs: "Because Holy Scripture is completely silent, we have no business affirming or denying anything here [in reference to Gen. 24:1–4]. What Scripture teaches, denies, or affirms, we can safely repeat and teach."[17] Luther insisted that the Holy Spirit gave the prophets and apostles all their words, so that even details that seem no more than trifles, including information about the biblical figures' lives that seem to have no spiritual significance, should be regarded as gifts of the Holy Spirit. He noted that such trivialities as Abraham's wealth (Gen. 13:2) were written

9. William A. Graham, *Beyond the Written Word: Oral Aspects of Scripture in the History of Religion* (Cambridge: Cambridge University Press, 1987), 7, 29, 63, 150; cf. Joachim Ringleben, *Gott im Wort: Luthers Theologie von der Sprache her* (Tübingen: Mohr Siebeck, 2010), 378–443; John A. Maxfield, *Luther's Lectures on Genesis and the Formation of Evangelical Identity* (Kirksville, MO: Truman State University Press, 2008), 12–16.

10. Robert D. Preus, *The Inspiration of Scripture* (Edinburgh: Oliver & Boyd, 1957).

11. WA 54:474.4.

12. WA 7:97.2–3.

13. WA 12:413.32–34; CP 2:23.

14. WA 43:618.31–33; LW 5:275.

15. WA 40/2:531.30–34; LW 12:242.

16. WA 42:23.23–24; LW 1:30.

17. WA 43:301.9–12; LW 4:230.

"for our instruction, reproof, and comfort" (Rom. 15:4; 2 Tim. 3:16) against false definitions of holiness, such as those of the monks.[18]

In 1541 Luther stated, "The Holy Scripture is God's Word, written and (in my way of speaking) spelled out, put down in letters. Just as Christ is God's eternal Word wrapped in humanity, and just as people touched and had transactions with Christ in the world, so it is with the written Word of God." By comparing the nature of Scripture with the nature of Christ's person, in his divine and human natures, Luther so depicted Scripture that he could recognize certain characteristics—indeed, certain problems—of Scripture in the framework of his "theology of the cross," part of which included insights gained from his distinction between God revealed and God hidden. Paul's description of the cross of Christ as a modus operandi and a message with terms like "weak" and "foolish" (cf. 1 Cor. 1:18–2:16) pointed to his working "under the appearances of the opposite [of what something seems to be]" (*sub contrario*). Thus, both the meaning and power of Scripture often cannot be perceived by human reason.[19] Luther mused of the biblical text, "It is a worm [cf. Ps. 22:6] and no book, considered in comparison to other books." He further declared that the Bible is either ignored or abused and crucified through misinterpretation.[20]

Luther's too-famous dictum labeling human reason "a whore" is misleading when not placed in the context of his larger perception of human reason as a creature and gift of God, bestowed on human beings for the exercise of their stewardship or dominion of God's world. Luther regarded reason as a necessary and useful tool for managing the affairs of daily life in creation. He even found it useful as a tool and servant in theology, guiding the understanding of Scripture and its application. Only in reason's presumption to judge God's Word does it lure and seduce human beings into resisting God's address to them.[21]

Satan, the father of lies, is always attacking God's truth (John 8:44). Scripture is a strategic point of conflict on the eschatological battlefield, where the Holy Spirit and Satan contend for the allegiance of human beings. The devil deceives by placing the vital questions of life under the judgment of human reason, this gift of God that is neither intended nor designed for judging what God is saying to his people in Scripture.

---

18. WA 42:494.29–33; LW 2:325.

19. Lectures on Psalm 51, 1532, WA 40/2:329.17–330.32; LW 12:312–13; cf. WA 40/2:386.31–387.27; LW 12:352.

20. WA 48:31.4–17.

21. Brian Gerrish, *Grace and Reason: A Study in the Theology of Luther* (Oxford: Clarendon, 1962).

The Holy Spirit, as Luther had experienced, acts in and through the biblical text. Just as the Spirit was present at the origin of the biblical text, he remains in and with the text to guide present interpretation. "Scripture is the kind of book which requires not only reading and preaching but also the true exegete, namely, the revelation of the Holy Spirit."[22] "The Holy Spirit himself must expound Scripture. Otherwise it remains unexpounded. Now if any one of the saintly fathers can show that his interpretation is based on Scripture, and if Scripture proves that this is the way it was to be interpreted, then the interpretation is right. If this is not the case, I dare not believe him."[23] "To understand the meaning of Scripture, the Spirit of Christ is required. But we know that this same Spirit, who was present before all things, will remain to the end of the world. We glory in having the Spirit of God and through him we have faith, some understanding of the Scriptures and some knowledge of other things that are necessary for pious living." The reformer's confidence in the guidance of the Holy Spirit sustained him as a teacher of the Bible. "Therefore, we do not invent new ideas but follow the rule of Holy Scripture and the rule of faith."[24] Luther did not address the theodical problem raised by contradictory interpretations apart from insisting that interpreters read the text with a knowledge of the usages of biblical language and customs and the history of the times for the proper understanding of what prophet or apostle, in conjunction with the Holy Spirit, meant. Why the Holy Spirit allowed false interpretations in his church was not a question Luther tried to answer apart from his insistence that God does not cause evil and that Satan is constantly warring with his deception against God's truth. Luther simply proclaimed and defended the text as he read it.

Biblical Difficulties

Luther did not, however, claim perfect understanding of the precise meaning of every text, nor did he let himself be troubled by seeming contradictions because he was convinced that human reason cannot completely grasp God's wisdom and way of speaking and that God's reliability does not depend on the reader's mastering every biblical passage. Genesis 11:27–28 appeared to him to be one of "the most obscure of the whole Old Testament" because the reckoning of the chronology did not agree with other passages. "Crosses of the grammarians" like this need not trouble interpreters: "In the Sacred Scriptures one should not stubbornly defend anything except what is true;

22. WA 21:230.21–23; LW 77:51.
23. Sermons on 2 Peter, 1523, WA 14:31.9–12; LW 30:166.
24. Lecture on Genesis 6:3, WA 42:272.37–273.2; LW 2:15–16.

about obscure and doubtful matters other people must be allowed their own judgment." Paul, too, had found that the rabbis of his time were raising questions that did not need to be answered (1 Tim. 1:4).[25] Luther puzzled over the dating of Terah and Abraham in Genesis 11, concluding that one should not "imitate the audacious minds who immediately shout that an obvious error has been committed whenever such a difficulty arises and who unabashedly dare alter books that are not their own. As yet, I have no real answer for this question although I have diligently computed the years of the world. Therefore, I confess my ignorance appropriately and humbly (for only the Holy Spirit knows and understands everything)." Luther thought that God denied readers information about the precise time the world would end to prevent speculation.[26]

Luther noted that the accounts of the apostle Andrew's call to discipleship differ significantly in Matthew 4:18–20, Luke 5:1–11, and John 1:35–42.[27] He hazarded a possible explanation that he granted might or might not be correct.[28] Because he not only believed in the presence of the Holy Spirit in the text but also that the human authors had acted as the Spirit's coauthors completely in their own personalities with their own experiences and perceptions, he found it only reasonable that the evangelists did not describe every single detail in the same way, "for no historical account is so precise that it is not told and described in a different way by others."[29]

This cooperation between the Holy Spirit and the human authors of Scripture imposes on the interpreters the necessity of knowing the human languages—their grammar, syntax, and vocabulary—well. The readers also need to recognize that the Holy Spirit developed his own grammar. "Grammar is necessary and proper, but it ought not govern the subject matter and should instead serve it," he reminded students.[30] Luther noted that Christians needed to learn the Hebrew language from Jews just as one would want to learn German from Germans, Italian from Italians, "but their faith, their understanding of Scripture, which God condemns, we avoid,"[31] precisely because the Holy Spirit has his own grammar.[32] "Just as a philosopher employs his own terms, so the Holy Spirit, too employs his." Astronomers speak of "spheres" and

25. WA 42:430.35–431.9; *LW* 2:237.

26. WA 42:431.40–432.9; *LW* 2:239.

27. Andrew is not explicitly mentioned in Luke's account.

28. WA 52:563.33–564.19.

29. EA[2] 4:435–36. Cf. Luther's resolution of the reports of Matthew and John on whether Jesus had disciples or not at his baptism, WA 46:694.33–697.17; *LW* 22:181–85.

30. WA 42:599.6–8; *LW* 3:70–71.

31. *On Shem Hamphoras*, 1543, WA 53:646.13–18.

32. Maxfield, *Genesis*, 48–63; cf. on Psalm 2:5, WA 40/2:20–28; *LW* 12:32–33.

"epicycles" as part of the movement of heavenly bodies. "On the other hand, the Holy Spirit and Holy Scripture know nothing about those designations and call the entire area above us 'heaven.' Nor should an astronomer find fault with this; let each of them speak in his own terminology."[33] Thus, human reason encounters its limits when the Holy Spirit expresses divine wisdom and the mysteries of God. The Holy Spirit's presentation of what God is doing is sometimes crystal clear, but at other times the glimpses or echoes of God's will and ways defy and overpower human grammar and syntax. Luther used the term "mystery" relatively seldom, but he was ever aware that much of the heart of the biblical message does not make sense within categories established by human reason. The Holy Spirit must bestow faith. One example of this is the inability of the human mind to perceive the deep-rooted defiance of the Creator that Luther labeled original sin.[34] Other truths that surpass human reason include the doctrines of the Trinity and the hypostatic union of the two natures of Christ.[35]

Luther's Canon

Some scholars who have assessed Luther's view of Scripture on the basis of his attitude toward the canon have come to the conclusion that "for Luther the boundaries of the canon were not definitively set in stone and could not be."[36] Such assessments ignore several factors. Luther gathered the "apocryphal" books or sections of the Old Testament together at the end of that Testament and labeled them "books that are not regarded as equal to the Holy Scripture and are nonetheless useful and good to read." Not at all radical or new, this judgment reflected Jerome's fourth-century appraisal of those parts of the Septuagint not found in the Hebrew Masoretic text and the opinion of many medieval scholars and some humanists, including Erasmus.[37] Furthermore, Luther's doubts about the authorship of Hebrews because its language is

---

33. WA 42:35.40–36.6; *LW* 1:47–48.

34. Lecture on Psalm 51:5, WA 40/2:383.34–37; *LW* 12:350; cf. the Smalcald Articles, *BSELK* 746/747; *BC* 311.

35. On the Trinity, see WA 39/2:287–88, 290–300; on the two natures of Christ, see WA 39/2:3–33 and 39/2:93–121, both of them disputations on these doctrines.

36. Bernhard Lohse, "Die Entscheidung der lutherischen Reformation über den Umfang des alttestamentlichen Kanons," in *Evangelium in der Geschichte: Studien zu Luther und der Reformation* (Göttingen: Vandenhoeck & Ruprecht, 1988), 233. See instead Mark D. Thompson, *A Sure Ground on Which to Stand: The Relation of Authority and Interpretive Method in Luther's Approach to Scripture* (Carlisle, UK: Paternoster, 2004), 124–38.

37. Henning Graf Reventlow, *A History of Biblical Interpretation*, vol. 2, *From Late Antiquity to the End of the Middle Ages*, trans. James O. Duke (Atlanta: Society of Biblical Literature, 2009), 40–41.

"much more embellished speech than Saint Paul uses in other places" did not inhibit his use of it as "a strong, powerful, and lofty epistle, which soars high and promotes the lofty article of faith in the deity of Christ."[38]

More problematic for many is Luther's evaluation of the Epistle of James. His 1522 preface to the New Testament regarded "John's gospel and his first epistle, Saint Paul's epistles, especially Romans, Galatians, and Ephesians, and Saint Peter's first epistle" as "books that show you Christ and teach you all that is necessary and salutary for you to know." It was in the context of evaluating the book's usefulness in proclaiming Jesus and the salvation he bestows that Luther characterized James's epistle as "an epistle of straw."[39] Those who try to see this passage as proof that Luther dealt with Scripture in a casual way that took its content but not its form or its nature as a place of God's presence seriously ignore his statement within the same body of prefaces to New Testament books that he considered James "a good book because it sets up no human teaching but vigorously promulgates the law of God." Luther recognized that many ancient authorities had not accepted the epistle's canonicity and that it fails to teach justification, Christ's passion and resurrection, and the Holy Spirit,[40] but he continued to preach on it occasionally.[41] Furthermore, scholars who try to use the label "epistle of straw" as an indication of Luther's operating with "a canon within a canon" fail to mention that this formulation from 1522 was not reprinted—the only omission—when this preface to the New Testament appeared in the complete translation of the Bible in 1534 and in subsequent editions. For reasons he did not mention, he seems to have believed that this passage did not represent his views clearly, and it is indeed true that this removal of the passage reflects "a conscious theological judgment."[42] Finally, Luther's use of Scripture indicates that he paid little attention to questions of canonicity and simply preached on the received canon as he had learned it, following the pericopal system of the medieval church on Sunday mornings and seeking those texts that he

---

38. EA² 7:144; *LW* 75:256.

39. Preface to the New Testament (1522), WA *DB* 6:20.33–35; *LW* 35:362. Luther later told students how to rank the books of the Old Testament: Daniel and Isaiah were in his opinion the most excellent among the prophets, probably because of the former's teaching on the end times and the latter's prophecies of Christ, WA *TR* 2:410 §2286b; cf. 3:266–67 §3320a–b.

40. Preface to James (1522), WA *DB* 7:384.1/385.1–386.30/387.30; *LW* 35:395–97.

41. On James 1:16–17, WA 45:77–81 (1537); 47:742–48 (1539); James 1:17–21, WA 41:578–90 (1536); James 1:21–27, WA 41:69–73 (1535); 47:748–56 (1539). See Jason D. Lane, "The Lutheran Interpretation of the Epistle of James in the Sixteenth and Seventeenth Centuries" (ThD diss., Universität Hamburg, 2015), 56–94.

42. Bernhard Rothen, *Die Klarheit der Schrift*, vol. 1, *Martin Luther: Die wieder entdeckten Grundlagen* (Göttingen: Vandenhoeck & Ruprecht, 1990), 47.

found most clear and important for the central message of Scripture concerning salvation in Jesus Christ for his lectures and preaching in other services.

Scripture's Clarity, Sufficiency, and Power

Therefore Luther believed that Scripture alone governs all proclamation and use of God's Word and that it must be interpreted from within its own pages. Every attempt to evaluate its message or its authenticity according to any other standard subjects the speaking God to human appraisal and thus dethrones the Creator. Luther affirmed the clarity of Scripture on two levels. First, Scripture possesses an external clarity, for the biblical writers expressed the mysteries of God in ordinary human language. Obscure passages certainly challenge and humble readers, but in general readers can ascertain what the prophets and apostles were saying. Second, Scripture provides believers with an internal clarity. The Holy Spirit may leave faithful readers puzzled at points, but he guides them into the truth of Christ's redeeming work, Luther insisted.[43] He also found Scripture to be fully sufficient as a source for God's will and ways and a means for his exercise of his saving power. In Michael Horton's judgment, the sufficiency of the Bible as authority and as interpreter of its own message was the central issue governing Luther's affirmation of its ultimate authority for faith and life.[44] As John Headley observes, "One of the most significant features that distinguishes Luther's understanding of history from humanistic reflections on the past is his rejection of any historical period, person, or event as normative. His successful avoidance of the lure provided by historical norms arose from his belief in the authority of Scripture and the activity of the Word in history."[45] Vitor Westhelle summarizes Luther's view of Scripture's sufficiency: "Is scripture alone enough? It is more than enough. . . . First, it exceeds anything we can bargain for, and in fact leaves our bargaining as worthless and detrimental insofar as it conveys us Christ. . . . And, second, it also exceeds in providing us with a plethora of examples that pertain to different circumstances of how this works out in our everyday life with its challenges, limits, circumstances, and possibilities."[46]

43. Friedrich Beisser, *Claritas scriptuae bei Martin Luther* (Göttingen: Vandenhoeck & Ruprecht, 1966), 9–37, 82–122; cf. Rothen, *Klarheit*, 55–69, 142–90; Ringleben, *Wort*, 252–71; Thompson, *Ground*, 191–247.

44. Michael Horton, "Theologies of Scripture in the Reformation and Counter-Reformation," in *Christian Theologies of Scripture: A Comparative Introduction*, ed. Justin S. Holcomb (New York: New York University Press, 2006), 87; cf. Thompson, *Ground*, 249–82.

45. John M. Headley, *Luther's View of Church History* (New Haven: Yale University Press, 1963), 163–64.

46. "Luther on the Authority of Scripture," *Lutheran Quarterly* 19 (2005): 389.

Because God is present and at work in and through his Word, Luther believed, the proclamation of this Word in its various forms actually is "the power of God for salvation" (Rom. 1:16). The power of God's Word serves his saving will, that all may "be saved and come to a knowledge of the truth" (1 Tim. 2:4).[47] The mystery of the continuation of sin and evil in the lives of the faithful necessitated for Luther that the assurance of being God's child rested in the promise of salvation on the basis of Christ's work alone, delivered by the Holy Spirit through oral, written, and sacramental forms of the promise. Because this Word creates the reality that the Author of reality sees, believers have confidence that the almighty saving God has determined that they really are righteous.

This re-creative Word exercises its power to forgive sins and thus create the new reality of the child of God in the form of God's promise, made in human language and made on the basis of Christ's sacrifice and resurrection. The promise is not only the substance of things hoped for but also the—indeed unseen—reality of what God bestows through his gift of faith in Christ. "For many preach Christ, but in such a way that they do not understand or articulate the use and benefit [of the message]. . . . For it is not a Christian sermon, if you preach only of the events in Christ's life, nor is it if you just preach the glory of God." It becomes a God-pleasing sermon "if you teach the story of Christ in such a way that it makes it useful for us believers for our righteousness and salvation, so that . . . we may know that all things which are in Christ are ours. This faith and knowledge of the Lord makes us love, magnify, and glorify him."[48]

Luther's Ockhamist background permitted him to view human language as a means or instrument through which God carries out his will. Just as God created through speaking in Genesis 1, so God has chosen to take biblical words and do more than point to a heavenly reality or describe from a neutral point what God has done or promised to do. The Holy Spirit places his Word in created vessels or instruments, delivering it to humankind in oral, written, and sacramental forms. Each "means of grace," as later sixteenth-century Lutherans labeled these ways in which the Word comes to people, rests on and proceeds from Scripture. The means of grace, Luther taught, actually convey and deliver God's grace and fashion a new reality in the person who hears

47. Although Luther translated 1 Tim. 2:4 "that all may have help" with the implication of earthly blessings being the meaning of the word also translated "saved," he used this passage in his *De servo arbitrio*, e.g., to give assurance that everyone might know that Christ had died and risen for him or her, WA 18:686.5–6; *LW* 33:140.

48. WA 5:543.12–22. Luther repeated this point in a sermon of March 21, 1521, WA 9:630.28–30.

and is moved by the Holy Spirit to trust in the gospel of Christ. They do so in parallel fashion to the creative Word of Genesis 1. Luther often used the language of "new creation" in explaining how God's Word actually reshapes reality, turning sinners into his faithful children from God's perspective.[49]

Although in a semiliterate society it is not surprising that oral and sacramental forms of God's Word played a more prominent role than written forms, Luther nonetheless treasured the ability to read the Word on the biblical page. His program for personal study of Scripture emerged from the monastic practice of the *lectio*, the readings for the assembled monks or nuns, above all at mealtime, which was to evoke *oratio* (prayer) and *meditatio* (meditation). Luther presumed the reading of the text and on the basis of Psalm 119 prescribed simultaneous prayer and meditation within the framework of the spiritual trials and assaults from Satan, the world, and the Christian's own desires that oppose God (*tentatio*; in German, *Anfechtung*).[50] These trials and satanic assaults Luther regarded as necessary for the formation of the Christian theologian. Engagement with God's voice in the biblical text could not take place apart from the devil's attempts to divert the believer's trust from Christ to some false god. Commenting on Mary's song of praise (Luke 1:46–55), Luther states: "No one can receive [a proper interpretation] from the Holy Spirit without experiencing, testing, and feeling it. In such experience the Holy Spirit instructs us in his own school, outside of which nothing is learned except empty words and idle fables."[51] Furthermore, Luther took the psychological process of reading seriously. Readers must caress the text and knead the words, by reading aloud and by connecting the passage at hand with the larger biblical context and with the challenges of daily life. Their minds must submit to the text. "Holy Scripture wants to have a humble heart [as reader], one who regards God's Word with respect, love, and esteem, and who remains with it alone and holds fast to it."[52] God's Word, faith in his Word, and the cross—the struggle with all that seeks to alienate from God

49. Among many examples, see WA 1:477.3–4; 2:430; 5:544.6, 672.7–15; 21:521.21–22; 36:327.22–328.11; 37:536.35–537.11; 45:173.21–22; 49:399.1–400.27. Cf. Johann Haar, *Initium creaturae Dei: Eine Untersuchung über Luthers Begriff der "neuen Creatur" im Zusammenhang mit seinem Verständnis von Jakobus 1,18 und mit seinem "Zeit"-Denken* (Gütersloh: Bertelsmann, 1939), 36–39.

50. WA 50:659.5–660.30; LW 34:285–86; cf. John Kleinig, *Grace upon Grace: Spirituality for Today* (St. Louis: Concordia, 2008); Oswald Bayer, *Martin Luther's Theology: A Contemporary Interpretation*, trans. Thomas H. Trapp (Grand Rapids: Eerdmans, 2008), 29–37; and Bayer, *Theology the Lutheran Way*, trans. Jeffrey G. Silcock and Mark C. Mattes (Grand Rapids: Eerdmans, 2007), 33–82.

51. WA 7:546.21–29; LW 21:299.

52. WA TR 4:617 §5017.

and the accompanying mortification of sinful desires—together constitute the Christian life, Luther concluded.[53]

Luther's Methods of Biblical Exposition

Luther believed that Scripture tells God's story in straightforward human language. However, although he rejected the medieval allegorical system as the chief method of biblical interpretation, he occasionally turned to allegory as an instrument of conveying basic biblical teachings. His commentary on Deuteronomy (1525) contained allegories that the lecturer offered his hearers in order "to prevent inept efforts of forging allegories in the manner of Jerome."[54] At the same time he asserted that allegory most often is uncertain and unreliable in conveying biblical teaching, because it reveals flights of fancy in the interpreter's mind, not the intent of the divine and human authors of the text.[55] The Latin edition of his lectures on Jonah accepted Jesus's making Jonah's being swallowed by the fish into an allegory of his own time in the tomb (Matt. 12:39–40),[56] but the German version labeled it simply "a sign which bears resemblance to an experience of Jonah" and added, "No one would be authorized to interpret it as we do if Christ had not done so himself."[57] In this German version of the Jonah lectures, Luther did develop two more elaborate figural interpretations on the basis of Jonah's name and of his actions in the story. Jonah means "dove" and thus points to the Holy Spirit and his assignment as a proclaimer of the gospel. Nineveh means "beautiful"; it typifies the world, with its wealth, pleasures, wisdom, and strength that cover its sin. Nineveh's repentance points to the power of God's Word. Jonah's troubles represent the persecution and temptations of every believer. In a second "allegory," Luther elaborated on those afflictions of temptation and persecution as Jonah's life modeled and symbolized them.[58]

Chiefly, however, Luther's exposition of texts began with knowing the linguistic devices used by the author and the historical circumstances in which the author had been bringing God's message to his people. Luther's students learned quickly that grammatical and syntactical usage were key to God's

---

53. WA 43:208.18–23; LW 4:101.

54. WA 14:500.10–20; LW 9:7; WA 14:561.26–564.25; LW 9:26–27; WA 14:650.19–654.19; LW 9:136–37; WA 14:659.25–660.32; LW 9:150–51; WA 14:672.12–673.15; LW 9:170–71; WA 14:676.29–678.19; LW 9:178–80; WA 14:689.18–691.3; LW 9:197–99; WA 14:693.23–695.9; LW 9:205–7; WA 40/2:548.22–551.32; LW 12:254–57.

55. WA 14:560.17–28; LW 9:24–25.

56. WA 13:257.40; LW 19:31.

57. WA 19:249.16–23; LW 19:102.

58. WA 19:245.1–251.2; LW 19:97–102.

communication of his truth[59] and that some knowledge of the historical setting of the text held the key to the author's precise application of his message to the original hearers.[60] His own linguistic abilities may have aided the Wittenberg professor in developing a high appreciation of God's gift of language as an integral part of his person and of every human creature shaped in his image.[61] His sense of God as the Creator of historical sequence and the guide of the historical unfolding of the human story, which is also God's story, led Luther to insist on the historical nature of the biblical narrative.[62] Each prophet and apostle wrote at a specific time in the course of history, and Scripture as a whole presents the account of God's critical actions in creation, redemption, and the recall of his people to himself. Thus, Scripture "contains the thread that is drawn from the first world to the middle and end of all things. . . . This knowledge the Holy Scriptures reveal to us. Those who do not have [this knowledge] live in error, confusion, and endless impiety."[63]

Most of Luther's sermons and lectures, however, focused on placing the text at hand into hearers' or readers' lives as the message that God intends to be the tool for reclaiming them in repentance, re-creating them as his children, and guiding them through life. Thus, the largest part of his preaching and lecturing had a catechetical nature. He placed the message of the biblical authors into the lives of his contemporaries within the framework of God's gift of life through Christ and of the demands placed on human beings by the Creator's design—Luther's distinction between law and gospel. Luther's literary skill led him to enrich his historical and catechetical exposition of texts through the retelling of biblical stories, sometimes dramatized to have the biblical figures speak directly to his own hearers.[64] Finally, his mode of exposition included the frequent use of typological interpretation, which exhibited his belief that the Old Testament testifies through figural parallels to Christ's work and to the church's life.

Luther's reluctant response to the monastic command to teach Bible turned into a joyful, exuberant immersion in and interaction with the biblical text, in his sermons and lectures, in his letters and conversations. He treasured the book as God's means of being present with his people, addressing them out of

59. WA 44:135.24–137.19; LW 6:182–83.

60. WA 44:259.7–8; LW 6:346.

61. Johannes von Lüpke, "Luther's Use of Language," in The Oxford Handbook of Martin Luther's Theology, ed. Robert Kolb, Irene Dingel, and L'ubomír Batka (Oxford: Oxford University Press, 2014), 143–55.

62. Mark Thompson, "Luther on God and History," in Kolb, Dingel, and Batka, Oxford Handbook, 127–42; Headley, History.

63. WA 42:409.21–29; LW 2:209.

64. Kolb, Luther and the Stories of God.

the historic situations of the prophets and apostles with his truth, his instrument to battle the deceptions of Satan. In the human characters of Scripture, he found people much like himself, despite their differing historical situations. From their stories in the pages of Scripture, which are also the stories of God's abiding faithfulness, Luther found his true identity as a child of God.

Holy Scripture in the Reformed Tradition

The Reformation was among other things a revolution of the book. There was, of course, a sociological dimension to this: the fifteenth-century invention of the printing press made books more readily available and set the foundation for a society in which literacy was to become more and more important. Yet the Reformation was no mere social transformation. At its heart lay the Bible.

Now, the Bible had always been important to Christianity. The Middle Ages produced a number of excellent expositors and preachers, and no man was deemed qualified to be a professor of theology in medieval times until he had lectured through significant quantities of the Bible. But the Reformation gave a new importance to Scripture. For the Reformers, God was present in his church primarily through his Word—the Word read and the Word preached. Pulpits came to occupy the focal point of attention, as altars had done in the past. To be a Reformer was to be someone who placed the Bible, its exposition, and its proclamation at the center of church life and who made the Bible the normative criteria for all theological discussion.

Yet it is clear that, for all this basic agreement, the issue of interpretation was one that ultimately divided the Lutherans and the Reformed, specifically as they came to focus on four little words, "This is my body." Nevertheless, we should not allow this serious and important disagreement to blind us to the substantial areas of common belief between the two traditions. Both Reformed and Lutherans sought to allow Scripture to regulate their confessions of the faith.

The Importance, Sufficiency, and Clarity of the Word

Like Luther, the Reformed regarded the Word, specifically the Word preached, as central to all they did. The most dramatic confessional expression of this occurs in chapter 1 of Heinrich Bullinger's Second Helvetic Confession: "Therefore when this word of God is today proclaimed in the Church through preachers who have been legitimately called, we believe that it is the very word of God which is proclaimed and received by the faithful; and that

no other word of God is to be invented nor to be expected from heaven."[65]
This is powerful language, and it needs to be properly understood. Bullinger
does not mean thereby to relativize the unique authority of Scripture as the
revelation of God and as the norming norm of theological formulation. That
would place him much closer to the Tridentine Roman Catholic camp. For
him, preaching does not stand independent from God's Word in Scripture or
alongside it with some kind of equal and supplementary authority. The act of
preaching is not some charismatic event whereby the preacher is inspired by
the Spirit in some way that is separate from the Word. As with the Lutherans,
the Reformed are adamant that Word and Spirit need to be kept together, and
that separation of the two leads to spiritual fanaticism.[66] In fact, the Spirit
works in and through the Word to accomplish God's purposes. The two work
together in a potent manner to convict of sin and to create faith in those who
hear the Word proclaimed. There is to be no separation of the two. Preaching is therefore to start with the text of Scripture and to be regulated by that
text and by the whole scope of scriptural teaching. It is not an act of liberal
improvisation but an activity disciplined by God's revelation of himself in
the words of the Bible.

What Bullinger means by this audacious statement in the Second Helvetic Confession is that preaching, when done faithfully by a legitimately
called pastor in accordance with what God has revealed in Scripture, is to
be received as an authoritative word from God. If the conceptual content of
the sermon is the same as that taught in the Bible, it is to be taken as God's
Word. Yes, we are to be like the Bereans and test all things by the standard
of Scripture. But we are also to come to hear the preaching of the Word
with a default position of trust in those who have been called to the teaching office, perhaps something we might characterize as a hermeneutic of
trust and obedience.[67] This involves ecclesiological assumptions, that there
is such a thing as the institutional church and that the church does have legitimate office-bearers who have ministerial authority, and also theological

---

65. My translation. The original reads: "Proinde cum hodie hoc Dei verbum per prædicatores
legitime vocatos annunciatur in Ecclesia, credimus ipsum Dei verbum annunciari et a fidelibus
recipi, neque aliud Dei verbum vel fingendum, vel cœlitus esse exspectandum."

66. Cf. Calvin, *Institutes* I.ix.1.

67. In our present age, shaped as it is in its epistemological tastes by those masters of suspicion
Marx, Nietzsche, and Freud, a hermeneutic of trust is likely to appear to be a naive interpretive
presupposition. Yet Christians, committed to the idea of a faithful and trustworthy God, are
required to set their faces against such knee-jerk cynicism when it comes to the reading and the
preaching of God's Word. For a useful response to postmodern cynicism relative to Scripture
from a Reformed perspective, see Timothy Ward, *Words of Life: Scripture as the Living and
Active Word of God* (Leicester: Inter-Varsity, 2009).

assumptions, that God has revealed himself clearly in Scripture and that persons trained with the right skills can expound Scripture in a manner that is accurate and faithful.

What this reflects is the general Reformed conviction that preaching is the central task of the church. Calvin makes this very clear when, in Luther-like fashion, he identifies the power of the keys with the proclamation of the Word:

> When we treat of the keys, we must always beware of dreaming of any power apart from the preaching of the Gospel. . . . Whatever privilege of binding and loosing Christ has bestowed on his Church is annexed to the word. This is especially true with regard to the ministry of the keys, the whole power of which consists in this, that the grace of the Gospel is publicly and privately sealed on the minds of believers by means of those whom the Lord has appointed; and the only method in which this can be done is by preaching.[68]

The Word both creates the church and regulates the church. God's speech through the preacher is the means by which the church is called into being and governed. The medieval church focused on the sacraments, since that was where God was present; the Reformed church focused on the preaching of his Word. This is why the preaching of the Word is regarded by the Reformed as one of the marks of the true church.[69]

This is not to say that the Reformed believed written Scripture preceded the existence of the church. The Word is the speech of God addressing his people and calling them into existence as the church. It thus preexisted its written form and was inscripturated in order to preserve the divine truth in a more reliable and stable form than that provided by oral tradition.[70] While God reveals himself in numerous ways, in his works of creation and providence, and in the incarnation of his Son, Scripture provides the basic, stable noetic

---

68. Calvin, *Institutes* III.iv.14; cf. IV.xi–xii.

69. While the Reformed varied somewhat on the marks of the church—whether there were two or three marks, and whether the third mark was discipline or pure worship, all agreed (as did the Lutherans) that the preaching of the Word, along with the administration of the sacraments, were nonnegotiable marks of the church: see Calvin, *Institutes* IV.i.9 (word, sacraments); Scots Confession 18 (word, sacraments, discipline); Westminster Confession of Faith (word, sacraments, public worship).

70. "When length of life was shortened and the state of wickedness was increasing daily, and Satan by means of his misleading oracles and apparitions with which he imitated God and his appearance was deluding the human race throughout the world, it pleased God from then until the end of the world to establish his Church also by means of the Scriptures, to preserve the divine truth more reliably, to widen its extent, and to restore it more easily where it had fallen into ruin." *Synopsis Purioris Theologiae*, disp. 2.4 (*Synopsis Purioris Theologiae/Synopsis of a Purer Theology: Latin Text and English Translation*, vol. 1, *Dispotations 1–23*, ed. Dolf te Velde, trans. Riemer A. Faber [Leiden: Brill, 2015], p. 51); cf. Turretin, *Institutes* II.2.

foundation for understanding God. Hence, Calvin uses his famous analogy of Scripture to eyeglasses:

> For as the aged, or those whose sight is defective, when any book however fair, is set before them, though they perceive that there is something written are scarcely able to make out two consecutive words, but, when aided by glasses, begin to read distinctly, so Scripture, gathering together the impressions of Deity, which, till then, lay confused in our minds, dissipates the darkness, and shows us the true God clearly. God therefore bestows a gift of singular value, when, for the instruction of the Church, he employs not dumb teachers merely, but opens his own sacred mouth; when he not only proclaims that some God must be worshipped, but at the same time declares that He is the God to whom worship is due; when he not only teaches his elect to have respect to God, but manifests himself as the God to whom this respect should be paid.[71]

When we speak of interpreting Scripture, then, there is a certain sense in which we misspeak: Scripture actually interprets us and the world around us, because it provides the framework for understanding reality as the creation of a sovereign God.

To return to the emphasis on the Second Helvetic Confession, for the Reformed Scripture and interpretation must always be understood as terminating in the task of proclamation. That is the primary act of the church, the point at which God confronts his people. This connects to everything from the understanding of what Scripture is to the nature of theological education to the expectations of pastoral ministry to the shape of the church service and the regular Christian life. All are to be regulated by the Word and practically oriented to the preaching of the Word.

Reformed pedagogical practice therefore reflects this. The Zurich prophesying meetings—gatherings to train preachers—and Calvin's company of pastors, as well as the Geneva Academy, all provide great examples of how preparing preachers and improving preaching were both high priorities in Reformed circles.[72] To survive and flourish, the church needed preachers. The training of men for that task, and the constant improving of those called to preach, were thus priorities for the Reformed churches of the Reformation.

Concerning preaching and theology, the Reformed confessions are emphatic that the Bible is authoritative and the sole normative source of proclamation

---

71. Calvin, *Institutes* I.vi.1.

72. See Daniel Timmerman, *Heinrich Bullinger on Prophecy and the Prophetic Office (1523–1538)* (Göttingen: Vandenhoeck & Ruprecht, 2015); Scott M. Manetsch, *Calvin's Company of Pastors: Pastoral Care and the Emerging Reformed Church, 1536–1609* (New York: Oxford University Press, 2012).

in the church. Thus the Thirty-Nine Articles of the Church of England suc-
cinctly declare the following: "Holy Scripture containeth all things necessary
to salvation: so that whatsoever is not read therein, nor may be proved thereby,
is not to be required of any man, that it should be believed as an article of
the faith, or be thought requisite or necessary to salvation."[73] The point is
clear and stands in obvious opposition to Roman Catholic claims regarding
the supplementary nature of tradition as a source of revelation proper rather
than merely an explication of its content. All theology, all proclamation, is
to be regulated by the content of the canon of Scripture. Scripture is thus the
norming norm of theological formulation. While it is necessary for the church
to express its teaching in extrascriptural language in creeds, confessions, and
sermons, all of these are to be regulated by the teaching of Scripture. As the
Synopsis Purioris Theologiae says, "The authority of Holy Scripture is much
greater than that of the Church" because "the Church is capable of erring
while Scripture cannot."[74]

The authority and sufficiency of Scripture therefore places the teaching
of Scripture in the position of being the criterion by which the tradition of
church teaching is to be normed. Herman Bavinck captures the Reformation
understanding of the relationship of Scripture and tradition well:

> The Reformation recognizes only a tradition that is founded on and flows from
> Scripture. To the mind of the Reformation, Scripture was an organic principle
> from which the entire tradition, living on in preaching, confession, liturgy,
> worship, theology, devotional literature, etc., arises and is nurtured. It is a pure
> spring of living water from which all the currents and channels of the religious
> life are fed and maintained. Such a tradition is grounded in Scripture itself.[75]

This is a very important point, because it separates the Reformed—and indeed
the magisterial Reformation as a whole—from both Tridentine Roman Catholicism and evangelical biblicism. The former allows for an extrascriptural
stream of authoritative revelation; the latter tends to ignore the tradition
of church teaching when it is more convenient to do so.[76] By contrast, the

---

73. James T. Dennison, *Reformed Confessions of the 16th and 17th Centuries in English
Translation, 1523–1693*, 4 vols. (Grand Rapids: Reformation Heritage Books, 2008–14), 2:755.
Hereafter Dennison.

74. *Synopsis Purioris Theologiae*, disp. 2.31 (p. 71).

75. *RD* 1:493.

76. For Trent's view, see Council of Trent, session 4, April 8, 1546: "The Decree on the
Reception of the Sacred Books and Traditions," in *Enchiridion symbolorum definitionum
et declarationum de rebus fidei et morum*, ed. Heinrich Denzinger, 43rd ed. (San Francisco:
Ignatius, 2012), 1501 (p. 370).

Reformed were assiduous students of the doctrinal and exegetical traditions of the church. Indeed, even the prooftexts provided for a document like the Westminster Confession were not prooftexts in the modern sense of the word, to be taken in isolation as knockout blows against opposing positions. Rather, they function as exegetical markers, directing the interested student back to the interpretive tradition surrounding those texts.[77]

In this context, it is also worth noting that the magisterial Protestants in general were committed readers of the commentary tradition on any given biblical book, and this was in no way restricted to Christian commentators only, as their extensive use of the rabbis demonstrated. Scripture alone did not function as cover for a narrow biblicism or a fundamentalist obscurantism. Quite the contrary. The unique authority of Scripture made it imperative that Protestants interpret it correctly, and a basic part of that task involved mastery of the biblical languages and a thorough acquaintance with the history of interpretation.[78]

This also connects to a basic commitment on the part of the Reformed (as with Luther) to the clarity and perspicuity of Scripture. Chapter 1 of the Westminster Confession expresses this neatly:

> 6. The whole counsel of God concerning all things necessary for his own glory, man's salvation, faith and life, is either expressly set down in Scripture, or by good and necessary consequence may be deduced from Scripture: unto which nothing at any time is to be added, whether by new revelations of the Spirit, or traditions of men. . . . 7. All things in Scripture are not alike plain in themselves, nor alike clear unto all: yet those things which are necessary to be known, believed, and observed for salvation, are so clearly propounded, and opened in some place of Scripture or other, that not only the learned, but the unlearned, in a due use of the ordinary means, may attain unto a sufficient understanding of them.

The basics of the Reformed position are here: Scripture is sufficient; Scripture is also clear on the essentials of salvation, either by direct statement or by legitimate inference; and the most vital truths are so plainly stated that even the ignorant and the unlearned should be able to grasp them.[79] We might

---

77. See Richard A. Muller and Rowland S. Ward, *Scripture and Worship: Biblical Interpretation and the Directory for Worship* (Phillipsburg, NJ: P&R, 2007), 70, 72.

78. See Katrin Ettenhuber, "The Preacher and Patristics," in *The Oxford Handbook of the Early Modern Sermon*, ed. Peter McCullough, Hugh Adlington, and Emma Rhatigan (Oxford: Oxford University Press, 2011), 34–53; also in the same volume, see Carl R. Trueman, "Preachers and Medieval and Renaissance Commentary," 54–71.

79. We do need to remember that in its teaching on scriptural clarity, the confession assumes a number of things that would require elaboration and defense today in the face of postmodern critiques: the existence of a clear canon, the possibility of producing accurate translations, and

add that interpretation, far from being the complicated matter that modern hermeneutical philosophers have sought to make it, was for the Reformed a rather straightforward affair. Doctrines such as the Trinity and the incarnation, as well as justification by grace through faith, were considered clearly evident to anyone with eyes to see. This connects to the development of lists of "fundamental articles" in Reformed orthodoxy—those doctrines that every Christian must come to believe because they are plainly taught by Scripture.[80]

This rests on the doctrine of Scripture's clarity, a necessary attribute of Scripture in the general Protestant polemic against Roman Catholic claims that the institutional church was necessary for correct interpretation. Instead, the Reformed asserted the basic clarity of Scripture in order to undermine papal claims and buttress their own emphasis on the ability and responsibility of all believers with respect to the Bible's teaching.

Reformed understanding of perspicuity is twofold, like that of Luther. First, there is the external clarity of the Bible in terms of the public accessibility of its teaching. The unregenerate person, endowed with the relevant natural skills in language and intellect, is able to grasp many things that the Bible teaches. Yet only regenerate persons who have the Holy Spirit can understand the meaning of Scripture in a way that applies its teaching to themselves in a salutary, saving manner. Nevertheless, scriptural interpretation, in extracting the basic sense of what the Bible says, is not a complicated or arcane matter.[81]

The assumption of Scripture's clarity also shapes the Reformed ideal for biblical commentary. In the preface to his commentary on Romans, Calvin (quietly reacting to the long-winded and therefore somewhat obfuscatory approach to commentating of his mentor and friend Martin Bucer) declares that "the chief excellency of an expounder consists in *lucid brevity*."[82] Commentators, like preachers, are to bring out the clear teaching of Scripture, not to hide it.

The Relationship between the Old and New Testaments

Perhaps the fundamental interpretive question for the Reformed—indeed, perhaps the fundamental interpretive question for the Christian church as a whole—is that of the relationship between the Old and New Testaments.

---

the congregation's ability to test the fidelity of expositions being offered by preachers. A fine example of such a defense is provided by Mark D. Thompson, *A Clear and Present Word: The Clarity of Scripture* (Leicester: Apollos, 2006).

80. See Turretin, *Institutes* I.xiv.

81. See *Synopsis Purioris Theologiae*, disp. 5 (pp. 128–49).

82. John Calvin, *Commentary on the Epistle of Paul the Apostle to the Romans*, trans. J. Owen (Edinburgh: Calvin Translation Society, 1849), xxiii.

Ever since Marcion attempted to construct a canon premised on the fundamental contradiction of the God of the Old and the God of (parts of) the
New Testament, this matter has been central to discussions of the meaning
of Scripture.

In book II of the *Institutes*, Calvin takes up this matter and outlines ways
in which the two Testaments are similar and different. While Calvin and the
confessional Reformed in general do hold to the law-gospel antithesis of
Luther, this is not their fundamental principle for understanding Scripture.
Instead, the Reformed approach is more oriented to a historical understanding
of the unfolding of God's redemption purposes.[83]

When Calvin addresses the issue of the similarity of the Testaments, his
focus is on the covenants made first with the patriarchs and then with the
New Testament church. Both pointed toward a blessing that was spiritual,
not material. Second, both were based on grace, not on human merit. And
third, both had Christ as Mediator of the covenant.[84]

As to differences between the Testaments, Calvin notes five. In the Old
Testament, the people of God receive a foretaste of their heavenly inheritance through earthly blessings.[85] Second, in the Old Testament the truth is
taught by types, whereas in the New the full substance is revealed.[86] Third,
the Old Testament was a dispensation of the letter, the New of the Spirit.
The former has an external quality to it; the latter is written on the heart.[87]
Fourth, the Old Testament is a dispensation characterized by bondage and
by fear (because it is not spiritual, as the third difference indicates), while
the New is characterized by the liberty that confidence and security bring
because of the full revelation of the work of Christ.[88] And the fifth distinction refers to the peculiar role of ethnic Israel under the Old Testament,
which has now been abolished through the inclusion of the gentiles into
God's gracious plan.[89]

Calvin's position on the relationship of the Old and New Testaments
might therefore be summarized in terms of promise and fulfillment, which
captures well the basic Reformed position. The Testaments are the same in
substance—the grace of God—but that substance is administered differ-
ently under each, with the New presenting the fulfillment of the Old in the

83. For the Reformed position on the law-gospel antithesis, see chap. 2 below.
84. Calvin, *Institutes* II.x.2.
85. Ibid., II.xi.1.
86. Ibid., II.xi.4.
87. Ibid., II.xi.7–8.
88. Ibid., II.xi.9.
89. Ibid., II.xi.11.

person and work of Jesus Christ and the giving of the Spirit at Pentecost. It also indicates that, while the Reformed generally regard allegorical exegesis as inappropriate and lacking sufficient textual and theological controls, nevertheless typological exegesis is crucial to understanding Scripture and biblical history. This is reflected in its most practical form in the practice of infant baptism, which depends on the identity of the covenant of grace in the Old and New Testaments but also on a change in administration in the New (see chap. 6).

In this context, we should also note the Reformed commitment to the literal sense of Scripture, in reaction to the medieval notion of the *quadriga*, or fourfold sense. While there was a perennial problem in defining exactly what constituted the literal sense of Scripture, Richard Muller has noted that in Calvin's exegetical works there is an increased emphasis on the "literal, grammatical meaning and even on a genuinely historical reading of the Old Testament," which evidenced itself in Calvin being far more cautious than Luther in advancing direct christological interpretations of Old Testament passages. This does not mean that Calvin and the later Reformed do not see Christ in the Old Testament, but their use of typology, and even more of allegory, is typically extremely cautious.[90] This led Lutherans to allege that Calvin's approach to the Old Testament involved a level of Judaizing.[91]

The Analogy of Faith

As the Westminster Confession acknowledges, the Reformed understand that not all passages in Scripture are equally perspicuous and that the obscure passages are to be interpreted in light of those whose meaning is clear. Interpretation therefore involves comparison of various passages, but it also involves the analogy of faith, a concept with a number of facets.[92] First, it assumes the coherence and consistency of the Bible's teaching, such that passages that appear to contradict each other should be understood as compatible. The failure to see how they cohere is a failure of interpretation or understanding, not a sign of a real problem resident in the text. As Turretin declares, after outlining what he considers to be inadequate responses to apparent contradictions in Scripture: "Finally others defend the integrity of

90. *PRRD* 2:469–72.
91. Ibid., 2:471.
92. See ibid., 2:493–97, where he demonstrates that there were some minor variations in the understanding of exactly what constituted the analogy of faith. In this chapter, I give a synthesis of its various aspects.

the Scriptures and say that these various contradictions are only apparent, not real and true; that certain passages are hard to be understood but not altogether inexplicable. This is the more common opinion of the orthodox, which we follow as safer and truer."[93]

Second, the analogy of faith assumes the essential clarity of Scripture relative to the basic elements of Christian catechesis: the Decalogue, the Lord's Prayer, and the articles of the ancient creeds. This is one reason why the Reformed were so concerned to produce catechisms: to provide the ordinary believer with the basic tools necessary for a correct understanding of Scripture. Catechizing, far from being an attempt to brainwash children or to impose a dogmatic grid on the reading of Scripture, was in fact designed to give believers the ability to read and interpret Scripture correctly. This point is made with some force by Ursinus, in the introduction to his commentary on the Heidelberg Catechism:

> There is a necessity that all persons should be made acquainted with the rule and standard according to which we are to judge and decide, in relation to the various opinions and dogmas of men, that we may not be led into error, and be seduced thereby, according to the commandment which is given in relation to this subject, "Beware of false prophets." "Prove all things." "Try the spirits whether they are of God." (Matt. 7:15. 1 Thess. 5:21. 1 John 4:1.) But the law and the Apostles' Creed, which are the chief parts of the catechism, constitute the rule and standard according to which we are to judge of the opinions of men, from which we may see the great importance of a familiar acquaintance with them. . . . Those who have properly studied and learned the Catechism, are generally better prepared to understand and appreciate the sermons which they hear from time to time, inasmuch as they can easily refer and reduce those things which they hear out of the word of God, to the different heads of the catechism to which they appropriately belong, whilst, on the other hand, those who have not enjoyed this preparatory training, hear sermons, for the most part, with but little profit to themselves.[94]

This is an important point, because it connects to the Reformed (and indeed also the Lutheran) understanding of the nature of creeds and confessions. These are ecclesiastical documents whose teaching is both drawn from Scripture and then used as a framework for interpreting Scripture. Therefore, they are neither separate forms of revelation that compromise the principle of Scripture alone nor are they dispensable by the church. Rather, they state

---

93. Turretin, *Institutes* II.v.3.
94. Zacharias Ursinus, *The Commentary of Dr. Zacharias Ursinus on the Heidelberg Catechism*, trans. G. W. Willard (Cincinnati: Elm Street, 1888), 15.

publicly what the church believes Scripture to teach and the assumptions by which the church believes Scripture should be interpreted.[95]

Third, the analogy of faith also assumes the legitimacy of drawing out doctrinal conclusions by good and necessary consequence from those passages that are deemed clear in order to provide interpretive insight into those that are obscure. Thus, the analogy of faith is not simply applied by interpreting one passage of Scripture in light of another; it can also involve interpreting one passage of Scripture in light of doctrinal conclusions drawn from another passage of Scripture.[96]

The most obvious example of this in the context of Lutheran-Reformed interaction is, of course, the question of the meaning of the words of eucharistic institution: "This is my body." When Calvin addresses this issue in the *Institutes*, he rests part of his argument for the rejection of the Lutheran position on the nature of Christ's body, which is, he argues, necessarily a claim for a localized body. If it were not so, he argues, it would not be a true body. Then, anticipating the objection that Christ's glorified flesh is not subject to the same limitations as our bodies, Calvin points out that Scripture indicates that the Lord's Supper took place prior to Christ's death and resurrection. Finally, preempting the fourth objection that Christ's preresurrection body also showed signs of its later glorification in the transfiguration, Calvin argues that that was simply to give the disciples a foretaste of glory and does not legitimate the far-reaching christological conclusions that the Lutherans wish to draw.[97] This is an excellent example of the Reformed use of both Scripture and logical reasoning.[98]

In his commentary on the Heidelberg Catechism, Ursinus addresses the same issue, that of the words of institution, and rejects both transubstantiation

---

95. See Carl R. Trueman, *The Creedal Imperative* (Wheaton: Crossway, 2012). Cf. *RD* 1:480. In his classic explication of the nature and method of preaching, William Perkins (*The Arte of Prophecying* [London: Felix Kyngston, 1607]) advises those seeking to interpret Scripture to grasp first of all the basic categories and divisions of theology (*Arte*, 26). In the same passage, Perkins also recommends reading the Scriptures in a certain order, beginning with the Letters of Paul, as the best means of grasping the basic structure of biblical teaching. Perkins's original work is available online at http://quod.lib.umich.edu/cgi/t/text/text-idx?c=eebo;idno=A09449.0001.001. For a modern reprint edition, see William Perkins, *The Art of Prophesying; with, The Calling of the Ministry*, ed. Sinclair B. Ferguson, rev. ed. (Carlisle, PA: Banner of Truth Trust, 1996).

96. For a good introduction to the Reformed use of consequences, see Ryan M. McGraw, *By Good and Necessary Consequence* (Grand Rapids: Reformation Heritage, 2012).

97. Calvin, *Institutes* IV.xvii.17.

98. Of course, the Lutherans would argue that extrapolating from the limitations of our bodies to those of Christ's body is a rationalist move without biblical sanction. That response goes to the heart of the hermeneutical issues that connect to the christological difference between the two traditions.

and consubstantiation on four grounds: the teaching of the text itself, the nature of sacraments in general, the implications for the text of other established elements of the faith, and the significance of parallel scriptural texts that shed light on the specific passage.[99] Of course, the question of which passages teach clearly and which are more obscure might itself be an issue that depends on one's doctrinal commitments, and that is again where the analogy of faith comes into play, as shaping such interpretive decisions. For Ursinus, the teaching that Christ's flesh is like ours in all things, sin excepted, is crucial for repudiating any idea that it might be infinite, omnipresent, or simply not localized in one place at any given moment.[100]

Fourth, and in connection with the third point, the analogy of faith assumes the basic interpretive dynamics of Scripture: the distinction between law and gospel and the overall redemptive scheme of biblical history as it culminates in Jesus Christ and the giving of the Spirit to the church.[101] These architectonic principles give Scripture its coherence and its fundamental message.

The Word Preached

As noted at the start of this section, for the Reformed the primary act of the Christian church is the preaching of the Word. Therefore, all biblical interpretation is tailored toward the goal of pressing the reality of God and the significance of Christ on those who hear.

The Reformed have typically adopted two basic approaches to preaching: consistent exposition of whole books of the Bible and catechetically framed sermons that follow a more topical ordering. The latter is exemplified by Bullinger's *Decades*, a cycle of sermons later published as a basic textbook of theology. More significantly for the long-term shape of Reformed homiletics was the decision to divide the Heidelberg Catechism into fifty-two Lord's Days and then to make it a practice in the continental Reformed churches to dedicate the afternoon or evening Lord's Day service to preaching on the specified section of the catechism for the day. This practice ensured that the basic doctrinal points of the catechism were reinforced on an annual basis.[102]

---

99. Ursinus, *Commentary*, 390–403.
100. Ibid., 396; cf. Perkins, *Arte*, 47.
101. See Ursinus, *Commentary*, 2–3; see also chap. 2 below.
102. This practice was stipulated by the Synod of the Hague in 1586 and reaffirmed at the Synod of Dort in 1618–19; the latter also stated that "the catechism sermons should be very brief and as intelligible as possible for the simple-minded people." Arie Baars, "'The Simple Heidelberg Catechism . . .': A Brief History of the Catechism Sermon in the Netherlands," in *Power of Faith: 450 Years of the Heidelberg Catechism*, ed. Karla Apperloo-Boersma and Herman J. Selderhuis (Göttingen: Vandenhoeck & Ruprecht, 2013), 159–67 (quote from 159).

Although fine in theory, it was not without its problems: some pastors proved unable to preach this way, and congregants sometimes complained that it made preachers lazy, since they could reuse the same sermons year after year.[103]

Preaching is also intended to be clear and practical, a point connecting to the Reformed commitment to the third use of the law (see chap. 2 below). In his classic handbook on preaching, *The Arte of Prophecying*, the Elizabethan Puritan William Perkins laid out a set of basic principles for the preacher to observe in any sermon. The preacher must not make a show of his learning but rather hide that in the pulpit. This is not for the purpose of preaching in an ignorant or unlearned manner—far from it—but in order to make the truth of God shine more clearly, unencumbered by human ostentation. He is to demonstrate the Spirit by his serious demeanor and to speak in a manner clear and easy to understand by ordinary people. This means that Latin and Greek words must be avoided, as well as the "telling of tales, and all profane and ridiculous speeches."[104]

For Perkins, true preaching involves "rightly dividing the word of truth" (2 Tim. 2:15), which consists of two parts: resolution or partition, and application. Resolution is proclaiming the doctrine that is either explicitly stated in the text or that can be legitimately derived therefrom.[105] Application is, in the words of Perkins, "that wherby the doctrine, rightlie collected, is diverslly fitted according as place, time, and person do require."[106] In short, if the doctrine is drawn from the text in a way determined by the objectivity of the text itself, application involves bringing that doctrine to bear on the specifics of the situation in which the preacher finds himself. Application can also be mental (i.e., teaching the mind doctrine is a form of application) or practical, referring to manner of life and behavior.[107] Again, this latter point really picks up on the Reformed commitment to the idea of the third use of the law as a positive, practical guide for Christian living in the present.

Perkins's treatise is one of the classics on Reformed preaching and is still in print today. This is because it captures so brilliantly the basic Reformed concern for preaching: the preacher is to move from the biblical text by correct principles of interpretation to a clear proclamation of the doctrine that the text teaches and thence to a practical application to the congregation, either in terms of aiding Christians to better understand the text and the doctrine or in terms of practical implications for life.

---

103. Baars, "'Simple Heidelberg Catechism,'" 160–61.
104. Perkins, *Arte*, 132–36.
105. Ibid., 90–92.
106. Ibid., 99.
107. Ibid., 122–23.

Conclusion

The Reformed commitment to correct biblical interpretation arises out of the belief that the Bible is the Word of God in written form and is the basis for God's saving action in the world. The basic means by which God acts through this Word is its proclamation in the church, a proclamation that, when done in a manner faithful to God's scriptural revelation, is used by the Holy Spirit to convict of sin, to inculcate faith, and to edify the body.

This has certain practical implications for church life. Believers are to be taught the basic catechetical categories of the faith so that they themselves will learn how to rightly handle the Word of truth and to be able to listen with discernment to what they hear from the pulpit. Preaching is to be central in the gathered worship of the church. Ministers who are called to this task are to be properly trained to handle the Word of God, which normally requires both linguistic and theological skills. Preaching is to draw attention not to the preachers themselves but to the God who speaks clearly through the preachers. Sermons are therefore to aid the believer in understanding Scripture better. But more than that: the Word preached is the Word of God and confronts individuals with the glorious Lord who saves, calling forth a response of faith and adoration.

2

Law and Gospel

At the very heart of Protestantism, both Lutheran and Reformed, lies the distinction between law and gospel. The tension between the two shapes everything, from the interpretation of Scripture to preaching to the practical understanding of the Christian life. It points to the two most basic aspects of God's relationship to his creatures: he commands them as their Lord and Sovereign to be holy as he is holy; and he promises them that he has acted on their behalf in Christ to fulfill his command and that all they therefore need to do is to trust in that promise. The law convicts me of my sin; the gospel gives me Christ and speaks peace to my soul.

This distinction is one of the basic elements of theology that gives Christianity and Christian doctrine an existential urgency. We can learn the facts of the Gospels, the events of Jesus's life, and the actions of God in history without ever understanding that these are not analogous to, say, the deeds of Napoleon. Napoleon's life is interesting and historically significant, but it does not address us in any urgent way or make any demands on us. Christianity, however, is deeply existential and confrontational in its very essence: God's Word commands and God's Word promises. It addresses us personally and demands a response. On this point, both Lutheran and Reformed agree and have much to say.

Law and Gospel in the Lutheran Tradition

As a friar, Luther heard God speaking from the pages of Scripture—almost without exception in a demanding voice. He experienced God's prescriptions for his daily behavior and attitude as requirements for the performance necessary to please God sufficiently to merit the grace needed to produce truly worthy good works. His instructors taught him that his eternal destiny depended on producing these works. As Luther delved deeper into Scripture, read Augustine's anti-Pelagian writings, engaged the devotional writings of the mystical monastic piety fostered by Johannes Tauler and others, and thought through what the psalmists, Paul, and the other biblical writers had written, he came to see that God was telling him two quite different things: first, what he had done for his human creatures as Creator and Restorer of life, and second, what he expects his human creatures to be and do.

Scripture's Two Messages

Alongside revealing God's plan for his human creatures' performance, his Word also tells readers about God's own activity. Luther found the center of Scripture in the benefits or blessings it conveys, which arise out of God's intervention in the world to rescue sinners from their own missing of his mark, or goal, for human life and to restore them to the kind of human lives he had designed them to live in the first place. God also reminds those who listen to him that he provides them the good things of life. He stands by them in their daily confrontations with evils of all kinds, their own transgressions of the boundaries he has set for the good life as well as the attacks of others and the misfortunes of the world's failing to function as he designed it. Distinguishing the commands and demands of God's plan for life from his promise of deliverance from sin and evil became absolutely essential for the Wittenberg Reformer if readers and hearers were to properly understand Scripture. Only through the appropriate distinction of command and promise could God's message in Scripture be properly absorbed and integrated into his people's lives. If these two fundamental modes of God's discourse with human beings are mixed, confusion results, and neither message is properly heard.

Luther presumed that the biblical metanarrative begins with God's gracious and unconditional gift of life to human creatures as he shaped Adam and Eve from the dust of the earth and breathed into them this gift (Gen. 2:4–7). The creative Word that made the first human beings did not demand but simply bestowed life; God was acting totally apart from any human assistance, contribution, condition, or merit. Along with that creative Word and the core identity as God's child that it bestowed came God's plan or design for truly human living, which set the standards for guiding and evaluating human performance. Like all parents, God has expectations for the children who owe their origin to his giving them life.

Although Luther recognized that biblical usage of the several Hebrew and Greek terms for "law" embraces a number of definitions, he labeled as "law" this design for human life that expresses God's intent and expectations for the attitudes and actions of his human creatures. Likewise, he recognized that "gospel" can embrace everything Mark has to tell about what Jesus said and did (Mark 1:1) and have other shades of meaning. But in distinguishing God's plan for human life from God's gift of human life and especially new life in Christ, Luther asserted narrow definitions for these two terms. He insisted on absolute clarity in using them if sin is to be recognized in all its seriousness and if consciences are to grasp the fullness of the comfort that Christ's death and resurrection give believers.

His *Short Form of the Ten Commandments, the Creed, and the Lord's Prayer* (1520) changed the order of these three core elements of the medieval program for instruction in the faith. Medieval Christians had followed Augustine, arranging these elements according to 1 Corinthians 13:13, beginning with the creed (faith) followed by the Lord's Prayer (hope), and either the Ten Commandments or lists of virtues and vices (love). Luther instead distinguished "three things [that] are necessary to know to be saved: first, what a person should do and not do [Ten Commandments]; second, when he sees that he cannot do or not do these things by his own strength, that he know where to seek and find it, so that he may do and not do these things [creed]; third, that he know how to pursue and gain it [Lord's Prayer]."[1] In his *Prayerbook* of 1522 Luther explained his new ordering of the catechism by noting that sick people must diagnose their illness (law), then seek the remedy (gospel), and as a result want to be healed and work toward that end (daily Christian living).[2] This embraced God's actions undertaken through his Word to make sinners his own, fostering repentance, trust, and new obedience.

Writing for his colleagues on the committee that composed the Formula of Concord in 1576–77, Jakob Andreae defined the law in this strict sense as "a divine teaching which gives instruction regarding what is right and God-pleasing and condemns everything that is sin and contrary to God's will." He defined gospel in the strict sense as that which "reveals what the human being who has not kept the law and been condemned by it should believe: that Christ has atoned and paid for all sins and apart from any human merit has obtained and won for people the forgiveness of sins, the righteousness which avails before God, and eternal life."[3] Andreae regarded this distinction

1. WA 7:204.13–27.
2. WA 10/2:376.12–377.14; *LW* 43:13.
3. *BSELK* 1248/1249.7–16; *BC* 500.

as "a particularly glorious light," since mixing or confusing law and gospel "obscures the merit of Christ and robs troubled consciences of the comfort that they otherwise have in the holy gospel when it is preached clearly and purely. With the help of this distinction these consciences can sustain themselves in their greatest spiritual struggles against the terror of the law."[4]

Penance and Repentance

In the 1510s Luther slowly sorted out these two orienting messages as he interpreted the Psalms and the Pauline Epistles, particularly Romans and Galatians. On a practical level, his struggle took place within the context of his pastoral concerns about the use of the sacrament of penance. In his personal experience, he gleaned only discouragement and despair from the sacrament's insistence on enumeration of mortal sins to qualify oneself for forgiveness. Its prescription of his performance of satisfactions for the completion of his deliverance from the punishments for sin crushed him. Luther's personal crisis that moved him toward his redefinition of being Christian sprang from his inability to find peace through the medieval system that ultimately rested on his own contribution to fostering his relationship with God through his own efforts. Particularly important for securing the relationship was the performance of critical sacred acts or ritual activities, centered on attending Mass and performing penance. Luther discovered that God was coming to him and claiming entire responsibility for his identity as child of God. This liberated him from the life-crushing burden he had been suffering. His own unrest reflected, at an intense personal level, a larger disquiet in the population of Germany at the time, a crisis of pastoral care that drove fifteenth-century theologians to make grace ever cheaper to obtain through human effort.[5]

Once Luther realized that the work of salvation was God's work and not his own, his life was transformed. Luther's fear of not enumerating all his mortal sins and his conviction that his performance of the satisfactions demanded after absolution was not pure and sufficient to put him right with God changed to relief and joy. He came to see that his entire relationship with God sprang from and was sustained by the absolution that conveyed forgiveness of sins and all the other benefits won for him by Jesus Christ. Like most of his contemporaries, Luther used one word, *poenitentia*, for the sacrament of penance, general acts of repentance, and the attitude of repentance, the desire to turn from sin to God. From Tauler's circle he had learned that

---

4. *BSELK* 1430/1431.21–30; *BC* 581.
5. Berndt Hamm, *Religiosität im späten Mittelalter: Spannungspole, Neuaufbrüche, Normierungen* (Tübingen: Mohr Siebeck, 2011), esp. 3–40, 244–98.

God's law casts sinners into despair and thus drives them to Christ as the only Savior.[6] Against this background, he presumed in his Ninety-Five Theses of 1517 that "the Christian's entire life is a life of repentance."[7] By the time he composed his catechisms a decade later, his conviction concerning repentance had deepened. He took ever more seriously the mystery of the continuation of sin and evil in the lives of the baptized.

Therefore, his Small Catechism teaches that baptism is one form of God's decisive promise to be the believer's Lord and that it establishes their relationship on the certainty of his saying so. In Paul's description of baptism as the burial of believers' sins and their resurrection to new life in Christ's footsteps (Rom. 6:3–11; cf. Col. 2:11–15), Luther also saw the basis for the Holy Spirit's daily forgiving of sin and restoring of righteousness. Luther wrote, "The old creature in us with all sins and evil desires is to be drowned and die through daily contrition and repentance, and daily a new person is to come forth and rise up to live before God in everlasting righteousness and purity."[8] In Luke 24:45–47 Luther found Jesus's command to bring this message of repentance and the forgiveness of sins to all people. He understood this to happen through the living, active words of God that present his condemnation on the basis of his design for human life and bestow his re-creative liberation from sin and restoration to a life of trust in God and love for neighbor. Thus Luther regarded repentance, involving both rejecting sin and trusting Christ, as the rhythm of the Christian's daily life. It embodied the application of God's law as a standard of evaluation and—for sinners—judgment, and of God's gospel as the liberating power of his forgiveness and restoration of life in trust toward him.

Luther's Definition of Being Human: Sin and Faith

To understand Luther's concept of sin and thus the ways in which the law of God impacts sinners, it is necessary to review his anthropology. Most Christian thinkers have presumed that perfect human righteousness consists in strict obedience to God's law, conformity to his plan for human life, and thus rests ultimately on human performance, even though most have also insisted that this is possible to attain only with some measure of help by

6. Volker Leppin, "Luther's Transformation of Medieval Thought: Continuity and Discontinuity," in *The Oxford Handbook of Martin Luther's Theology*, ed. Robert Kolb, Irene Dingel, and L'ubomír Batka (Oxford: Oxford University Press, 2014), 121–22; Leppin, "Luther's Roots in Monastic-Mystical Piety," in ibid., 55–60.

7. WA 1:233.10–11; LW 31:25.

8. *BSELK* 884/885.14–17; *BC* 360.

God's grace. From reading the psalms and Paul, Luther learned that there are two aspects to human righteousness, quite distinct, in two dimensions of human life. In the vertical relationship with God—that is, in God's sight (which is the determining factor in the reality of human identity and existence)—righteousness, or being God's child, is completely a gift from the Creator and Father. Adam and Eve did not have a probation period in which they had to prove their worthiness; the Creator simply gave them their humanness out of love beyond human fathoming. Luther labeled this gift of our core identity *iustitia aliena*—that is, righteousness from outside ourselves. This righteousness, our identity as God's children, is God's undeserved gift, bestowed unconditionally on the basis of his unfathomable love. On the human side, this righteousness takes form in trust in God and hearkening to his Word.

Luther's understanding of being human placed trust at the heart of humanity—most important, trust in God above all else. As the modern psychologist-philosopher Erik Erikson also held, Luther regarded trust as fundamental to human personhood and personality. Without trust, little is possible in life. Trust in an ultimate and absolute object that anchors our sense of identity, security, and meaning is at the foundation and heart of human living. If that trust is placed in the Creator, as the "source of all good and haven in times of need," then the human being is functioning as God designed humanity to be.[9] This trust, the human side of righteousness in relationship to God, produces *iustitia propria*, righteousness we perform in conformity with God's plan for human life, both in praise and prayer to God and in service and love for others. He later called the former aspect of human identity "passive righteousness" and the latter "active righteousness." The former expresses itself naturally in the latter. Faith becomes active in love. Those who are confident that God regards them as righteous demonstrate that righteousness in their life in his world.

The fall into sin destroyed human righteousness before God and seriously damaged every person's ability to perform active righteousness in this world, although some measure of civil righteousness, or external adherence to God's plan for life, remains, according to Luther. His understanding of unrighteousness or sin reveals the breakdown of human creatures' ability to be all they were designed to be. L'ubomír Batka notes that Luther's adoption of the several biblical words for sin can be seen. Luther understood the Hebrew *pesha'* as "sin," "unrighteousness," or "transgression"; *'awen* as

9. Luther's Large Catechism, explanation of the first article of the creed, *BSELK* 930/931.10–940/941.20; *BC* 386–90.

"unrighteousness in God's sight" or "misdeeds"; *khatta'* as "original sin," the root rejection of God; and *rasha'* as "rude Godlessness, pride and a lack of fear of God, an active self-confidence of one's own righteousness and denial of sin"—evil.[10]

All disobedience against the particulars of God's law arises from the fundamental denial of God's lordship and doubt of his Word that Luther regarded as the root sin, the original sin. Luther's lectures on Genesis 3 in 1535 made this clear. "Satan here attacks Adam and Eve in this way to deprive them of the Word and to make them believe his lie after they have lost the Word and their trust in God. . . . Unbelief is the source of all sins; when Satan brought about this unbelief by driving out or corrupting the Word, the rest was easy for him. . . . The chief temptation was to listen to another word and depart from the word that God had already spoken."[11] Thus, "the fountain from which all sin flows is unbelief, doubt, and abandonment of the Word," which are idolatry, denial of God's truth, the invention of new gods.[12] Luther noted that Eve had not only rejected God's command but also distorted it by adding to it (Gen. 3:3).[13] "When Satan had separated them from and deprived them of God's Word, nothing was not easy for him."[14] "All evils result from unbelief or doubt of the Word and of God."[15] For doubt eradicates the trust that constitutes the foundation of the human relationship to God, who by nature is faithful to his promises.

"Inherited sin" or "root sin" designated for Luther what he also called "original sin," using the medieval term. As with certain other terms, the Wittenberg theologians continued its medieval use as a confession that from the fall of Adam and Eve, humans are born sinful. That universally experienced fact of life, encountered first as a diagnosis, and only then perceived as an accusation by sinners who have turned in on themselves and thus wish to take responsibility for what they are and do, becomes concrete in the failure of all to "fear, love, and trust in God above all else." This failure is the origin of sin every day of life. Luther's colleague Philip Melanchthon agreed: in his 1532 Romans commentary, he defined sin as "the struggle against the first table of the law, the wish not to know God, the lack of fear, love, and trust in God" along with the proper and justifying core of humanness, trust

10. "Luther's Teaching on Sin and Evil," in *The Oxford Handbook of Martin Luther's Theology*, ed. Robert Kolb, Irene Dingel, and L'ubomír Batka (Oxford: Oxford University Press, 2014), 234–43, cf. 233–53.

11. WA 42:110.38–111.3; *LW* 1:147.

12. WA 42:112.20–22; *LW* 1:149.

13. WA 42:116.40–117.14; *LW* 1:154–55.

14. WA 42:111.2–4; *LW* 1:147.

15. WA 42:111.18–25; *LW* 1:147–48.

in God.[16] In treating Psalm 51:5, Luther described original sin by repeating David's words: "Before you [God], I am such a sinner that my nature, my very origin, my conception, is sin, to say nothing of the words, works, thoughts, and life which follow. . . . I am an evil tree and by nature a child of wrath and sin." This "old" Adam must die and decay before Christ can arise completely.[17]

The proper coordination and application of law and gospel accomplish this purpose: "This inherited sin has caused such a deep, evil corruption of nature that reason does not comprehend it," Luther observed. All people notice wrongdoing in others, even if not in themselves. But apart from the Scripture sinners cannot recognize the God whom they are denying and what this denial means for disruption of the perfect functioning of their entire lives. Although the law's crushing power pushes sinners toward the abandonment of false gods, the perception of the root of their problems depends on hearing the gospel and learning to know Jesus Christ as God and Savior.[18]

Therefore, Luther rejected the medieval argument that baptism abolishes original sin; for him, God's forgiveness means that he does not take original sin into consideration in recognizing the reality of the faithful believer's being his child. But original sin does explain for Luther how Christians fail to conform perfectly to God's expectations, both those of the first commandment, which define being human as trusting God, and those of the other commandments, which sketch the performance that our heavenly parent expects from his children.

Luther's students and later followers continued to teach that original sin provoked and caused all other sins. In his Genesis commentary, the seventeenth-century Jena professor Johann Gerhard explicitly criticized the contention of "Scholastics and Jesuits" that human pride had been the original sin. He defined it instead as "doubt of God's Word and unbelief; pride results from doubt and unbelief, and the root and beginning of conversion to God after the fall is faith (Heb. 11:6)."[19] In paradise God's human creatures enjoyed "bliss and the most blessed condition" of the full richness of God's gift; sin placed them under his curse.[20] Satan led them to hate God and abuse other creatures. Nonetheless, human beings are responsible for their sins. Gerhard joined Luther and all his followers in rejecting any suggestion that God is responsible for sin and evil.[21]

16. CR 15:62.
17. WA 18:501.31–502.3; LW 14:169.
18. BSELK 746/747.27–29; BC 311.
19. Commentarius super Genesin (Jena: Steinmann, 1637), 86.
20. Ioannis Gerhardi Loci theologici, ed. Eduard Preus, vol. 2 (Berlin: Schlawitz, 1864), 142a.
21. Ibid., 142b–43a, 144a–47a.

The Uses of the Law

Luther's understanding of the law and its accusation against sinners must be interpreted in light of this anthropological analysis of being human and his understanding of sin. The law's content is well summarized in the Ten Commandments, Luther held. Indeed, early in his career, as he was combating the medieval view that fulfilling divine and ecclesiastical laws contributed in some way to salvation and a similar legalism in his former colleague Andreas Bodenstein von Karlstadt, Luther perceived the same dangerous religious pattern in both scholastic theology and Karlstadt. Both regarded human performance based on the demands of God's law as the key to the relationship between God and human creatures. In this context Luther argued that even the Ten Commandments, which God gave Israel after leading his people out of Egypt in Exodus 20, are binding on gentiles only because they agree with the New Testament and natural law, in which God sets forth his plan for all human life.[22] He later abandoned any emphasis on this point and indeed, for instance in his catechisms, used the Decalogue as the basis for sketching what God expects of his creatures according to his design for human life.

The content of the law is precisely those commands that God gave for all people to observe; this content goes beyond the words of the Ten Commandments or any other specific Bible passages, though it is expressed in Scripture in reliable form. Furthermore, the commands God gives governing specific kinds of action found their place for Luther within the structure of callings that God had created to ensure the proper functioning of human life. In the family, in economic activity, in societal and political relationships, and in the religious life of his people, God had established tasks, roles, and responsibilities for each individual human being. These callings coupled with his commands to direct human performance of the good life.[23]

The law is a good gift of God, Luther taught, for it helps preserve order in the affairs of this world and leads sinners to the despair that prepares them to be drawn to Christ.[24] Some medieval theologians had spoken of "uses" of the law, but such a categorization was not an axiomatic element of scholastic treatments of the law. In 1535 Luther's colleague Philip Melanchthon had fashioned a third "use" of the law while struggling with challenges to the Wittenberg insistence that the law continues to function in the Christian life. That principle had been challenged by one of Melanchthon's and Luther's brightest students, Johann Agricola, who had the impression

---

22. WA 16:371.13–375.29; LW 35:164–66.
23. E.g., WA 36:30.24.
24. WA 40/1:519.5–521.26; LW 26:335–37; cf. WA 36:13.28–14.21.

that the gospel alone works both command and promise in believers' lives. Luther and Melanchthon alike rejected this as a confusion of law and gospel and adamantly maintained that Christians need the disciplining force of God's law, its call to repentance, and its instruction in the details of faithful godly living.[25]

In early 1537 Luther did record his description of two uses of the law in his agenda for the papal council, the Smalcald Articles. First, the law "curbs sin by means of the threat and terror of punishment and also by means of the promise and offer of grace and favor." This has worked with only limited success, he observed. Some—the spiritual equivalent of the "terrible twos"— do the opposite of God's plan simply to assert their own independence from his claims, seeking to establish an identity of their own making. Others take their conformity to the law as grounds for God's necessary acceptance of them, falling into defining their ultimate righteousness in God's sight on the basis of their own performance. "This attitude produces hypocrites and false saints," Luther stated. To this he added "the foremost function or power of the law": "it reveals inherited sin and its fruits. It shows human beings into what utter depths their nature has fallen and how completely corrupt it is."[26]

Melanchthon introduced the expression "third use of the law," defining it as that application of God's law that "pertains to the regenerate," qualifying its use immediately by noting that "insofar as the regenerate have been justified by faith, they are free from the law, . . . that is, from the curse and the condemnation and God's wrath which are set forth in the law." However, they are righteous and sinful at the same time. Thus, the law "points out the remnants of sin, in order that the knowledge of sin and repentance may grow and the gospel also must proclaim Christ in order that faith may grow." Melanchthon also embraced an instructive use of the law for Christians. "The law must be preached to the regenerate to teach them certain works in which God wills that we practice obedience." "When human reason is not directed by God's Word, it is very likely to lack something." The input of the law is necessary, because the justified are indeed made righteous in forgiveness so that they may live in obedience to God.[27] The Formula of Concord reiterated Melanchthon's position. In addition to maintaining external discipline and bringing the disobedient to recognition of their sins, the law "is also used

25. Timothy J. Wengert, *Law and Gospel: Philip Melanchthon's Debate with John Agricola of Eisleben over Poenitentia* (Grand Rapids: Baker, 1997).

26. *BSELK* 750/751.1–21; *BC* 311–12.

27. *CR* 21:719; Philip Melanchthon, *Loci communes 1543*, trans. J. A. O. Preus (St. Louis: Concordia, 1992), 74.

when those who have been born anew through God's Spirit, converted to the Lord, and had the veil of Moses removed for them, live and walk in the law. . . . The Holy Spirit, who is given and received not through the law but through the proclamation of the gospel, Galatians 3 [vv. 2, 14], renews the heart. Thereafter, the Holy Spirit uses the law to instruct the reborn and to show and demonstrate to them in the Ten Commandments what is the acceptable will of God, Romans 12 [v. 2] and in which good works, which God prepared beforehand, they are supposed to walk, Ephesians 2 [v. 10]."[28] In the Christian life the law continues to discipline sinful desires and to call to daily repentance, but it also supplies instruction for those in the daily struggle with sinful temptation.

Luther did not use the phrase "use of the law" frequently and did not develop a formal third use or employ that terminology. But from his first postil onward, and particularly after visiting rural and town congregations in the formal Saxon visitation in 1527 and 1528, he frequently commented in sermons on the positive instruction of the law as well as on its negative message as a call to repentance.[29] In his 1535 A Simple Way to Pray, he commented, "I divide each commandment into four parts. . . . That is, I think of each commandment as, first, instruction, which is really what it is intended to be, and I consider what the Lord demands of me so earnestly. Second, I turn it into a thanksgiving; third, a confession; and fourth, a prayer."[30]

Examples of his giving positive instruction in Christian behavior abound, as do corresponding critiques of the sinful behavior that he encountered in Wittenberg or observed in reports from afar. "A man is to live, speak, act, hear, suffer and die for the good of his wife and child, a wife for the husband, the children for the parents, the servants for their master, the masters for their servants, the secular authorities for their subjects, the subjects for the secular authorities, every person for other people, even for enemies, so that one is the other's hand, mouth, eye, foot, even heart and mind," Luther wrote in his model sermon for the first Sunday in Advent in 1522.[31] Perhaps more frequently the positive and negative are intertwined. In his Small Catechism, he explains that "You are not to kill" means that we are "to fear and love God so that we neither endanger nor harm the lives of our neighbors but instead help and support them in all of life's needs."[32] The Large Catechism's comment focuses, for example, more specifically:

28. *BSELK* 1442/1443.31–33/27–30; *BC* 587.
29. *BSELK* 1444/1445.17–1448/1449.21; *BC* 587–89.
30. *WA* 38:364.28–365.3; *LW* 43:200.
31. *WA* 10/1.2:41.7–14; *LW* 75:44.
32. *BSELK* 864/865.13–18/25–34; *BC* 352.

Many people, although they do not actually commit murder, nevertheless curse others and wish such frightful things on them that, if they were to come true, they would soon put an end to them. . . . Therefore, God wishes to remove the root and source that embitters our heart toward our neighbor. He wants to train us to hold this commandment always before our eyes as a mirror in which to see ourselves, so that we may be attentive to his will and, with heartfelt confidence and prayer in his name, commit whatever wrong we suffer to God. . . . Thus we may learn to calm our anger and have a patient, gentle heart, especially toward those who give us cause to be angry, namely, our enemies.[33]

Such words could both accuse and instruct. Perhaps Luther recognized that no matter how the one who is presenting elements of God's plan for human life to others intends hearers to receive it, its impact on them—or its function in their hearts and minds—may be quite different from the speaker's intent. What we offer as instruction may be heard as accusation, or our accusations may only curb people into outwardly proper behavior without effecting repentance at all.

While Melanchthon and Luther were convinced that the law "always accuses," because of the mystery of sin's continuation in the lives of the faithful, Luther realized that the accusation is not always heard.[34] Nonetheless, he asserted that the law crushes even those who do not feel guilty, because it keeps hammering away at the sensitivity that all have to the absence of the true God in their lives. God reveals his will for his human creatures and his wrath that functions as a "thunderbolt of God, by means of which he destroys both the open sinner and the false saint and . . . drives them into despair." He further compared this action of the law to "a hammer that breaks a rock in pieces" (Jer. 23:29). Although Luther certainly viewed himself and all other sinners as guilty before God for not observing his law, he emphasized the fear, even terror, that they feel when they notice that things are falling apart, as cracks open up in their lives. That terror may spring from the sinner's being a victim of "war, pestilence, poverty, and shame," along with being a perpetrator of transgressions against God's law.[35] In the end Luther brought his hearers and readers to confront their guilt. When the law puts its claim on the conscience, every believer is vulnerable. The fulfilling of the law is never perfect and complete in Christians' lives, the Wittenberg theologians contended, because "all that is done apart from faith is sin" (Rom. 14:23), and faith is always incomplete.

33. *BSELK* 996/997.2–14; *BC* 411.
34. Melanchthon's phrase in the Apology of the Augsburg Confession, *BSELK* 336/337.4–9; 378/379.3–6; *BC* 148; 166.
35. WA 36:15.30–16.25.

The mystery of the continuation of sin and evil in believers' lives means that even their hearts are not totally trusting in God above all else. Therefore, the preacher exercised his pastoral sensitivities and told the Wittenberg congregation, "In this situation a person must grasp the promise, and so that you do not fall under his justice, do not leave it with the law, for whoever denies the gospel must thrash about in the hope that God does have a gospel, that he will not play with you according to the standards of justice, but rather will deal with me on the basis of grace for Christ's sake, that he forgives you all that you have failed to do out of grace, and that he will give you what you cannot do."[36] When he edited the sermon for publication, Luther's amanuensis Georg Rörer moved beyond the notes taken as Luther preached: "See to it that you grasp the promise and not let the law gain the upper hand and rule in your conscience. That will bring you under judgment if you deny the gospel. You must cast yourself upon and grasp the word of grace or the gospel of the forgiveness of sins."[37]

Luther analyzed the social (or political) and instructional functions of God's law less than its crushing or theological function. He left its political function largely to secular authorities. His sermons and catechisms[38] are filled with examples of the law's instructional use, both in positive exposition of what God expects in every sphere of life from his human creatures and in negative criticism of what has gone wrong with the human performance. The latter instruction functions, of course, as accusation as well. The fact that the law functions apart from the intended use may explain why Luther did not indulge in extensive treatment of its uses.

The Gospel

Although the proclamation of God's providing and preserving love as he demonstrates it within the structures of creation played a prominent role in Luther's preaching and teaching,[39] his definition of the gospel in the strict sense focused alone on Jesus Christ and the Holy Spirit's delivery of Christ's "benefits," the new life won through Christ's death and resurrection. Luther could label his theology "a theology of the cross."[40] Matthias Flacius Illyricus,

36. WA 36:22.30–23.12.
37. WA 36:41.37–42.21.
38. E.g., his Small Catechism, both in its exposition of the Decalogue and of the Table of Christian Callings, BSELK 862–71, 894–99; BC 351–54, 365–67; and in the Large Catechism's treatment of the Decalogue, BSELK 912–1049; BC 386–431.
39. E.g., cf. his treatment of the first article of the creed, Small Catechism, BSELK 870/871; BC 354–55; and Large Catechism, BSELK 1050–55; BC 432–33.
40. WA 1:362.15–19; LW 31:53.

one of the most intellectually gifted of Luther's and Melanchthon's students, if also one of the most controversial, reinforced this simple point in his most enduring contribution, the initiation of modern efforts to construct a biblical hermeneutic.[41] Flacius titled his discussion of hermeneutics *The Key to the Sacred Scripture* (*Clavis Scripturae sacrae*, 1567). His key to all of the biblical text was Jesus Christ, as redeemer of sinners, presented to readers and hearers within the framework of distinguishing the law that prescribes human action and the gospel that delivers God's saving action.[42] Scripture revealed many things, but above all its witness to Christ as the Lord and Savior of the faithful stood at the center of God's revelation: he inspired the biblical text to make sinners wise regarding their salvation in and through Christ and thus to provide comfort for troubled consciences. Flacius faithfully followed his mentors, Luther and Melanchthon, in placing Christ as Savior at the center of God's message for his fallen human creatures.

Luther's treatment of the story of God's restoration of the relationship between himself and his human creatures embraced the incarnation of the Second Person of the Trinity—Jesus's perfect life, suffering, and ascension—but at the heart of the delivery of humankind from sin and evil stood, for him, Christ's death and resurrection. The Lamb of God takes away the sin of the world (John 1:29). In his death Christ dealt with our sin; in his resurrection he restored our righteousness (Rom. 4:25; 1 Cor. 15:3–5).[43] In explaining the distinction of law and gospel to the Wittenberg congregation in 1532, Luther commented that the person who is being turned from sin and the law to the gospel believes that Christ "is truly God's lamb, who takes away the sin of the world, reconciles his heavenly Father, and freely gives eternal righteousness, life, and salvation to all who believe, totally without condition, out of grace."[44] His defining the gospel continued:

> The gospel or faith is something that does not demand our works or tell us what to do, but tells us to receive, to accept a gift, so that we are passive, that is, that God promises and says to you: "this and that I impart to you. You can

41. As asserted by Wilhlem Dilthey, *Die Entstehung der Hermeneutik* (1924), in *Gesammelte Schriften*, 3rd ed. (Göttingen: Vandenhoeck & Ruprecht, 1980–), 3:324–25; and Hans-Georg Gadamer, "Logik oder Rhetorik? Nochmals zur Frühgeschichte der Hermeneutik," *Archiv für Begriffsgeschichte* 20 (1976): 7–16.

42. *Clavis Scriptvrae S., seu, De sermone sacrarum literarum . . . Pars prima . . .* , and *Altera pars Clavis Scriptvrae . . .* (Basel: Paul Quiecum, 1567); see esp. Rudolf Keller, *Der Schlüssel zur Schrift: Die Lehre vom Wort Gottes bei Matthias Flacius Illyricus* (Hannover: Lutherisches Verlagshaus, 1984), 11, 120–27, 157–61.

43. See the Lutheran section of chap. 3 below.

44. WA 36:36.13–21.

do nothing for it; you have done nothing for it, but it is my doing." Just as in baptism, I did nothing; it is not of my doing in any way. It is God's doing, and he says to me, "Pay attention. I baptize you and wash you of all your sins. Accept it, it is yours." That is what it means to receive a gift. This is the distinction of law and gospel. Through the law a demand is made for what we should do. It presses for our activity for God and the neighbor. In the gospel we are required to receive a gift. . . . The gospel is pure gift, freely bestowed, salvation.[45]

An analogy from the sixteenth-century political world served to emphasize the unconditionality of God's gift. In the feudal system of the time (comparable to what twentieth-century scholars discovered in the ancient Near Eastern suzerainty covenants), Luther found his illustration. When a prince bestows property on a noble, the noble has done nothing to compel his superior to give this gift. When the noble goes to serve his lord, however, he acts, doing something for the prince.[46]

Through five centuries Luther's followers have continued to rely on the language of the distinction of law and gospel, applying it in their differing situations in different ways. Some Lutherans have criticized the distinction, because they have failed to recognize how lively and dynamic Luther's and Melanchthon's actual usage of it was. Not intended as a straitjacket or an automatic formula that applies one pattern to every homiletical or pedagogical presentation of God's Word, it is intended to function as a diagnostic tool for assessing the human problems and divine solution across the spectrum of experiences that Christians encounter in conversation with others. It asks why the person (or persons) with whom we are in conversation is asking the question being posed or is puzzled or troubled by the situation at hand. It aids in searching the Scriptures for the proper words to address the problem immediately at hand. The distinction of law and gospel prepares believers to share both God's call for repentance and his gift of forgiveness, life, and salvation. It applies both God's plan for human performance and God's magnificent deliverance from sin and the gift of new life in Christ's footsteps to the grand variety of experiences of human life in this world.

Law and Gospel in the Reformed Tradition

One of the most interesting and significant doctrinal points for understanding the relationship between Lutheran and Reformed theology is the

45. WA 36:14.22–32.
46. WA 36:14.8–15.29; 36:34.5–10, 22–29.

connection between law and gospel. It is here that Reformed dependence on Luther's thinking can be very clearly discerned but also where its independence from him is very noticeable. Certainly, as we note in the chapter on justification and sanctification, there is considerable overlap between Lutherans and Reformed on issues of personal salvation, particularly in the emphasis on the need for faith and repentance. But there are also differences, and these are most noticeable in the understanding of the law. This was perhaps inevitable, given the complexity of connecting the biblical teaching on justification with what the New Testament mandates, particularly in Paul's Letters, for Christians to show forth their identity in Christ in public, practical ways.

The role of the law is also an important topic for Christians as they think of their position within society as a whole. Indeed, it is set to become more so in the coming years, as the outward values of Western society depart further and further from the traditional norms that were so profoundly shaped by Christianity and even come to stand in stark and militant opposition to such. In the world that is emerging before us, the question of ethics, specifically the question of what Christian behavior is to look like and by what criteria it is to be assessed, is going to be crucial. The question of sanctification (see chap. 5) and the role of the law are the two most obvious theological places where this needs to be discussed.

Before addressing the connection between law and gospel, however, it is worthwhile noting the framework within which the Reformed discussed Old Testament law.

The Divisions of the Law

The Reformed typically divide Old Testament law into three categories: moral, ceremonial, and civil. The moral law is embodied in the Decalogue. The Reformed regard this as teaching transcendent moral truths applicable to human beings in general and not simply to the specific people of Israel prior to the coming of Christ.

In addition to this, there is also the ceremonial law pertaining to the sacrificial system and pointing both to Christ and to certain moral obligations. Finally, there is the civil law pertaining to the political administration of ancient Israel. Of these three divisions, the latter two have been abrogated with the coming of Christ.[47] The ceremonial law in particular found its fulfillment in Christ, because its sacrifices and rituals were types of his life and work.

---

47. See Westminster Confession of Faith 19.

They pointed forward to him, giving the people of Israel indication of God's overall redemptive plan.[48]

This way of distinguishing aspects of the law under the Old Testament is not original with the Reformed or with the Reformation. For example, Thomas Aquinas distinguished moral, ceremonial, and judicial elements in his discussion of law in the *Summa theologiae*.[49] It served the Reformers, as it did Aquinas, as a means of carefully delineating the nature of the relationship and the continuities between the Old Testament epoch and that of the New.

Nevertheless, despite the fact that the ceremonial law pointed to Christ in a peculiarly powerful manner, the Reformed understand the whole system of Mosaic law in terms of God's promise to Abraham as fulfilled in Christ. On that level, there is no law-gospel antithesis: the law points toward the need and the advent of Christ. Calvin makes this clear in the *Institutes*:

> The Law was not superadded about four hundred years after the death of Abraham in order that it might lead the chosen people away from Christ, but, on the contrary, to keep them in suspense until his advent; to inflame their desire, and confirm their expectation, that they might not become dispirited by the long delay. By the Law, I understand not only the Ten Commandments, which contain a complete rule of life, but the whole system of religion delivered by the hand of Moses. Moses was not appointed as a Lawgiver, to do away with the blessing promised to the race of Abraham; nay, we see that he is constantly reminding the Jews of the free covenant which had been made with their fathers, and of which they were heirs; as if he had been sent for the purpose of renewing it.[50]

Thus, we might say that the whole of the law has an ultimately gracious purpose: it is designed to point to Christ. But we should add that certain elements of this—specifically the ceremonial and the civic aspects—were fulfilled and/or abrogated at the coming of Christ and the transformation of Israel from a political and ethnic entity into a spiritual body. The coming of Christ changes the nature of the relationship of God's people to God's law.

The moral law, however, remains in place because this reflects the character of God and also the obligations of men and women made in his image. The coming of Christ does not disrupt that, and Christ's fulfillment of the terms of the moral law does not mean that the moral law has no further relevance to the Christian. The Westminster Confession, chapter 19, summarizes the Reformed position:

48. See Belgic Confession 25.
49. See *Summa theologiae* 1a2ae.99.4.
50. Calvin, *Institutes* II.vii.1.

1. God gave to Adam a law, as a covenant of works, by which he bound him and all his posterity to personal, entire, exact, and perpetual obedience, promised life upon the fulfilling, and threatened death upon the breach of it, and endued him with power and ability to keep it.

2. This law, after his fall, continued to be a perfect rule of righteousness; and, as such, was delivered by God upon Mount Sinai, in ten commandments, and written in two tables: the first four commandments containing our duty towards God; and the other six, our duty to man.

Thus, the Decalogue, as an express summary of the principles and obligations of the moral law, remains in place.

To this remaining moral law the Reformed assign three functions. The first use of the law is that of exposing sin. The second is that of restraining wickedness. The third is that of providing moral principles for guiding the life of the Christian believer.

Of these three, it is the first and the third uses that are of most significance. The second use of the law, that of restraining wickedness, is often seen by the Reformed as providing the basic principles by which civil authorities should frame their law codes. The Westminster Confession (19.4) refers to the principle of general equity, which underlay the civil laws of Old Testament Israel, and clearly regards this as still relevant for the framing of civil law codes, though it is careful to avoid giving precise case-law examples of what that might look like. The Old Testament civil law in terms of its details may have been specifically intended for the ethnic nation of Israel, but it was built on general principles that apply to all good governments everywhere.

Law and Gospel: The First Use of the Law

On the first use of the law, that of revealing sin, there is no real disagreement between the Lutherans and the Reformed. Indeed, Zacharias Ursinus, in his commentary on the Heidelberg Catechism, makes this his principal point in the prolegomena: "The doctrine of the church consists of two parts: the Law, and the Gospel; in which we have comprehended the sum and substance of the sacred Scriptures. The law is called the Decalogue, and the gospel is the doctrine concerning Christ the mediator, and the free remission of sins, through faith."[51] By setting this distinction at the start of the commentary,

---

51. *The Commentary of Dr. Zacharias Ursinus on the Heidelberg Catechism*, trans. G. W. Willard (Cincinnati: Elm Street, 1888), 2.

Ursinus is making a clear statement: the law-gospel distinction is foundational to understanding the Christian faith.

That this foundational doctrine is common to both Lutherans and Reformed should not be a surprise. First, there is the obvious and unique significance of Luther for all magisterial Protestants as an authority and source on the matter of justification and its concomitant hermeneutical and theological principles. Second, given their shared anthropological and hamartiological understanding, both traditions see the law as a vital component in convicting individuals of the seriousness of their situation before God and of the need for divine grace. Human beings, fallen in Adam, are incapable of performing good works that would merit salvation, yet they are supremely confident that they are capable of so doing. The law thus acts as a means of demonstrating that they are mistaken.

We should note, however, that this agreement on the first use of the law is not agreement on its priority and relative importance. For the Reformed, it is the third use, which encourages and guides the behavior of the believer, that is the most prominent.[52] For this reason, the so-called law-gospel dialectic is present in Reformed thought in terms of its substance, but it plays a much less prominent role for the Reformed than for Lutherans.

Calvin deals with the division and use of the law in his *Institutes*, book 2, after discussing the fall of Adam and the consequent impotence of the will in matters of salvation. In terms reminiscent of Luther's response to Erasmus's claim that the law reveals ability, Calvin asserts rather that the law simply shows us our responsibility.[53] The fact that we are required to act in certain ways does not imply that we have the power so to do. The law simply reminds us of our obligations, while giving no power toward their fulfillment.

In showing us our responsibility, the law also reveals to us our sin. Because the law exposes us to what we are supposed to do, we become acutely aware that we cannot do it. Indeed, it is a vital part of the process of conviction of sin. Calvin, who always liked to use images connected with vision, such as his famous analogy between the Scriptures and eyeglasses, compared the law to a mirror:

> The Law is a kind of mirror. As in a mirror we discover any stains upon our face, so in the Law we behold, first, our impotence; then, in consequence of it, our iniquity; and, finally, the curse, as the consequence of both. He who has no power of following righteousness is necessarily plunged in the mire of iniquity,

---

52. Louis Berkhof, *Systematic Theology* (Edinburgh: Banner of Truth Trust, 1971), 615; Calvin, *Institutes* II.vii.12.

53. Calvin, *Institutes* II.vii.4–5.

and this iniquity is immediately followed by the curse. Accordingly, the greater the transgression of which the Law convicts us, the severer the judgment to which we are exposed.[54]

Here is the first use of the law stated clearly. It sets before fallen men and women their moral obligation toward God. It shows them who they should be and how they are impotent in themselves to be so. That they can never be such because of their fallen sinful nature is precisely the point, because it thus drives them to despair in themselves. On this point, the Reformed and the Lutherans would have no disagreement.

This brings us to the relationship between this function of the law and the gospel.

The first thing that needs to be clearly understood on this issue is that the antithesis between law and gospel is not that one commands and the other promises. Both law and gospel offer promises; the difference is that the law's promises are conditioned on our obedience, but the latter is unconditional because of the life and work of Jesus Christ.[55] In short, law and gospel offer fundamentally different ways to be justified before God: the one requires works, the other requires faith.

This then leads to a further observation. In the chapter on justification, I note that the Reformed typically placed faith prior to repentance in their understanding of the order of salvation, on the grounds that true repentance assumes faith in Christ, for otherwise it would merely terminate in despair. This has practical implications, in that the preaching of the law in isolation as a necessary means of preparing people to receive God's grace in Christ is thereby excluded. The law in itself does not encourage faith, because it does not present individuals with Christ as an object of faith. It simply demands obedience that the fallen cannot possibly give and reminds them of how desperate their plight is. Mere conviction of sin through exposure to the law is therefore not true repentance, because repentance involves both a turning from our own works to Christ and a dying to self and a turning to newness of life. We might characterize despair at sin brought about simply by the law as remorse or penitence, but that does not involve the turning away from sin and self-righteousness and the turning to Christ in which true biblical repentance

54. Ibid., II.vii.7.

55. Cf. the comment of Bavinck (RD 4:454): "Law and gospel, viewed concretely, do not so much differ in that the law always speaks with a commanding voice and the gospel with a promising voice, for also the law makes promises and the gospel utters admonitions and imposes obligations. But they differ especially in content: the law demands that humans work out their own righteousness, and the gospel invites them to renounce all self-righteousness and to accept the righteousness of Christ and even offers the gift of faith to that end."

consists. Yes, the law exposes sin. But it gives no power to do anything else and offers no hope to the one under conviction.

For the Reformed, the solution to this practical issue is to be found not through theoretical consideration of the concepts of law and gospel but through the manifestation of these in the preaching of the church. Preaching is the primary means by which the Word of God comes to individuals, and this preaching, while assuming the antithesis between law and gospel, has to take account of the fact that biblical repentance is not a function of the law in and of itself. Therefore, the moral demands of the law should never be preached in a way that is isolated from the clear declaration of the gospel promises as manifested and fulfilled in the Lord Jesus Christ. The law's demands and the gospel promise in Christ need to be coordinated, such that the former is always set within the larger context of God's grace as revealed in the latter. Failure to do so will lead to despair, to legalism, or to some combination of the two.

This is one of the main burdens of the famous *Marrow of Modern Divinity*.[56] Asked by Nomista, the legalist participant in the dialogue, if there is a repentance that precedes faith, Evangelista, the exponent of the true Christian gospel, replies as follows:

> Yes indeed, I think there is. As, for example, when a profane, sensual man (who lives as though, with the Sadducees, he did not believe any resurrection of the dead, neither hell nor heaven) is convinced in his conscience, that if he go on in making a god of his belly, and in minding only earthly things, his end shall be damnation; sometimes such a man thereupon changes his mind, and of a profane man, becomes a strict Pharisee, or (as some call him) a legal professor; but being convinced, that all his own righteousness will avail him nothing, in the case of justification, and that it is only the righteousness of Jesus Christ that is available in that case, then he changes his mind, and, with the apostle, "desires to be found in Christ, not having his own righteousness which is of the law, but that which is through the faith of Christ, even the righteousness which is of God through faith" (Phil. 3:9). Now I conceive, that a man that does this, changes his mind from false ways to the right way, and his heart from evil to good; and so consequently, doth truly repent.[57]

The implications of this passage are clear. The law, standing in antithesis to the gospel, cannot be proclaimed in isolation from the gospel because to do so, even if apparently effective, can only produce a kind of legal repentance that at best leads to a superficial renovation of behavior. The law on its own

56. This is discussed more fully in chap. 5 below.
57. Edward Fisher, *Marrow of Modern Divinity* (Fearn, UK: Christian Focus, 2009), 164.

produces Pharisees. Ironically, this will then fuel a sinful self-righteousness that simply makes the person much worse.

Gospel and Law: The Third Use of the Law

For the Reformed, salvation is by union with Christ, and that union brings about two realities. The first is justification by grace through faith by the imputed righteousness of Christ; the second is sanctification, or the gradual restoration of the image of God in the believer by the work of the Holy Spirit—begun but never completed in this life (see chap. 5 below).

In this context, the first thing to note is that Reformed theology wants to take seriously the typical structure of Paul's Letters. So often when Paul writes, the order is not law-gospel but gospel-law. The identity of the believer logically precedes the ethical obligations of a believer. Because one is in Christ, therefore one is to act in certain ways.

Take, for example, Paul's Letter to the Colossians. The early chapters are clearly motivated by a desire to counter the influence of certain heretical groups that have some kind of contact with the church in Colossae. But the content of those chapters is overwhelmingly positive: this is what Christ has done, and this is who you are as those who identify with Christ by faith. You have died and been raised with him (Col. 2:11–14). This is then followed by specific practical applications. What Paul is doing is arguing from the indicative (what is true for those in Christ) to the imperative (what should characterize their lives as those in Christ). You should forgive each other, be compassionate, kind, meek, and patient (Col. 3:12–13). Paul does not simply operate with a binary opposition of law and gospel, whereby the one drives the individual to despair and the other offers comfort in Christ. The structure of his argument is more complicated than that: Here is what you are in Christ; these thoughts, attitudes, and actions should therefore characterize how you live your lives.

Given this New Testament background, we can perhaps understand some of the peculiar pressure on this and related issues that Protestants faced at the Reformation. Since its inception Protestantism has faced the challenge not only of maintaining the imperative of sanctification but also of describing exactly what sanctification looks like. A number of factors make this complicated. First, there is the fact that salvation is focused on justification by imputation, which detaches it in a significant way from actual good works. Second, sanctification does not progress at the same rate in everybody. Some seem to become godly in a short period of time; others struggle with the same sins for many years. Second, sanctification is not a process whereby there is continual, incremental growth. Christians fall into sin, sometimes very serious sin; the Christian life is not an ongoing story of increasing triumph over temptation.[58] Third, there is the question of identifying the ethical norms by which sanctification is to be judged.

One answer to this last question is that a Christian's sanctification is motivated and shaped by love. This certainly seems to be the position advocated by Luther, for example, in his 1520 treatise *On the Freedom of the Christian Man*. The Christian, in gratitude to God for the freedom of his mercy and grace shown in Christ, responds in gratitude to God by serving him in love and also doing the same for his neighbor.

The strength of this approach is that it preempts any notion that works might be done in order to merit eternal life in some kind of legalistic way. Indeed, the emphasis on works as rooted in part in the joy of the believer's new life in Christ is an important part of the Reformed understanding of good works.[59]

The problem with this approach is not only that it weakens the whole notion of the biblical function of imperatives (why would Paul need to press home the need for good works if they simply flow out of gratitude to God for his work in Christ?) but also that it leaves practical ethics as a rather vague, if not positively subjective, phenomenon. In terms of ethical norms, if the sole guiding principle is love, then this needs to be given specific shape, or else it will rapidly degenerate into a mere sentiment or emotional state.

Paul, of course, never leaves love as such an ethically shapeless concept but rather gives it solid content. Thus, in Ephesians 5 he declares that husbands are to love their wives as Christ loved the church. In that context love clearly has a specific content: it involves the husband giving his life, metaphorically

---

58. See questions 77 and 78 of the Larger Catechism:

Q. 77. Wherein do justification and sanctification differ? A. Although sanctification be inseparably joined with justification, yet they differ, in that God in justification imputeth the righteousness of Christ; in sanctification his Spirit infuseth grace, and enableth to the exercise thereof; in the former, sin is pardoned; in the other, it is subdued: the one doth equally free all believers from the revenging wrath of God, and that perfectly in this life, that they never fall into condemnation; the other is neither equal in all, nor in this life perfect in any, but growing up to perfection.

Q. 78. Whence ariseth the imperfection of sanctification in believers? A. The imperfection of sanctification in believers ariseth from the remnants of sin abiding in every part of them, and the perpetual lustings of the flesh against the spirit; whereby they are often foiled with temptations, and fall into many sins, are hindered in all their spiritual services, and their best works are imperfect and defiled in the sight of God. (*The Westminster Confession of Faith and Larger and Shorter Catechisms with Proof Texts* [Willow Grove, PA: Orthodox Presbyterian Church, 2005])

59. See Heidelberg Catechism 86.

at least but perhaps in some extreme cases literally, for the well-being of his wife. Marital love has a Christlike shape, as Paul's analogy makes clear.

This point is particularly relevant today. "Love" as a term has become utterly debased in our modern society. It is a synonym for sex or an emotion. It is rarely, if ever, considered in terms of specific moral content exhibited in specific actions, and where it is such, it typically serves some sentimental or therapeutic cause. For the Christian, however, this is not an option: Paul's Letters are replete with practical applications, specific practical applications, of what Christian love is to look like.

To do justice to this, the Reformed developed a doctrine of sanctification as the work of the Holy Spirit in the life of the Christian guided by the law of God as the aspirational norm of behavior. This is perhaps most clearly set forth in the structure of the Heidelberg Catechism. Following typical catechetical practice from the Middle Ages, the Heidelberg Catechism contains an exposition of the Decalogue. The placement of this exposition is significant. Of the three sections of the catechism—grief, grace, and gratitude—it is located in the latter. Thus it is intended as the ethical guide and framework for the regenerate Christian life. The catechism describes the good works performed by the believer as follows:

> Q. 91. What are good works? A. Those only which proceed from true faith (Rom. 14:23), and are done according to the Law of God (1 Sam. 15:22; Eph. 2:10), unto His glory (1 Cor. 10:31), and not such as rest on our own opinion (Deut. 12:32; Ezek. 20:18, 20; Isa. 29:13) or the commandments of men (Matt. 15:9).[60]

The law is thus the guide for the Christian in order to avoid both the subjectivity of determining our own ethics and the temptation of simply following human commandments. In the Reformation, these latter would have been the various ceremonies that the Roman Catholic Church had developed over the years without any clear scriptural warrant. Today the danger is more likely to be that our understanding of a good work is shaped by the canons and criteria of the secular world around us.

---

60. Dennison 2:790. Cf. the Second Helvetic Confession 63:
It was said before that the law of God, which is the will of God, prescribes unto us the pattern of good works. And the apostle says, "This is the will of God, even your sanctification, that ye abstain from all uncleanness, and that no man oppress or deceive his brother in any matter" (1 Thess. 4:3, 6). But as for such works and worship of God as are taken up upon our own liking, which St. Paul calls "will—worship" (Col. 2:23), they are not allowed nor liked of God. Of such the Lord says in the gospel, "They worship Me in vain, teaching for doctrine the precepts of men" (Matt. 15:9). (Dennison 2:842)

It is probably the case that, in terms of practical ethics, the Lutherans and the Reformed differ little on most things. A comparison of the exposition of the Decalogue in Luther's Small and Large Catechisms with that found in the Heidelberg Catechism or the Westminster Standards reveals considerable overlap. The two key differences in terms of content would be attitudes toward images and toward the Sabbath, or Lord's Day. The Reformed would typically reject the use of images and affirm the ongoing importance of the Sabbath. Yet the function of the law in its third use is one that distinguishes the two communions.

No doubt the emphasis on the law as an external guide looks legalistic to Lutherans, a means by which works righteousness is being smuggled back in to the salvific equation. This is where the Reformed doctrine of sanctification is important: the Spirit internalizes the law—writes it on the believer's heart—in a manner that makes obedience to its requirements something the believer can and does do. This is part of the order of salvation, grounded in the will of God.[61] It is perhaps not appropriate to refer to this obedience as natural, as that would be too strong a statement and would weaken the notion of struggle, which sanctification still demands within the believer. But it is something that Christians desire and, even as the law goads them with their sin, it does so in a manner designed to allow them to understand how they might enjoy their heavenly Father's approval. Following are some quotations from leading Reformed theologians who make this point.

> The third use of the Law (being also the principal use, and more closely connected with its proper end) has respect to believers in whose hearts the Spirit of God already flourishes and reigns. For although the Law is written and engraven on their hearts by the finger of God, that is, although they are so influenced and actuated by the Spirit, that they desire to obey God, there are two ways in which they still profit in the Law. For it is the best instrument for enabling them daily to learn with greater truth and certainty what that will of the Lord is which they aspire to follow, and to confirm them in this knowledge; just as a servant who desires with all his soul to approve himself to his master, must still observe, and be careful to ascertain his master's dispositions, that he may comport himself in accommodation to them. Let none of us deem ourselves exempt from this necessity, for none have as yet attained to such a degree of

---

61. See the comment in *RD* 3:528: "Inasmuch as the good works in which believers must walk are prepared by God in Christ [Eph. 2:10], faith cannot stop at the forgiveness of sins but reaches out to the perfection that is in Christ, seeks to confirm itself from works as from its own fruits, girds itself with courage and power not only to live in communion with Christ but also to fight under him as king against sin, the world, and the flesh, and to make all things serviceable to the honor of God's name."

wisdom, as that they may not, by the daily instruction of the Law, advance to a
purer knowledge of the Divine will. Then, because we need not doctrine merely,
but exhortation also, the servant of God will derive this further advantage from
the Law: by frequently meditating upon it, he will be excited to obedience, and
confirmed in it, and so drawn away from the slippery paths of sin.[62]

Here we see how Calvin connects the law, the work of the Spirit, and the
responsibility of the believer. The law is internalized through the work of
the Spirit, not simply in pressing its demands on human beings—that is part
of what being made in God's image means anyway—but also in the spiritual
desire and strength to strive to conform to it.

> And this is the main difference between the old covenant of works and the new
> one of grace, that in that the Lord did only require the fulfilling of the condi-
> tion prescribed, but in this he promiseth to effect it in them himself with whom
> the covenant is made. And without this spiritual efficacy, the truth is, the new
> covenant would be as weak and unprofitable, for the end of a covenant (the
> bringing of us and binding of us to God), as the old.[63]

Here Owen makes the same point but in terms of the difference between the
old covenant and the new, specifically with reference to Jeremiah 31:31–32 and
Hebrews 8:9–11. The externality of the old is replaced by an internal spiritual
dynamic in the new. This is not legalism, for it is rooted in the very nature of
the regenerate Christian. The believer acts in (albeit imperfect) conformity
with the law because of the indwelling of the Holy Spirit. This has historical
significance, in that God promised in the Old Testament that this internal-
izing of the law through the Holy Spirit would be a sign of the fulfillment of
his great saving purposes for his people. Thus, this is a characteristic of the
Christian life in the church age. It also has immediate existential significance,
because it is the lived, experienced reality for the believer.

This spiritual principle also has a christological reference that connects to
the role of Christ as king.

> And as Christ doth . . . suppress all other governors but himself in the heart
> of a believer, so doth he raze out and deface all other laws, and writes his own
> there, according to his promise (Jer. 31:33) and makes them pliable and willing
> to do and suffer his will; and that because it is his will. So that the mind and will
> of Christ, laid down in his word, and manifested in his works, is not only the

---

62. Calvin, *Institutes* II.vii.12.
63. John Owen, *The Works of John Owen, D.D.*, ed. William H. Goold, 17 vols. (Edinburgh:
T&T Clark, 1862), 10:236–37.

rule of a believer's obedience, but also the reason of it, as I once heard a godly minister say in the pulpit; so that he does not only do that which is Christ's will, but he does it because it is his will.[64]

Thus, the law stands as something in line with the believer's new nature that reflects the fact that Christ is king and rules over the believer's life. To be united to Christ is to be united to him as Mediator, with its prophetic, priestly, and kingly aspects. The kingly dimension has an existential impact, making Christ king of the heart from which he rules the conscience and the moral will. Yes, the old nature still fights, and sanctification is a struggle. But the law's function is a positive one: goading and guiding the one who loves its principle by the power of the indwelling Spirit toward good works regulated by Christ's law. We might draw an analogy to a household: it is not legalism that makes a son respect his father and act accordingly. It is a result of his identity as son. To respect his father is to act in accordance with who the son actually is.[65]

This is important for understanding why the Reformed conception of the third use of the law is not a type of legalism. Legalism involves an external imposition of law and the principle that obedience to the law is what merits salvation. Under the kingship of Christ, the law is written in the heart of the believer, and the Holy Spirit gives the desire and power to obey, to a certain and still imperfect extent, the provisions of the law. For the Reformed, this is simply a faithful exposition of the theology of Paul and of the logic of his letters.

Two Practical Implications of the Third Use

In concluding this topic, it is worth noting two particular ways in which the law leads to significant practical differences between Lutherans and Reformed. First, the second commandment (in the Reformed numbering of the Decalogue) is understood as forbidding the use of any images of Christ or any pictorial representation of God. This is discussed in more depth in chapter 8, but the central point is this: the literal stipulation of the command still applies, so the aesthetics found in a Roman Catholic or Lutheran church are absent from their Reformed equivalent. Today, of course, many Reformed churches meet in buildings that were not purposely built for Reformed worship, so ideal and reality may differ.

The second is the fourth commandment, that on Sabbath observance. This became a particular hallmark of Reformed and Presbyterian church life. The

---

64. Fisher, *Marrow of Modern Divinity*, 251.
65. See *RD* 4:87–88.

Heidelberg Catechism in question 103 clearly marks off Sunday as a day on which the absolute priority for the Christian is church attendance for hearing the Word, partaking of the sacraments, prayer, and giving of alms. The Westminster Standards are somewhat more detailed and prescriptive, in part due to the way in which Sabbatarianism came to function as a distinctive marker within English church life in the latter part of the sixteenth century, inspired in part by Nicholas Bownde's *The Doctrine of the Sabbath* (1595). By the time of the Westminster Assembly, an elaborate and strict Sabbatarianism was a hallmark of many English Reformed clergy, as exemplified in the extremely detailed prescriptions for behavior on Sunday as laid out in the Larger Catechism questions 116 to 121.[66] But in both traditions, the imperative nature of some form of Lord's Day observance is quite clear.

Conclusion

The Reformed are indebted to Luther for his sharp articulation of the antithesis of the law and gospel in salvation. The law demands and convicts where the gospel promises and fulfills. As with justification, there is a basic foundational agreement between both traditions on this point. Where the Reformed differ is in the articulation of the third use of the law, which has a much more robust role for them than within the Lutheran tradition. The third use is the key to the practical expression of Christian identity.

To a Lutheran this might look like legalism or pietism. To the Reformed it is no more than the teaching of the New Testament, where the logic of Paul's Letters in particular is to move from being in Christ to acting like Christ, from the indicative to the imperative. Those imperatives have a shape—specifically the shape of conformity to the Decalogue. The Reformed avoid legalism by connecting this to the inward work of the Holy Spirit and the overall structure of the order of salvation.

In an era like ours, when relativism rules and there is significant ethical chaos in the wider world, there is a need for a clear and coherent Christian ethic rooted both in salvation in Christ and in the moral framework provided by the Bible. Reformed theology, by giving specific shape and content to the believer's response to salvation and identity in Christ, offers a significant means of meeting this challenge.

---

66. Strict Sabbatarianism is not as universally observed in practice in modern Presbyterian and Reformed churches as would have been the case even a hundred years ago. Changing patterns of life and the rise of Sunday entertainment play a part. Some, however (including the author), find the provisions particularly of the Larger Catechism to go beyond that warranted by Scripture and, where appropriate, seek permission from their presbyteries not to teach such a strict view.

3

The Person and Work of Christ

At the very center of the Christian faith stands the figure of Jesus Christ. The question of his identity is the most important question any Christian—in fact, any human being—can address. The orthodox Christian belief that he is God manifest in the flesh, the very incarnation of the God of Israel, is audacious in its claims and stupendous in its implications. And the church, from its very inception in the book of Acts, has focused its beliefs, its piety, and its practices on him.

The basic understanding of who Christ is was hammered out in the early church. The Councils of Nicaea (325) and Constantinople (381) established the parameters for discussions of his person in relation to God the Father and God the Holy Spirit. The Council of Chalcedon (451) set the framework for understanding how the divine nature and the human nature in the incarnation should be understood. The Reformers had no desire to tamper with the creedal Christology of the ancient church. They saw themselves as catholic Christians, faithfully teaching the biblical traditions of the church in this matter and thereby passing the truth on to the next generation.

Nevertheless, Christology became a serious point of contention between the Lutheran and Reformed traditions and remains so today. If the two communions are ever to come to a more sympathetic understanding of each other on, for example, the Lord's Supper, then they must wrestle with the differences that exist between them on Christ and come to appreciate the concerns that drive them to their different positions, even as they seek to be faithful to the Bible's teaching as expressed in the great catholic creeds of the ancient church to which both adhere.

Christology in the Lutheran Tradition

In 1528 Martin Luther issued his *Confession on the Lord's Supper*, in which he engaged the criticism of his understanding of Christ's presence in the Lord's Supper in detail. He concluded this work with a simple confession of his faith outlined, according to the Apostles' Creed, as a summary of biblical teaching. It affirmed his belief that "the second person in the Godhead, the Son, alone became a true human being, conceived by the Holy Spirit without human cooperation, and was born of the pure, holy Virgin Mary as of a real natural mother." Luther rejected the Apollinarian heresy, writing "that God the Son assumed not only a body without a soul . . . but also the soul, that is, full, complete humanity and was born the promised true seed or child of Abraham and David and Mary's son by nature, in every way and form a true human being, as I am myself and every other human being, except that he came without sin." He rejected Nestorianism by acclaiming Mary as the "mother of God" as decreed by the Council of Ephesus (431) and continued with a summary of Christ's atoning work.[1]

The Hypostatic Union

Throughout his teaching career, Luther's Christology exhibited his commitment to the formulations of the ancient councils, particularly Chalcedon (451), and to his understanding of its explanation that the divine and human natures of Christ are so united in the one person who is both the Second Person of the Trinity and Jesus of Nazareth (hypostatic union). He understood that in this union, although each nature retains its own integrity and the characteristics of one nature never become the possession of the other, they do nevertheless share these characteristics (*communicatio idiomatum*). To posit any separation of the two natures, which always remain distinct, destroys the unity of the person of the God-man and therefore undermines the proclamation of salvation through him.

This confession reflected what Luther was preaching quite apart from the sacramental controversies that led him to refine his understanding of the hypostatic union of the divine and human natures of Christ. Such a presentation of the Savior's person had been a natural part of his proclamation of the incarnation in the 1520s. In 1522 he had prepared a homiletic treatment of Hebrews 1:1–12. On verse 2 he explained what it meant that Jesus is called "the Son of God": "Christ is true God and a true human being, and sometimes Scripture and he himself speak [of him] according to his divine nature,

1. WA 26:500.33–501.35; *LW* 37:361–62.

sometimes according to his human nature. When he says, 'Before Abraham was, I am,' John 8[:58], that is said about the deity. But when he says to James and John, 'To sit at my right hand and my left is not mine to grant,' Matthew 20[:23], that is spoken of his humanity, just as he could not help himself on the cross." Luther continued with the example of Jesus's saying that he did not know the hour of the end of all things as an example of his humanity speaking. Having established the integrity of each nature, he continued with an affirmation of the hypostatic union of the two natures, inseparable but ever distinct, in the one person Jesus Christ.

> We must believe that Christ is over all things not only according to the deity but also according to the humanity. Thus all creatures are subject and subjugated to Christ the human being. As God he creates all things, but as a human being he creates nothing, and yet all are subject to him. . . . Thus Christ is our God and our Lord. . . . Although the two natures are distinct, there is one person, so that all Christ does or suffers God has certainly done and suffered even though only one nature is encountered [in a given action].[2]

This view guided Luther's proclamation to the end of his life. In 1537 he treated John 1 from the pulpit. "God himself took on this poor, feeble, and corrupt human nature. . . . The dear fathers, I say, were amazed that the divine majesty assumed every aspect of this bag of worms, our human nature, except sin and guiltiness of death. He ate, drank, slept, woke up, etc., but he was not born in sin as we were."[3] Luther told the Wittenberg congregation,

> The same Word [of God], which became human, Mary breastfed and carried in her arms as any other mother does her child. He came to human beings, lived and dwelt among them. Thus it was no spirit but a true human being, 'taking the form of a servant,' as Saint Paul says [Phil. 2:7], 'being born in human likeness,' with regard to seeing, hearing, speaking, eating, drinking, sleeping, and walking, so that all who saw and heard him were constrained to confess and say that he was a true, natural human being.[4]

He continued by paraphrasing John's "He dwelt among us" (1:14). The evangelist was saying that Christ, in contrast to Gabriel, who quickly disappeared after giving Mary the news of her impending pregnancy, "remained with us according to his human nature, which was inseparably united with the divine nature since his incarnation. Into his thirty-fourth year he ate and drank with

---

2. WA 10/1.1:148.19–150.24; *LW* 75:259–60.
3. WA 46:626.20–29; *LW* 22:104.
4. WA 46:633.2–8; *LW* 22:112.

us, was angry and sad, prayed and wept. He accomplished his Father's mission, suffered persecution and death finally at the hands of his own people. Thus the Jews crucified the true Son of God, the Lord of glory, and we saw his blood oozing forth and flowing to the ground." This teaching, Luther observed "is our greatest consolation, and through it we become God's children." Whether the incarnation glorifies God or was a disgrace is an irrelevant question since salvation and comfort depend on his becoming human flesh.[5]

In 1541 Luther asserted that he was anchoring his Christology in the biblical report of Jesus's words and deeds, concluding that the decision in Ephesus rejecting what the council viewed as Nestorius's teaching was scripturally grounded. He summarized the biblical teaching repeated at the council:

> Mary is the true natural mother of the child called Jesus Christ and she is the true natural mother of God and bearer of God. Whatever else can be said of children's mothers, such as breast-feeding, bathing, feeding [can be said of her as the mother of the person who is God and human]—that Mary breastfed God, rocked God to sleep, prepared broth and soup for God, etc. For God and this human being are one person, one Christ, one Son, one Jesus, not two Christs, not two sons, not two Jesuses.[6]

Luther recognized the paradoxical nature of the incarnation as he explicated John 3:16.

> It sounds plausible that the Son of Man might be crucified, but that he should bestow eternal life does not seem reasonable. It seems just as incongruous that God's Son should die and give his life for the life of the world. But we must bear in mind that when we speak of Christ, we are thinking of his two natures in one person and that what is ascribed to the two natures individually is really comprehended in one person. Thus, I can very properly say that the Son of man created heaven and earth, just as I say that the Son of God is the creator of heaven and earth. We dare not follow the Nestorians, . . . who alleged that only Mary's Son, not God's Son, died for us. . . . "God gave his Son for the world." . . . When Christ was delivered to Pilate to be crucified, . . . he [Pilate] took hold of the hand not only of the man Jesus but also of the Son of God, whom he crucified.

Luther cited 1 Corinthians 2:8 to ground his proclamation that "it was God's Son who was conceived by the Virgin Mary, who suffered and died, was buried,

---

5. WA 46:634.21–36; *LW* 22:113–14. Passages affirming the hypostatic union in a variety of ways are found throughout his preaching, e.g., at the end of his life: WA 51:8.39–9.23; *LW* 58:254–55; WA 51:172.6–16; *LW* 58:439; WA 51:150.18–151.15; *LW* 58:414; WA 51:152.30–153.21; *LW* 58:416.

6. WA 50:587.6–16; *LW* 41:100.

descended into hell, and rose again from the dead."[7] The orthodox claim, since the Council of Ephesus in 431, that Mary is the "God-bearer" was Luther's claim too.

The distinction of the divine and human natures within the one person of Jesus served as a hermeneutical aid for sorting out what is meant by the seemingly contradictory claims that Jesus makes about himself, sometimes speaking of himself in thoroughly human terms, sometimes describing himself and his actions in ways that are only possible to be said of God. Preaching on John 14:16 in 1537, Luther compared the relationship of the two natures in the person of Christ to the relationship of Father and Son within the Trinity: both distinct but united as the one and only God. Thus, "the natures must always be distinguished, the person must remain undivided." This means that "all that Scripture says of Christ covers the whole person, as if God and this human being were one essence. Often Scripture uses expressions interchangeably and assigns the attributes of both to each nature. This is done because of the personal union in what we call the communication of attributes."[8] Preaching on Matthew 23:39 in the same year, Luther asserted the following about the word "Lord":

> God cannot die or be born if you wish to speak according to the properties of the natures. Likewise, God cannot rise from the dead or ascend into heaven. All such things are said of him as a true man, which he also is. For he also does everything, eats and drinks, etc. like another man. The dear Lord uses both natures and wields all of their properties, at times only properties of the divine nature, and at other times also properties of the human nature, so that we know that both natures are participating.[9]

Luther's teaching on the person of Christ related closely to his understanding of his work as Savior. Citing 1 Corinthians 1:21, Luther noted that "true Christian theology . . . does not present God to us in his majesty as Moses and other doctrinal systems do, but Christ born of the virgin, our mediator and high priest." The "weak and foolish" preaching of the Word, which reveals God's power and strength, comes from the topic of that preaching, "Christ crucified, a stumbling block to the Jews and folly to the Gentiles." This compels preachers to "begin where Christ began—in the Virgin's womb, in the manger, and at his mother's breasts. For this purpose he came down, was born, lived among human beings, suffered, was crucified, and died, so that

---

7. WA 47:76.33–77.16; LW 22:351; cf. WA 47:86.3–87.8; LW 22:361–62.
8. WA 45:555.32–557.38; LW 24:104–6.
9. WA 47:542.6–13; LW 68:251–52.

in every possible way he might present himself to our sight. He wants us to fix the gaze of our hearts upon himself and thus to prevent us from climbing into heaven and speculating about the divine majesty."[10]

The Hypostatic Union and the Atonement

An editorial expansion of Luther's sermon for Easter Tuesday in his church postil expounded his understanding of the personal union of the Second Person of the Trinity with the human Jesus of Nazareth and tied that to the atoning work of the Savior:

> If this Christ (through whom this covenant was made) is truly a human being—as he promised David, of his blood and flesh—and is to bring and give eternal grace, then he also must be God, who alone is capable of giving this. Then he could not remain in death even though he dies like a natural human being, but he must himself rise from the dead so that he can also redeem others from death and give them eternal life. In this way he would accurately be called and be an eternal king of grace, righteousness, and life, as God has firmly promised to perform.[11]

Luther did not reproduce a strict Anselmian satisfaction theory of the atonement in presenting his interpretation of God's decision to restore sinful humanity to himself through the incarnation; his emphasis fell on Jesus's divine power that could overcome death and other enemies of the believer though he did not discount the divine ability to compensate for sin.

> God became human, a natural man, our flesh and blood, but without any sin, [not under] the power of the devil, so that he could trample on [the devil's] head. . . . If he is to be the Lord over sin and death, subdue the devil, and snatch us from his power, then this requires divine, almighty power. Human strength and ability are not enough. . . . He had to take our place, become a sacrifice for us, and bear himself the wrath and curse that had fallen upon us and under which we lie. He had to make satisfaction for [sin], but he did not remain under it.[12]

Death and the devil thought they could gobble Jesus down, but he devoured them through his innocent suffering and death.[13]

Closer to medieval explanations of the incarnation was that of Martin Chemnitz in his sermons on Christ's suffering and death:

10. WA 40/1:77.11–78.13; LW 26:28–29; cf. also WA 45:234.14–248.20; LW 12:122–34.
11. WA 22:446.24–32; LW 77:69.
12. WA 21:234.5–27; LW 77:55; cf. WA 21:484.4–19; LW 77:369.
13. WA 17/1:189.18–35; cf. his sermon on John 3:16, WA 47:87.9–24; LW 22:362–63.

If a mere human being had suffered for us, a transaction sufficient for the sins of the whole world could not have taken place. Because it had to be divine suffering that paid for sin, God's Son had to take human nature upon himself. The whole Christ, God and human being, became our redeemer and savior. What that means is that when Christ's human nature died and suffered, God's body, God's blood, God's suffering, God's wounds accomplished it. . . . Because of that, this suffering of Christ has the power to make alive, to redeem from sin, because the one who suffered for us is the Son of Man and at the same time the Son of the living God. This person alone could tread the winepress of God's wrath, as in Isaiah 63[:3].[14]

Luther was accused of the Eutychian heresy of denying the continued existence of Christ's human nature, because he maintained that it can exercise the characteristics of the divine nature even if it never possesses them. Yet few Christian preachers have so dramatically and clearly affirmed the humanness of Jesus. Preaching on Luke 2, Luther noted how miserable the circumstances of Christ's birth were. No one took pity on the young woman, his mother; no one was concerned about her pregnant body. No one in this foreign village had seen to providing the minimum that parents need, a cradle for the child. Without preparation, without light, without fire, in the middle of the night, in total darkness, no one offered aid. He then affirmed that Mary suffered the curse of Eve and indeed bore Jesus in pain, in a completely natural human way even though the child had been conceived by the Holy Spirit and was without sin. She nourished the baby Jesus with milk from her breasts. Through this birth he plunged deeply into human nature, flesh and blood.[15] He was thoroughly human from conception onward.

The Christologies of Luther and Zwingli

A significant presuppositional gulf divided Luther's Ockhamist-shaped belief that God works comfortably within his creation and with selected elements of it from the realist position of others, such as Ulrich Zwingli. Zwingli's engagement with Platonic and Neoplatonic writings reinforced his realist training, which laid parameters for his understanding of the personal (hypostatic) union of divine and human natures in the person of Jesus. Luther insisted that the two natures retain their own characteristics and do not take possession of the characteristics of the other nature. But he did believe that the Second Person of the Trinity had become the human being

14. Martin Chemnitz, *Historia der Passion unsers lieben Herrn und Heilands Jesu Christi* . . . (Wolfenbüttel: Konrad Horn, 1590), 333a.
15. WA 10/1.1:65.14–69.3.

named Jesus Christ and that Jesus of Nazareth was God the Word in human flesh. The Wittenberg Reformer held that the hypostatic union of Christ's two natures bound them so tightly together in his person that neither nature exists or acts alone. The two remain forever distinct, for Luther's doctrine of creation demands a sharp distinction between the Creator and all that he has made, but in the union of the two natures, that distinction never leads to separation.

In discussing the presence of Christ in the Lord's Supper, Luther relied fundamentally on the biblical text, the words of the institution of the Supper (Matt. 26:26–29; Mark 14:22–24; Luke 22:17–20; 1 Cor. 11:23–25). Acknowledging metaphorical usage throughout Scripture, he argued for a literal interpretation whenever possible. He believed that the only reason for not interpreting the words of the institution of the Supper literally was the false impression that God could not mysteriously make his body and blood present with the elements through the power of his Word. Luther's opponents, including Zwingli and Johannes Oecolampadius, presumed that the material and spiritual realms were so distinct that "the finite cannot bear [or deliver] the infinite" (*finitum non est capax infiniti*), a phrase later used in polemics between Reformed and Lutheran theologians but which expresses the assumption of Luther's critics in the 1520s. Luther's Ockhamist understanding of the power of the almighty Creator led him to believe that if God wanted to have certain selected elements of his created order come together with the divine, he could do so. The hypostatic union of Christ's divine and human natures demonstrates that principle most profoundly. Since the two natures are so tightly bound together that, while always distinguishable, they are now inseparable, they share their characteristics. Nonetheless, human nature as such, apart from Christ's person, never has the ability to be in more than one place in more than one form at the same time, and divinity, apart from Christ's person, is by definition unable to die.

In his *Confession concerning Christ's Supper*, Luther introduced three presuppositions based on this view of God's power and presence to give background or support his belief that Christ's body and blood are sacramentally present in and with the bread and wine of the Supper. These supporting axioms involved the Chalcedonian christological framework with which he was working. "The first is the article of our faith, that Jesus Christ is essential, natural, true complete God and human being in one person, undivided and inseparable." Second, he presumed that the Hebrew understanding of God's right hand did not refer to a physical location within or outside the bounds of the created order but rather to the position that shared God the Father's power and glory. Therefore, he rejected Zwingli's argument that

Jesus's body and blood could not be present in any form on the altar: he held instead that God's power and glory are indeed everywhere, albeit revealed in varying ways. Finally, he presumed that more than one definition of "presence" is used in Scripture to describe how God is in and with his people and his whole creation. He gave three examples from the Aristotelian concept of presence: local, definitive (through which "an object or body is not palpably in one place and is not measurable according to the dimensions of the place where it is," as is the case with angels' and spirits' presence throughout an entire city or was the case as Christ came to the disciples through a closed door [John 20:19]), and repletive, as God is, filling the universe. There is no reason, Luther concluded, why this particular sacramental presence cannot bring the whole person of Christ in his special "sacramental" way to the bread and wine of the Lord's Supper.[16]

Luther did not find his convictions regarding the communication of attributes to be of use only in supporting his case for the true presence of Christ's body and blood in the Lord's Supper. He also brought the concept into his argument against the doctrine of the celestial flesh of Christ as advanced by Caspar Schwenkfeld. In a disputation drafted in 1540, Luther began with the axiom "Those things that are attributed to the human being may rightly be asserted with respect to God; and, on the other hand, those things that are attributed to God may rightly be asserted with respect to the human being," adding the proviso on which Melanchthon also insisted, "These things are not valid in the abstract"—that is, about divinity or humanity in general—but only in the concrete case of the person of Christ.[17] He rejected Schwenkfeld's contention that Christ brought his flesh with him from heaven and did not receive it as normal human flesh from his mother Mary.[18] In the disputation itself, Luther affirmed that "in Christ there is a divine nature and a human nature, and those two natures are in one person, so that no other thing is conjoined and nevertheless the humanity is not the divinity nor is the divinity the humanity, nor does that distinction hinder anything but rather confirms the unity."[19] Specifically, that meant, among other things, that "insofar as the human being cries out, God also cries out, and the Lord of glory is crucified [1 Cor. 2:8], which is something impossible according to the divinity; however, it is possible according to the humanity

---

16. WA 26:326.29–330.28; *LW* 37:214–16; cf. WA 26:326.29–378.27; *LW* 37:214–30.

17. WA 39/2:93.2–19; English translation in Mitchell Tolpingrud, "Luther's Disputation concerning the Divinity and the Humanity of Christ," *Lutheran Quarterly* 10 (1996): 151–78 (quote from 152–53).

18. WA 39/2:95.1–2; Tolpingrud, "Luther's Disputation," 154, thesis 31.

19. WA 39/2:97.9–14; Tolpingrud, "Luther's Disputation," 157.

and, because there is the unity of the person, that attribute [to be crucified] is attributed also to the divinity."[20]

Christ in the Old Testament

Toward the end of his life, in 1543, Luther engaged Christian exegetes who were repeating interpretations gained from Jewish commentators on the subject of Old Testament prophecies of Christ. His exposition of "the last will and testament of David"[21] (2 Sam. 23:1–7) cited Old and New Testament passages that he believed brought the human being, prophesied as Messiah, born as Jesus of Nazareth, together with the Second Person of the Trinity. This argument focused on the mysteries of the Trinity and the incarnation and the saving work that takes place because God the Son became human. The human being called "ruler" in Psalm 8:4–6 exercises dominion over God's kingdom and must therefore be equal to God—that is, God himself. The psalmist, Luther argued, brought together "the two most sublime teachings of our faith so aptly, that there are three distinct persons in God, and that one of these, the Son, was to become a human being, receiving honor and dominion over everything from the Father, and that the Holy Spirit, who has previously proclaimed this through the mouth and lips of the prophets, should inscribe this into the human heart by faith."[22] He called on Daniel 7:13–14 to support this contention.[23] By sheer force of words Luther maintained his defense against patripassianism: he maintained that the human nature of Christ "is a real creature created by the Father, the Son, and the Holy Spirit. We would not permit the Creed to state that the Father alone or the Son alone or the Holy Spirit alone created this creature." The incarnation is a work of the entire Trinity. Furthermore, "of this human being, you cannot say that this is God the Father or that is God the Holy Spirit, but you must say that this is God the Son, although God the Father, the Son, and the Holy Spirit are one God, and there is no other god beside him." In Jesus dwells the fullness of the Godhead bodily (Col. 2:9), and that truth lies alongside the distinction and inseparability of the persons of the Trinity.[24] Luther again rejected any attempt to reconcile or harmonize in rational terms how the mysteries of the Trinity and the incarnation fit together. He could only conclude, "Jesus of Nazareth, who died for us on the cross, is the God who says in the First

20. WA 39/2:103.24–31; Tolpingrud, "Luther's Disputation," 162.
21. WA 54:31.10–23; LW 15:270.
22. WA 54:36.32–40; LW 15:277.
23. WA 54:47.38–50.24; LW 15:291–94.
24. WA 54:60.16–30; LW 15:305; cf. WA 54:63.14–64.21; LW 15:309–10.

Commandment, 'I am the Lord your God.'"[25] Luther added an argument from Genesis 3:15. "It is certain that this seed of a woman is to be a human being. But, in addition he must also be God . . . for [Moses] imputes to this seed the power which is proper to no creature but to God alone, namely, to abolish death and the murderer, sin, and God's wrath, and to restore righteousness and life."[26]

Alternative patristic interpretations of the communication of attributes (as he understood them from his scholastic studies) attracted Luther's critique.

> He who is called a human being and who was born of the Virgin Mary and was crucified by the Jews must also be called the Son of God. And we must say that God was born of Mary and was crucified by the Jews, for God and this human being are one person. There are not two sons, one of God, the other of Mary, but he is just one Son, God's and Mary's. If you were to concur with Nestorius and say that God, or Jesus, God's Son, was not born of Mary nor crucified by the Jews but that this death was experienced only by the human being, Mary's son, you would create two persons, you would split the one person into two. . . . On the other hand, if you were to say with Eutyches that the man Jesus, Mary's son, is not Creator of heaven and earth, or that he is not God's Son, who is to be worshiped, you would again divide the person and split it into two persons.[27]

This led Luther to confess,

> therefore, we exult and rejoice that God's Son, the one true God together with the Father and the Holy Spirit, became a human being, a servant [Phil. 2:7], a sinner, a worm for us; that God died and bore our sins on the cross in his own body [Col. 1:19–22], that God redeemed us through his own blood. For God and this human being are one person. Whatever the human being does, suffers, and speaks, that God does, suffers, and speaks, and conversely what God does and speaks, that the human being does and speaks. He is both God's and Mary's Son in one undivided person and in two distinct natures.[28]

Subsequent Lutheran Christology

The controversies over the Lord's Supper during the 1550s and 1560s involved the related christological questions as well.[29] Chief among the Lutherans

25. WA 54:67.10–16; *LW* 15:313–14.
26. WA 54:71.1–11; *LW* 15:317–18.
27. WA 54:90.14–91.14; *LW* 15:341–42.
28. WA 54:92.13–20; *LW* 15:343.
29. Theodor Mahlmann, *Das neue Dogma der lutherischen Christologie: Problem und Geschichte seiner Begründung* (Gütersloh: Gütersloher Verlagshaus, 1969). On the use of patristic

who formulated the implications of Luther's teaching was Martin Chemnitz. His work *On the Two Natures in Christ*[30] was intended to refute the position of the crypto-Philippist theologians in Wittenberg, who—like Chemnitz and his ally David Chytraeus—believed themselves to be most faithfully representing Melanchthon's position.[31] Chemnitz avoided some of the language employed by Johannes Brenz and Jakob Andreae of Württemberg, who had attracted the epithet "ubiquitarian" from Reformed opponents because they insisted that Christ's human nature is present throughout the creation. Like Luther, Chemnitz argued for the presence of Christ's body and blood in the elements of the Lord's Supper chiefly on the basis of a literal interpretation of Christ's words of institution of the Supper. But he also defended the belief that God, because of his omnipotence, could make the divine and the human natures of Christ united in the one person of the Son present wherever, whenever, and in whatever form he wished. In his treatise *On the Two Natures*, Chemnitz laid down three principles (*genus/genera* in Latin) to guide thinking about the sharing of the characteristics of the two natures. The principle of properties (or characteristics or attributes, *genus idiomaticum*) affirmed that the characteristics belonging to one nature or the other shall be used to describe the entire person of Christ, whether one nature or both are in fact mentioned. The second principle posited that the actions that Christ performed as he carried out his specific tasks, particularly his activities on behalf of the salvation of sinners, are to be attributed to the whole person of Christ, on the principle of

argument in these controversies, see Esther Chung-Kim, *Inventing Authority: The Use of the Church Fathers in Reformation Debates over the Eucharist* (Waco: Baylor University Press, 2011); Irene Dingel, "Das Streben nach einem 'Consensus Orthodoxus' mit den Vätern in der Abendmahlsdiskussion des späten 16. Jahrhunderts," in *Die Patristik in der Bibelexegese des 16. Jahrhunderts*, ed. David Steinmetz (Wiesbaden: Harrassowitz, 1999), 181–204; and Dingel, *Concordia controversa: Die öffentlichen Diskussionen um das lutherische Konkordienwerk am Ende des 16. Jahrhunderts* (Gütersloh: Gütersloher Verlagshaus, 1996), 230–79.

30. *De duabus naturis in Christo* (Jena, 1570). This work was extensively revised and expanded in response to the developing Wittenberg Christology in a second edition, Leipzig, 1578. For an English translation, see *The Two Natures in Christ*, trans. J. A. O. Preus (St. Louis: Concordia, 1971).

31. Because they believed that Melanchthon had not departed from Luther's point of view, Chytraeus and Chemnitz held that their common viewpoint taught the presence of Christ's body and blood in the elements of the Lord's Supper and given to communicants with the bread and wine. Others, led by Melanchthon's son-in-law, medical professor Caspar Peucer, believed that Christ is only spiritually present, while his human body is at God's right hand in heaven, and that this was also Melanchthon's position. On Melanchthon's Christology toward the end of his life, as expressed in comments on Col. 3:1, which appeared to contemporaries and later scholars to endorse a Zwinglian understanding of Christ's sitting at the Father's right hand, see the cautionary qualification of Timothy J. Wengert, in "Philip Melanchthon's 1557 Lecture on Colossians 3:1–2," in *Philip Melanchthon: Theologian in Classroom, Confession, and Controversy*, by Irene Dingel et al. (Göttingen: Vandenhoeck & Ruprecht, 2012), 209–35.

the actions of his offices (*genus apostelismaticum*). The third principle, that of majesty (*genus majesticum*), maintained that within the personal union that is Jesus Christ, the Second Person of the Trinity shares with the human nature all of his divine attributes. These characteristics are shared in such a way that what can be said of one can be said of both, even though they do not become the possession of the other nature. In this way the integrity of the coming together of God and this human being Jesus is preserved.[32]

Together Andreae and Chemnitz composed the eighth article of the Formula of Concord in 1576–77, working together with four colleagues on its text. It confessed "that there are now in this one, inseparable person of Christ two distinct natures, the divine, from eternity, and the human, which was assumed into the union of the person of God's Son in time." Using the language of the Council of Chalcedon (451), it continues, "These two natures can never again be separated nor mixed together with each other, nor can one be transformed into the other. Rather, each remains in its own nature and essence within the person of Christ into all eternity." After affirming that characteristics such as omnipotence, eternality, and omnipresence belong naturally only to the divine nature, and that flesh and blood, finiteness, suffering and dying, suffering from hunger, and so on belong naturally to the human nature, and that neither nature ever takes possession of the other nature's characteristics, the Formula confesses, "After the incarnation neither nature in Christ exists in and of itself, so that neither is or acts as a separate person, but they are so united that they constitute one single person, which at the same time consists of both natures and in which both the divine nature and the assumed human nature are personally present." This means that the two natures in the person of Christ share their characteristics, so that the power and majesty that belong only to the divine nature by its nature are shared with the human nature as the person of Jesus, truly God and truly a human being, exists and acts, and that the Second Person of the Trinity is inseparable from the person Jesus who died on the cross.[33]

The Christology of the Formula of Concord shaped the ways in which Lutheran dogmaticians and preachers taught and proclaimed the person of Christ throughout the seventeenth century. Johann Gerhard's locus on Christ demonstrates this, with his detailed account of three *genera*, a part of his development of the communication of attributes, which occupied more than half of his exposition of the topic.[34] In the discussion regarding the question of whether

---

32. Chemnitz uses the principles throughout *De duabus naturis*.

33. *BSELK* 1508.23–1513.6; *BC* 617–18.

34. Johann Gerhard, *Locorum Theologicorum . . . Tomus Primus* (Jena: Tobias Steinmann, 1610); ET: *On the Person of Christ*, trans. Richard J. Dinda, ed. Benjamin T. G. Mayes (St. Louis: Concordia, 2009).

Christ "emptied" his person of the exercise of his divine attributes during his time on earth (*kenōsis*) or hid his divine attributes (*krypsis*), the former position, held by the theologians of the University of Giessen, was opposed by those at the University of Tübingen. The *Saxon Decision* of 1624 incorporated elements of both and warned against extending dogmatic debate beyond the limits of what is given in Scripture. This judgment was intended to discourage further construction of metaphysical defenses of fundamental biblical teaching.[35]

Another controversy broke out over the relationship of Jesus's two natures in the late nineteenth century as the Erlangen University professors Gottfried Thomasius and F. H. R. Frank, among others, proposed that Jesus had completely emptied himself of the divine characteristics belonging to his divine nature and did not exercise them in any way. This view failed to gain support among most Lutherans.

Today Luther's words in his hymn adapted from the words of Ambrose of Milan, "Savior of the nations, come," express for most Lutherans the union of God and this human being as the source of comfort in the midst of sin and evil:

> Savior of the nations, come. Show yourself the virgin's son.
> Marvel, wonder, all the earth that our God chose such a birth.
>> No human power of mind or blood but the Spirit of our God
>> Made the Word of God a man, the fruit of woman's womb.
> This virgin's body, filled with child, remained so pure, so undefiled.
> Her many virtues shining bright, God on his throne was there in
>> might.
>> He left his chambers far behind, his royal hall for humankind,
>> God by nature, human, too, he hastened on his way to you.
> To earth he came from Father's side, and goes back heavenwards to
>> abide.
>> Went to hell below alone, returned to God's eternal throne.
>> Equal to the Father, you won for us the victory, too,
>> In flesh, with God's eternal might, heal us from ev'ry fleshly blight.

For this incarnation of the Second Person of the Trinity, Luther could only react with thanks and praise.[36]

---

35. Jörg Baur, "Auf dem Wege zur klassischen Tübinger Christologie: Einführende Überlegungen zum sogenannten Kenosis-Crypsis-Streit," in *Luther und seine klassischen Erben* (Tübingen: Mohr Siebeck, 1993), 204–89; Ulrich Wiedenroth, *Krypsis und Kenosis: Studien zum Thema und Genese der Tübinger Christologie im 17. Jahrhundert* (Tübingen: Mohr Siebeck, 2011); and Joar Haga, *Was There a Lutheran Metaphysics? The Interpretation of the* Communicatio Idiomatum *in Early Modern Lutheranism* (Göttingen: Vandenhoeck & Ruprecht, 2012).

36. WA 35:430.1–431.15; translation adapted from that of F. Samuel Janzow, *Lutheran Worship* (St. Louis: Concordia, 1982), 13.

Christology in the Reformed Tradition

The Reformation was a multifaceted phenomenon, but at its heart lay a revised understanding of the person and work of the Lord Jesus Christ and his significance for salvation and for the church. The practical displacement of the Mass as the central point of Christian devotion and its replacement by the preached Word was a direct corollary of the emphasis on God's promise being fulfilled in his Son in his once-for-all death on Calvary and made available by its proclamation and reception by faith. A new understanding of Christ's work lay at the heart of the magisterial Protestant project. On this, Lutheran and Reformed were and are agreed.

While the most famous difference between Lutherans and Reformed is that on the Lord's Supper, that difference is itself rooted in significant differences over Christology. Indeed, the formal point of rupture at Marburg may have been the understanding of the words of eucharistic institution, "This is my body" and "This is my blood," but the interpretation of those words depended to a large extent on prior christological commitments. Specifically, the difference lies in the different understandings that Lutheran and Reformed have of the communication of attributes. Yet there is much more to Christology than that for both sides, so we will address that issue as part of a larger exposition of Reformed Christology.

The Foundation of Christology

For the Reformed, the foundation of Christology is the divine decision to save humanity in the light of its fall in Adam into sin.[37] The incarnation is thus only necessary in light of this. Many later Reformed theologians came to discuss this decision in terms of what they called the "covenant of redemption" or, to use the Latin term, *pactum salutis*. This was the idea that the Father and the Son entered into a covenant with each other in eternity whereby the Son would accept the role of Mediator and be appointed as the second and last Adam, federal head of all those the Father would give to him. As this terminology became commonplace only after about 1645, however, the idea of a covenant of redemption between the Father and the Son does not have confessional status in either the German/Dutch Reformed churches that subscribe to the Three Forms of Unity or Presbyterian churches that subscribe

---

37. Calvin, *Institutes* II.xii.1. Calvin does make the statement in this chapter that the distance between God and humanity even prior to the fall was such that a mediator would have been necessary. This may well be symptomatic of the roots of Calvin's theology in late medieval voluntarism, though rhetorically the statement functions here more as a way of arguing that a fortiori in the wake of the fall a mediator was even more necessary.

to the Westminster Standards. The idea of a covenant of redemption is not universally accepted by Reformed theologians but remains a matter of intra-confessional discussion.[38]

Within this framework, the Reformed typically used an argument with an Anselmic structure to argue for the incarnation, thereby tying together both the person and the work of Christ. This is clear in questions 12 through 15 of the Heidelberg Catechism:

> Q. 12. Since, then, by the righteous judgment of God we deserve temporal and eternal punishment, how may we escape this punishment and be again received into favor? A. God wills that His justice be satisfied; therefore, we must make full satisfaction to that justice, either by ourselves or by another (Rom. 8:3–4).
>
> Q. 13. Can we ourselves make this satisfaction? A. Certainly not; on the contrary, we daily increase our guilt.
>
> Q. 14. Can any mere creature make satisfaction for us? A. None; for first, God will not punish any other creature for the sin which man committed; and further, no mere creature can sustain the burden of God's eternal wrath against sin and redeem others from it.
>
> Q. 15. What kind of mediator and redeemer, then, must we seek? A. One who is a true and righteous man, and yet more powerful than all creatures, that is, one who is also true God.[39]

This is not, of course, pure Anselm. Anselm's thinking was predicated primarily on the notion of God's honor and only secondarily on God's justice, and it was clearly couched in the concepts of medieval feudal society. Further, Anselm's Christ needed to obey the law to fulfill his own obligation, as a human being, to God. This then qualified him to die as a kind of work of supererogation for others. We might therefore say that for Anselm, the real significance of the incarnation was that it was instrumental to the death of Christ. As with the Apostles' Creed, there is a sense in which the details of the incarnate life of Christ do not seem to have great theological significance.

Further, for Anselm God had to make atonement because it was more fitting that he satisfy his honor that way than by, say, simply starting all over again. But the basic Anselmic logic was easy to adapt to the categories of justice and righteousness. As the section from the Heidelberg Catechism makes clear, the essentials are there: only God can pay the price for sin and satisfy God's righteousness, but only a human being ought to pay the price

---

38. See J. V. Fesko, *The Covenant of Redemption: Origins, Development, and Reception* (Göttingen: Vandenhoeck & Ruprecht, 2015). For a more popular treatment by the same author, see *The Trinity and the Covenant of Redemption* (Fearn, UK: Mentor, 2016).

39. Cf. Calvin, *Institutes* II.xii.

for sin and satisfy God's righteousness. But the Reformed emphasis on the contingency of incarnation with regard to the divine will cut away the more necessitarian emphasis in Anselm's original construction; and the Reformed also in general saw the satisfaction as extending to the whole of Christ's life and not simply his sacrifice on Calvary. The active righteousness of Christ, his positive fulfillment of the law, was a component part of what most Reformed theologians believed was imputed in justification (see chap. 5). Nevertheless, the basic dynamic of the argument from Anselm as to why Christ had to be both divine and human remained of perennial theological importance.

The Catholic Framework

While the Reformed (like the Lutherans) sought to make Scripture alone the norming norm of their faith, they were also conscious of the importance of the church and its historic creedal statements for the formulation of doctrine. Thus, in the matter of Christology, they sought to operate within the broad categories established in the ancient church for thinking of both God as Trinity and Jesus Christ as God incarnate. Central to such is the Nicene Creed (381), the Chalcedonian Definition (451), and the later developments that flowed from these, such as the assertion of christological dyothelitism at the Third Council of Constantinople (681). While the Reformed would regard none of these councils as in principle infallible, the assumption has always been that the burden of proof lies with those who seek to break with a council's basic teaching. On the negative side, this commitment to catholic, ecumenical trinitarianism and Christology also means that perceived christological deviations are typically categorized using the taxonomy of patristic heresy: Arianism, Apollinarianism, Eutychianism, Nestorianism, and others.[40] This Nicene-Chalcedonian framework is clear from the concise statement of Christology found in the Westminster Confession (8.2):

> The Son of God, the second person in the Trinity, being very and eternal God, of one substance and equal with the Father, did, when the fullness of time was come, take upon him man's nature, with all the essential properties, and common infirmities thereof, yet without sin; being conceived by the power of the Holy Ghost, in the womb of the virgin Mary, of her substance. So that two whole, perfect, and distinct natures, the Godhead and the manhood, were inseparably joined together in one person, without conversion, composition, or confusion.

40. J. van Genderen and W. H. Velema, *Concise Reformed Dogmatics* (Phillipsburg, NJ: P&R, 2008), 446–48; Louis Berkhof, *Systematic Theology* (Edinburgh: Banner of Truth Trust, 1971), 308; *RD* 3:256–59.

Which person is very God, and very man, yet one Christ, the only Mediator between God and man.[41]

Two distinct natures in one person, without conversion, composition, or confusion: that is Nicene-Chalcedonian orthodoxy and is typical of the Reformed christological position.[42]

The Communication of Attributes

As noted above, central to the division between Lutherans and Reformed on the Lord's Supper is the question of the communication of properties between the two natures of Christ. In brief: the Lutheran doctrine of the real presence of the whole Christ in, with, and under the eucharistic elements assumes that Christ's body is not spatially limited in the manner typically associated with human embodiment. This in turn rests on the notion that certain properties of Christ's deity are communicated directly to his human nature.[43]

At this point Reformed theology operates with a number of axioms. First, it desires to take seriously the Chalcedonian point that the natures are not to be commingled in such a way as to produce a third nature that is neither human nor divine but an amalgam of the two.[44] Second, it holds to the principle that what is finite cannot comprehend or contain the infinite. This idea was expressed in classical Reformed theology with the Latin maxim *finitum non capax infiniti* (lit., the finite is incapable of the infinite). Christologically, this was used to indicate the finitude of all humanity, including the humanity of Christ himself, and therefore the fact that it was incapable

---

41. *The Westminster Confession of Faith and Larger and Shorter Catechisms with Proof Texts* (Willow Grove, PA: Orthodox Presbyterian Church, 2005). Cf. The Thirty-Nine Articles II; Belgic Confession X and XVIII.

42. The framing of christological questions using patristic heresies is evident, for example, in Turretin's treatment of the hypostatic union in which he affirms his position in explicit opposition to those of Nestorius and Eutyches. See Turretin, *Institutes* XIII.vii.

43. Robert Kolb, *The Christian Faith: A Lutheran Exposition* (St. Louis: Concordia, 1993), 133–34:

> Lutherans regard the sharing of the characteristics of the two natures as an important insight into God's coming into human flesh. We use it to help us confess how the human body and blood of Jesus Christ can be present in a mysterious way in the bread and wine of the Lord's Supper. His body and blood share with the divine nature that characteristic of being able to be present wherever, whenever, and in whatever form God wills. It is also of great comfort to us to know that he who shares our human nature is sitting in the councils of the Trinity. God not only knows our human experience through his divine omniscience but also through the human experience of the second person of the Trinity.

44. Berkhof, *Systematic Theology*, 322.

of receiving divine attributes such as omnipresence and omniscience—the so-called incommunicable attributes.[45] This in turn underlay the concept that Lutherans polemically dismissed as the so-called *extra calvinisticum*. This was the idea that the Logos was not fully contained within the humanity of Christ but, while truly united to it in the person of the Mediator, continued also to exist beyond the physical limits of the flesh.[46] Clearly both of these points are of central importance to the different understandings of the Lord's Supper held by Lutherans and Reformed and point to the fact that exegesis of the words of institution is also connected to assumptions about Christology.

Because the Lord's Supper was the point of division between Lutheran and Reformed, the matter of Christology formed a central part of the history of dogmatic developments within the two communions. The increasingly acrimonious and technical debate between Lutherans and Reformed in the later sixteenth and seventeenth centuries led to elaborate discussion of the nature of the communication of properties, with the Lutherans developing a particularly technical taxonomy to deal with the issue. In comparison, the Reformed offered a relatively simple approach. What is crucial for us to understand is that the debate about the Lord's Supper is at its foundation a debate about Christology, with discussion of the meaning of the words of institution playing out against a background of radically different understandings of the nature of the incarnation.

Anhypostatic/Enhypostatic

The concern at the heart of the Reformed position was a focus on the person of Christ. The human nature, considered abstractly in itself, was anhypostatic—that is, not possessing intrinsic personhood but receiving its personhood from its union with the divine.[47] Joined with the Logos, the human nature receives the personal subsistence of the Second Person of the Godhead and is thus enhypostatic. This point is vital to avoid falling into the heresy of Nestorianism, of ascribing two persons to the incarnation. Further, the human nature never existed outside of its union with the divine but is united with the Logos at the moment of conception. Were this not so, then the Nestorian error of two persons would be unavoidable. Thus, from the moment of its creation, Christ's human nature is in union with, and receiving its personhood from, the Logos. All predicates are therefore spoken of the

45. See *DLGTT*, s.v. "Finitum non capax infiniti."
46. See *DLGTT*, s.v. "extra calvinisticum."
47. Turretin, *Institutes* XIII.vi.5.

person of the Mediator as a whole, but this should not be misconstrued as meaning that all predicates apply to both natures.[48]

This christological position is extremely important, marking a major point of distinction between Lutheran and Reformed, and has profound implications for how language about Christ is understood. Calvin makes this point in *Institutes* II.xiv.2, where he cites a number of biblical passages and explains how they should be understood. When Paul says in Acts 20:28 that God purchased the church with his own blood, he is speaking of God incarnate in the person of the Mediator and not ascribing physical blood to the being of God in himself. The ascription is a linguistic one, appropriate because it refers to the Mediator, but not to be given properly metaphysical significance as far as the nature of God is concerned.[49] It also aids the Reformed in ascribing to the incarnate Christ real growth in knowledge during his time on earth. If the hypostatic union in itself did not lead to the direct communication of divine properties to the human nature, then there was scope for the Mediator to learn and develop intellectually and morally as a real human being. The boy Jesus could enter Joseph's workshop, see his father planing a piece of wood, and actually learn something he had not known before. This dynamic understanding of the incarnation allows the Reformed to do justice to the historical narratives contained in the Gospels while still respecting the structures of catholic Christology.[50]

The Two States of Christ

The historical dynamic of the gospel as it focuses on the incarnate Christ is a central concern of Reformed theology. Building on the catholic christological foundation, the Reformed divide the work of Christ in the economy of salvation into two: his state of humiliation and his state of exaltation. The division was an attempt both to capture something of the theological significance of the historical drama of salvation and to integrate basic Christology with the Gospel narratives and the teaching of Paul.

48. It is interesting to note that Turretin (*Institutes* XIII.vii.11) defends the anti-Nestorian title for Mary, *Theotokos*, on the grounds that she gave life to him who was also God, using Luke 1:43 as textual support.

49. Cf. Ursinus, *The Commentary of Dr. Zacharias Ursinus on the Heidelberg Catechism*, trans. G. W. Willard (Cincinnati: Elm Street, 1888), 199.

50. See *RD* 3:311–16. The definitive exposition of this point is by John Owen in his treatise *Pneumatologia*, where he argues that the only direct act of the Logos on the human nature was the hypostatization of the latter by assuming it into union with himself. All other acts of the Logos on the human nature are thereafter voluntary and the direct action of the Holy Spirit. This is a subtle point but allows both for placing the incarnation in trinitarian context and for the growth of real knowledge of Jesus Christ. See John Owen, *The Works of John Owen, D.D.*, ed. William H. Goold, 17 vols. (Edinburgh: T&T Clark, 1862), 3:159–88.

The understanding of the twofold state, connected as it is to the communication of attributes, is thus another point of distinction between Lutheran and Reformed. For the Lutherans, the state of humiliation is not the incarnation in itself, and the subject of humiliation is Christ's human nature as it is united with the divine, and not the divine person.[51] The Reformed, however, make a distinction between the *kenōsis* of Christ, in which he laid aside his divine majesty and took human flesh, and the *tapeinōsis*, which consists in his being subject to the law and obedient unto death.[52] On this basis, the Reformed disagree with Lutherans and see the incarnation itself as the first, preliminary stage in the state of humiliation and include the "descent into hell" clause of the Apostles' Creed (however it is understood) as part of this.[53] Incarnation is itself a gracious act of God's condescension to his people. The Lutherans, by contrast, see the descent as the first stage of the exaltation.[54]

For the Reformed, the state of exaltation begins with the resurrection and continues in the ascension, the session at God's right hand, and the second coming and final judgment.[55] The incarnation continues, but the state of humiliation no longer applies; Christ as incarnate Mediator is now exalted, because the postresurrection human nature of Christ now shares in the glory that the Son has had with the Father from all eternity.[56]

The two states are thus two sides of the same coin, two historical phases in the work of Christ, both vital parts of Christ's one mediatorial office, with the one leading to the other. As Bavinck so beautifully yet concisely expresses it, "The death of Christ, the end of his humiliation, was simultaneously the road to his exaltation."[57] Between them, the two states offer a comprehensive account of the nature and necessity of his saving work and also bind together both the Christ of the Gospels and the Christ of Paul's Letters, the former

51. See John Theodore Mueller, *Christian Dogmatics* (St. Louis: Concordia, 1934), 287: This condition of self-renunciation we designate as "Christ's state of humiliation" (*status exinanitionis*). The humiliation of Christ did not consist essentially in the act of the incarnation, although it was a most gracious condescension for the Son of God to assume our human nature; for while the state of humiliation ceased with His burial, Phil. 2:8f., the personal union resulting from the incarnation never ceased, Eph. 1:20–23; 4:10. Again, while in the incarnation the Son of God entered into a true and real union with human nature, the state of humiliation does not pertain to Christ's divine, but only to His human nature (against modern kenoticism).

52. Berkhof, *Systematic Theology*, 332.

53. For a brief survey of the various understandings of the clause, see Berkhof, *Systematic Theology*, 342. For a discussion of the theological implications of the clause from a Reformed perspective, see *RD* 3:410–17.

54. Compare Berkhof, *Systematic Theology*, 341–43, with Mueller, *Christian Dogmatics*, 292.

55. See Berkhof, *Systematic Theology*, 344–55.

56. *RD* 3:432.

57. *RD* 3:421.

setting forth in narrative form what the latter explicates more doctrinally.
Turretin expresses it this way:

> The necessity [of the twofold state] is evinced on the part of both God and
> Christ, and on our part, and on the part of the salvation to be bestowed on
> us. (1) On the part of God because to reconcile God to us and to obtain the
> fruits of saving grace, two things were to be done: first, satisfaction was to
> be made to offended justice by the suffering and death of Christ; second, the
> gifts of grace were to be poured out on men (which was done in the exalta-
> tion, Eph. 4:8). (2) On the part of Christ because he must sustain a twofold
> relation of surety (to satisfy for us) and of head (to vivify and govern us in
> union with himself).[58]

This then points toward the second major structural pattern of Reformed
Christology: the threefold division of the office of the Mediator into prophet,
priest, and king.

The Threefold Office

The Reformed share with many Lutheran theologians (and indeed the Socin-
ians!) the taxonomy of prophet, priest, and king relative to Christ's work of
mediation.[59] Key to this is Christ's being anointed by the Holy Spirit, which
ties him in with the historical antecedents not only of the kings of Israel but
also with the priests and (given that it is the Spirit who anoints) the prophets.[60]

The threefold office is central to the Reformed catechetical tradition, as a
means of teaching the various aspects of Christ's saving work. The Heidelberg
Catechism expresses the matter thus in question 31:

> Q. 31. Why is He called "Christ," that is, Anointed? A. Because He is ordained
> of God the Father and anointed with the Holy Ghost to be our chief Prophet
> and Teacher, who has fully revealed to us the secret counsel and will of God
> concerning our redemption, and our only High Priest (Ps. 110:4; Heb. 7:21),
> who by the one sacrifice of His body, has redeemed us, and ever lives to make
> intercession for us with the Father (Rom. 5:9–10); and our eternal King, who
> governs us by His Word and Spirit, and defends and preserves us in the redemp-
> tion obtained for us (Ps. 2:6; Luke 1:33; Matt. 28:18).[61]

58. Turretin, *Institutes* XIII.ix.3.
59. Cf. Berkhof, *Systematic Theology*, 356; and Mueller, *Christian Dogmatics*, 302.
60. Calvin, *Institutes* II.xv.2.
61. Cf. the Larger Catechism: "Q. 42. Why was our mediator called Christ? A. Our mediator was called Christ, because he was anointed with the Holy Ghost above measure; and so set
apart, and fully furnished with all authority and ability, to execute the offices of prophet, priest,

CHRIST AS PROPHET

The prophetic office is necessary for three reasons. First, the nature of salvation requires a special revelation, because natural revelation is insufficient in this regard. Second, the method of salvation is therefore grasped solely by faith. Third, it fulfills Old Testament prophecies about the coming of the great prophet, as indicated by Hebrews 1:1–2.[62]

Thus, in his *Commentary on the Heidelberg Catechism*, Ursinus notes a number of aspects to this office. Christ reveals God and his will to human beings and to angels, and he institutes and effects the ministry of the church. He then teaches the church internally and effectively via this outward ministry.[63] This is important since it creates a clear connection between Christology and the church. Although not a priest in the Roman Catholic sense, the minister does represent God to the people. The role is, as the title suggests, ministerial but nonetheless real and special. Turretin distinguishes between Christ's immediate work of prophecy—the preaching that he himself performs directly in his earthly ministry—and his mediate work of the same. This is where the message of Christ is proclaimed by those who act in his name. In the Old Testament these were the prophets such as Moses, Isaiah, and others. In the postascension period, these were the apostles and then later the ordinary ministers of the gospel.[64]

Given the basic identity of the church, that body of people united to Christ, it is not surprising to find this christological connection relative to the ministerial office. Christ continues to work in the church by his Spirit, and the church's ministers act in a Christlike capacity, not in any ontological or mystical sense, but as those who proclaim his prophetic Word to the people week by week. Their power in this regard, as in all other aspects of their calling, is purely ministerial. They have authority only so far as they are given it by Christ and represent him faithfully to the people.

CHRIST AS PRIEST

Christ's priesthood is typically the aspect of his mediatorial office to which the Reformed devoted most attention. In part this was driven by polemical exigencies. Roman Catholic notions of the Mass and of the role of the

---

and king of his church, in the estate both of his humiliation and exaltation" (*The Westminster Confession of Faith and Larger and Shorter Catechisms with Proof Texts* [Willow Grove, PA: Orthodox Presbyterian Church, 2005]).

62. Turretin, *Institutes* XIV.vii.iii.

63. Ursinus, *Commentary*, 173–74.

64. Turretin, *Institutes* XIV.vii.xii.

contemporary priesthood, Socinian rejection of vicarious atonement, and, from the early seventeenth century, Arminian reconstructions of the efficacy of Christ's atonement—all these issues served to focus Reformed attention on this topic.[65] Yet also the basic impulse of Reformation theology, which made Christ the center of salvation and the one who acts on behalf of his people before a holy and righteous God, also served to place his priesthood in a position of priority.

Following the Old Testament paradigm, the Reformed see Christ's priesthood as consisting of two actions: his sacrifice and the offering of that sacrifice to the Father. We noted earlier that the incarnation is rooted in God's decision to save; a certain diversity of opinion within the Reformed tradition exists regarding specific elements of this central tenet. Thus, within the confessional consensus there have been supralapsarians and infralapsarians, as well as those who avoid the question altogether (see chap. 4 below). Further, drawing perhaps on more Anselmic and Thomistic patterns, some regard the incarnation and atonement as necessarily required once God had decided to save; others, reflecting more Scotist/voluntarist thinking, regard it as necessary simply because God willed that it should be accomplished in such a way.[66]

Central to the notion of Christ's sacrifice is the propitiation of God's justice or righteousness. The Reformed take to heart the idea that Christ's death on Calvary is offered to propitiate God's wrath once and for all for the sins of the people. God is holy and righteous. Sin is an affront to him that can be dealt with only via blood sacrifice. A sacrificial victim is needed in order to satisfy God's wrath.

In Reformed theology this connects to the covenants. Important here are Romans 5 and 1 Corinthians 15:22, with their parallels between Adam and Christ, because the figure of Adam provides the paradigm for understanding the work of Christ. This is understood in terms of covenants. Adam was created and placed under the terms of a covenant of works as a representative of all his progeny. When he sinned, he became subject to death and to the penal sanction of the law. This defines the moral and existential problem of all subsequent human beings and thus determines the shape of the salvation wrought by Christ. Christ comes as the second and last Adam, placed under the same Adamic terms of obedience demanded by the covenant of works but now acting on behalf of his spiritual progeny, who will be united to

65. See Carl R. Trueman, *The Claims of Truth: John Owen's Trinitarian Theology* (Carlisle, UK: Paternoster, 1998), 187–88.

66. See the discussion in Carl R. Trueman, "John Owen's *Dissertation on Divine Justice*: An Exercise in Christocentric Scholasticism," *Calvin Theological Journal* 33 (1998): 87–103.

him by faith under the terms of the covenant of grace.[67] It is this covenantal structure that makes his sacrifice meritorious before God. Christ obeys the law on his people's behalf and suffers the penalty that they deserved. This he then presents before his Father as he intercedes in heaven for his people.

Within the bounds of the confessional Reformed faith, there is some diversity on the details of the priesthood. Debates about the extent of the atonement became increasingly acrimonious in the mid-seventeenth century, even though it is hard to tie down those debates in a clear manner. Hypothetical universalists like James Davenant offered a model of divine willing that saw some level of genuine universal intention to save in the atonement.[68] The Amyraldians, such as John Cameron, reconfigured the covenantal ordering of the decrees in order to establish a universal atonement that yet respected a particular and limited election, while theologians such as John Owen and Patrick Gillespie used the covenant of redemption to argue for much stricter particularity and efficacy in Christ's priestly office.[69] It is important to note that these divisions, though not insignificant in themselves, can generally be embraced within the broad Reformed confessional consensus in a way that, say, Arminian notions of the atonement, which deny its inherent efficacy, cannot.

The issue of the extent of the atonement also became a point of significant historiographical debate, dominated by the question "Did Calvin believe in limited atonement?" The question itself is fraught with problems, from the contentious term "limited atonement" to the apparent (and erroneous) assumption that Calvin has some kind of normative confessional status in the Reformed world. The so-called Calvin against the Calvinists debate has been put to rest over the last two decades, as the deeper roots of Reformed theology in ongoing Western paradigms have been explored and as the diverse influences shaping Reformed theology in the sixteenth and seventeenth centuries have become clearer.[70]

67. *RD* 3:200; Shorter Catechism: "Q. 20. Did God leave all mankind to perish in the estate of sin and misery? A. God having, out of his mere good pleasure, from all eternity, elected some to everlasting life, did enter into a covenant of grace, to deliver them out of the estate of sin and misery, and to bring them into an estate of salvation by a redeemer" (*Westminster Confession of Faith* [OPC edition, 2005]).

68. John Davenant, *Dissertationes duae prima de morte Christi* (Cambridge: Roger Daniel, 1650).

69. See John Owen, *Death of Death in the Death of Christ*, in *Works*, vol. 10; Patrick Gillespie, *The Ark of the Covenant Opened* (London: Thomas Parkhurst, 1677).

70. The work of Richard Muller has been crucial in this regard. On the atonement in Reformed theology, see his *Christ and the Decree: Christology and Predestination from Calvin to Perkins* (Grand Rapids: Baker Academic, 2008); on reframing the historiography of Reformed theology in a way that avoids a naive prioritizing of Calvin, see his *After Calvin: Studies in the Development of a Theological Tradition* (New York: Oxford University Press, 2003).

Perhaps the most powerful arguments in favor of efficacious (or "limited") atonement derive from emphasizing the unity of the sacrifice and the intercession, the idea that Christ does not die for any for whom he does not intercede. This is not a speculative notion, since it is rooted in the Bible's teaching that the Levitical priests sacrificed a goat for the people in Leviticus 16 and then offered the blood for precisely the same people. As Christ is the antitype to the Old Testament priesthood, so too he offers his blood for the people for whom he died.[71]

Whatever the variations among the Reformed on the extent of the atonement, one thing is clear: the priesthood of Christ, as that which deals with human sin, is the foundational aspect of his mediatorial office. It is as priest that Christ addresses the issue of God's wrath against sin and thus removes the impediment preventing human beings from enjoying communion with God. As question 43 of the Heidelberg Catechism makes clear, the death of Christ means that our old man, our sinful nature, is crucified; sin cannot have ultimate power over us; and we can now offer ourselves as living sacrifices in God's service.

CHRIST AS KING

The third aspect of Christ's office for the Reformed is that of Christ as king. The Westminster Shorter Catechism describes this role as follows:

> Q. 26. How doth Christ execute the office of a king? A. Christ executeth the office of a king, in subduing us to himself, in ruling and defending us, and in restraining and conquering all his and our enemies.

The kingly role therefore falls into three basic parts. First, Christ subdues us to himself. This clearly connects to the Reformed view of sanctification, in which God works in the believer by his Holy Spirit to put to death the deeds of the sinful flesh and to cultivate and strengthen an increasing Christlikeness.

Second, Christ rules believers here and now. There is in Reformed theology a twofold aspect to this. Christ rules believers from the perspective of setting the rules by which they are to live as individuals; he also rules them corporately through the church, over which he is king and over which ministers and elders govern in a ministerial capacity. The church is God's creation, and he has established the means by which it is governed; he is the ultimate ruler to whom even ministers and elders must be accountable.

---

71. See Carl R. Trueman, "Definite Atonement View," in *Perspectives on the Extent of the Atonement: 3 Views*, ed. Andrew David Naselli and Mark A. Snoeberger (Nashville: B&H Academic, 2015), 19–61, esp. 44–47.

Third, Christ rules by protecting his people from evil. As the catechism notes, he defends the church and subdues all enemies. In a wonderfully pastoral way, the catechism defines these enemies as "his and our." The emphasis is significant, because it reminds the church that Christ loves his people and cares for them in such a way that he is active in protecting them from those who would seek to do them harm. Too often we can reduce Christ's work to his sacrifice for sin or to his moral teachings. The kingly office reminds us that Christ's work is ongoing here and now and, while sometimes it might appear that the enemies of the church are in the ascendant, Christ is still king and still protects his own, both as individuals and as a body.

In this context, of course, we must remember that Christ's own kingship was inaugurated through suffering and death. He rules over death, because he went through death and showed that it had no hold over him. Thus, his rule and protection in the here and now should not be confused with a guarantee of earthly prosperity or comfort. As Bavinck reminds us, believers should expect to follow in his footsteps. To the world, his kingdom might therefore be invisible, but it means that Christians can overcome suffering and persecution because Christ has already overcome these for them.[72]

Finally, we should note that Christ's kingship will only be fully consummated in the future. As Bavinck states, the kingdom exists now in a very real sense but also in only a spiritual and moral sense, yet it has as its end the glorious and eternal city of God from which all evil will be banished.[73] Thus Christ's kingship gives us confidence now based on what God has promised he will ultimately do. Calvin expresses it well: "Christ, therefore, to raise our hope to the heavens, declares that his kingdom is not of this world (John 18:36). In fine, let each of us, when he hears that the kingdom of Christ is spiritual, be roused by the thought to entertain the hope of a better life, and to expect that as it is now protected by the hand of Christ, so it will be fully realised in a future life."[74]

Conclusion

Christology is the locus about which there is the most disagreement between the Reformed and the Lutherans, primarily because of the way in which it connects to the heated debates over the Lord's Supper and the meaning of the words of institution. This is both understandable—the Lord's Supper is an important aspect of Christian faith and practice—and also unfortunate, given

72. *RD* 3:480.
73. *RD* 3:366.
74. Calvin, *Institutes* II.xv.3.

the fact that on many key points of Christology there is much common ground between the two traditions. The Reformed, like the Lutherans, understand Christ's office of Mediator to be multifaceted and ongoing. The incarnation manifests God's merciful grace toward a fallen world. Christ points consistently to both the holiness and the love of God. On the cross, he crushes the power of sin and evil. And by his death he inaugurates a kingdom in which Christians already live. The Reformed also understand that the full consummation of the kingdom lies in the future and that suffering and contradiction and even invisibility are to characterize the Christian life in the present age. Christ is a perfect Savior, and the Christian faith can be confident precisely because he is God manifest in the flesh, God for us.

4

Election and the Bondage
of the Will

Any Christians who reflect on the question of salvation will soon find themselves raising a number of related issues. How does the creaturely status of human beings affect how they act in this world? What impact does their sinful nature have on their ability to make decisions? What is the relationship between the eternal God's plan of salvation and the execution of that plan in history?

The church first wrestled in depth with these matters in the so-called Pelagian controversy of the fifth century, when the great bishop of Hippo in North Africa, Augustine, clashed with a British monk, Pelagius, and then with Pelagius's numerous followers, debating the nature of salvation. At stake were a number of issues—such as the nature of human freedom, the understanding of biblical references to election and predestination, the impact of the fall on subsequent humanity, and the definition of grace.

Debates and discussions on these matters long outlived Augustine and continued throughout the Middle Ages. Indeed, they continue down to the present day. But they reached a peculiar intensity at the time of the Reformation, when the Protestant Reformers sought to articulate an understanding of salvation that drew deeply on the writings of Augustine and attempted to set their theology within a tradition emphasizing the powerful and decisive sovereignty of God in Jesus Christ. Both Lutheran and Reformed knew that God was sovereign and that men and women were dead in trespasses and sins and therefore in need of God's decisive, unilateral saving action. This brought questions of election and the bondage of the will to the fore in discussions of salvation.

Election and the Bondage of the Will in the Lutheran Tradition

His scholastic instructors at the University of Erfurt taught Martin Luther that he could earn sufficient grace to make his imperfect works count for merit in God's sight if he would only first do his best. Gabriel Biel, the University of Tübingen professor who had taught Luther's instructors, held that God gives (initial) grace to those who do what is in them (*facere quod in se est*, or "do what they can").[1] Luther found his own will too weak to do his best at all times and so became convinced that he did not have God's grace. His instructors, largely shaped by one stream of the thought of William of Ockham, also maintained that the will controls human activity and identity. Luther's own experience convinced him that the sinner's will, active though it is, is bound to turn away from God to false gods.

Erasmus versus Luther

When Desiderius Erasmus sought an issue on which to distinguish his own position from Luther's and thus ward off Roman Catholic attacks on his own reform program, he chose Luther's insistence that the will is bound. Erasmus had treated this issue seldom and lightly in previous works and generally had emphasized God's grace in granting salvation to sinners. He also shared fears that the idea of complete abandonment of any freedom accorded the human will would result in libertinism and a breakdown of moral order. Erasmus chose to attack Luther in the form of the academic disputation, which he had practiced only seldom, in contrast to Luther, who knew well how to engage critics in this forum. Luther thanked Erasmus for his choice of topic: "It is not irreverent, inquisitive, or superfluous, but essentially salutary and necessary for a Christian to find out whether the will does anything or nothing in matters pertaining to eternal salvation. . . . This is the cardinal issue between us, the point on which everything in this controversy turns."[2]

Luther's decision to follow Erasmus in shaping their discussion in the form of a disputation did not allow for him to express as clearly as he did in other genres the fundamental pastoral concern that shaped his argument. His own

---

1. Heiko Augustinus Oberman, *The Harvest of Medieval Theology: Gabriel Biel and Late Medieval Nominalism*, 3rd ed. (Grand Rapids: Baker Academic, 2000), 132–34.
2. WA 18:614.3–6; *LW* 33:35. Cf. similar passages, WA 18:602.22–32; *LW* 33:18; WA 18:786.39–40; *LW* 33:294–95.

experience compelled him to insist that sinners could find no comfort when wrestling with their own sinfulness if even the slightest part of their deliverance rested on themselves. He had felt that his own will had interfered with his best efforts to concentrate his entire attention and life on God and God's will. Therefore, he marshaled all his debating skills to demonstrate that Erasmus's ambiguous embrace of much grace and a modest human effort could ultimately lead only to despair for those sincerely struggling with their own attempts to turn their wills toward God. Only through the power of the Holy Spirit could the will be restored to trust and godliness.

The outcome of this soul-wrenching dilemma led Luther to distinguish the hidden God (*Deus absconditus*) from the revealed God (*Deus revelatus*). He did so most clearly in his *On Bound Choice* (*De servo arbitrio*). God hidden was acting, Luther concluded, when he seemed to be acting contrary to the loving intentions for his people revealed in Scripture. Luther found it logical that because the Creator is greater than the creature, human beings even apart from sin would not understand everything that God is and does apart from his revelation. Sin had only compounded the absence of clear understanding of much that God is doing in a fallen world.[3] But Luther also told his students that God hidden and God revealed do not contradict each other and that what God does that confounds human rationality does not controvert his intentions revealed in Christ.[4] This distinction enabled him to affirm the total omnipotence of God, which he had also learned from his Ockhamist teachers, while confessing the unconditional and total love of God as he found it revealed in God's coming into human flesh to die and rise for sinners as well as in the praise of the psalmists and prophets. Thus, his honest confrontation with the boundness of his own natural choosing of false gods rather than the true God, together with his conviction that God had chosen him apart from any merit or worthiness of his own to be his faithful child, became foundational for his entire theology.

Thus, even though the disputation form, which he employed in *On Bound Choice*, did not require Luther to speak of Christ often, since the issue under dispute was the relative powers and responsibilities of God and the sinner, Klaus Schwarzwäller accurately identified the theme guiding the reformer's argument there as "Christ alone."[5] Luther's confession that God is almighty and loving guided his confrontation with Erasmus regarding the degree to which the human will might need to contribute to building the relationship

3. WA 18:634.14–638.11; LW 33:64–70.
4. WA 43:459.24–32; LW 5:45.
5. *Theologia crucis: Luthers Lehre von Prädestination nach De servo arbitrio, 1525* (Munich: Kaiser, 1970), 109.

with God. The Wittenberg Reformer was not attempting to assert an abstract eternal principle but trying to reproduce the biblical confession of God's reliability and the certainty of his promise of salvation to his chosen people. "Luther stops at the boundary that God's Godness draws; . . . he surrenders himself completely to the God that meets him there. On the other hand, Erasmus is forced by his conclusions to know something *about* God that is not from God . . . but from himself, or more precisely, from a metaphysical principle that gives human beings the possibility of making a judgment about what is God, what belongs to God, what divine is, and what is not."[6]

On Bound Choice

In his reaction to the storm of attacks from papal supporters that had greeted his Ninety-Five Theses on indulgences (1517), Luther wrote in 1521 that, "After the fall of Adam, or after the commission of actual sin, free will exists only in name, and when it does what it can [as Biel had asserted], it is [actively] committing sin." He quoted Augustine to support his belief that only with God's help can sinners escape living with wills bound to wrong choices regarding God.[7] That same year Luther's critique of Jacob Latomus, theologian at the University of Louvain, summarized the view Luther opposed: "Thus, free will reigns not merely in acting rightly but even in fulfilling the intention of him who commands—that is, to put it plainly, [it extends its domination] over the very grace of God; for it is certainly [according to Latomus] in the free will's hand whether grace comes [to the willing person] or not." Luther found Latomus's opinion blasphemous and contrary to Romans 8:3–4, where Paul says that the law, weakened by human desire, cannot accomplish salvation, that God sent Christ to fulfill the demand for righteousness that the law sets forth.[8]

Luther's response to Erasmus, often labeled *On the Bondage of the Will*, was more literally titled *On Bound Choice*, for Luther held that the will continues to be active in its bondage to sin. Its ability to choose God is bound to make false choices by its sinfulness: it continues to will and to move human beings to place trust in objects God created rather than in the Creator himself. Therefore, *On Bound Choice* is first of all a discourse on the nature of the Creator. In line with the Ockhamist convictions of his instructors, Luther presented God as almighty and absolute in his power. Nothing in his creation can hinder or redirect his will or keep him from achieving what he wills.

6. Ibid., 160.
7. WA 7:444.31–451.7; *LW* 32:92–94.
8. WA 8:54.22–55.38; *LW* 31:154–55.

For the will of God is effectual and cannot be impeded since it is the power of God's nature itself; moreover, it is wise, so that it cannot do something wrong. Now, if his will is not impeded, there is nothing to prevent the work itself from being done, in the place, time, manner, and measure that he himself both foresees and wills. If the will of God were such that, when what he was doing was completed, what he had accomplished would remain but the will stopped functioning, as is the case with the human will, which ceases to will when the house it wanted is built, just as it also comes to an end in death, then it could be truly said that things happen contingently and mutably. However, the opposite is the case; God completes what he is doing and his will continues to function.[9]

God's will is immutable—Luther uses this term from his scholastic instructors—but the God whose will does not change is himself wise and loving. "Immutability" means reliability or trustworthiness in the case of the One who created humankind. Luther refused to allow Erasmus to separate God's foreknowledge from his willing. What God foreknows proceeds from what he wills, and therefore his entire engagement with his creation is totally in his hands. Luther could not imagine God's ever being in a passive relationship with his creation and merely observing something independent of his creative hand. God's foreknowing is creative and creating.

Luther constructed an argument that was designed to provide comfort by asserting that God's promises are unchanging. He dismissed the scholastic distinction between a necessity of consequence (*necessitas consequentiae*), an absolute necessity, and a necessity of what is consequent (*necessitas consequentis*), what follows one or another contingency. He accepted only the former.[10]

He abandoned the use of the concept of absolute necessity after writing *On Bound Choice*. It is not to be found in his writings from 1526 on. Luther's focus was not on the philosophical concept of necessity but on the dependability and constancy of God, as is shown by the Bible passages he cited in this connection (Rom. 3:4; 9:6; 2 Tim. 2:19; Titus 1:2).[11] It is unclear whether Luther himself wrote the note of clarification that appeared in the republication of *On Bound Choice* in 1546, the year of his death, in regard to the term "absolute necessity." It reads as follows:

I could wish indeed that another and better word had been introduced into our discussion than this usual one, "necessity," which is not rightly applied either to the divine or the human will. It has too harsh and incongruous a meaning for this purpose, for it suggests a kind of compulsion, and the very opposite of

9. WA 18:615.33–616.6; *LW* 33:38.
10. WA 18:614.27–620.37; *LW* 33:36–44.
11. WA 18:619.6–25; *LW* 33:42.

willingness, although the subject under discussion implies no such thing. For neither the divine nor the human will does what it does, whether good or evil, under any compulsion, but from sheer pleasure or desire, as with true freedom; and yet the will of God is immutable and infallible, and it governs our mutable will, as Boethius sings: "Remaining fixed, you make all things move"; and our will, especially when it is evil, cannot of itself do good. The reader's intelligence must therefore supply what the word "necessity" does not express, by understanding it to mean what you might call the immutability of the will of God and the impotence of our evil will, or what some have called the necessity of immutability though this is not very good either grammatically or theologically.[12]

This particular line of defense of his concept of the bound will is not necessary for his observation and conviction that the human will is bound to create idols and cannot "by its own reason or strength come to Jesus Christ" or trust in him, as Luther taught children to confess in explaining the third article of the Apostles' Creed in his Small Catechism.[13] These thoughts are consistent with Luther's warning to his students against logical maneuvers with the concept of absolute necessity as he lectured on Genesis 26 and 27 in 1541–42.[14]

Luther's certainty that the will is totally bound to seek and rely on false gods did not mean that he regarded the human creature as a puppet or automaton propelled here and there by an arbitrary Creator. The human will remains active but is driven by its own refusal to look toward God to find a source for fundamental identity and instead seeks a safe haven in creatures fashioned by God and refashioned into idols by these sinners. Although he did not describe being human in precisely this fashion, it is clear that Luther did not endeavor to fathom the mystery of humanity, a creature totally in God's hand but also, because created in God's image, with active reasoning, will, and emotions. Therefore, the Wittenberg Reformer lived with the tension between God's omnipotence and the human will's activity and thus responsibility for rebellion against and rejection of God and his Word. In defense of his chief concern, arguing against Erasmus, Luther concluded, "Free choice does many things, but these are nonetheless 'nothing' in the sight of God."[15] He further explained that God "does not work in us without us"—that is, without our functioning as the human creatures he created and preserves as human even when we are defying and doubting him. He is active while directing human

---

12. WA 18:616. See Robert Kolb, *Bound Choice, Election, and Wittenberg Theological Method: From Martin Luther to the Formula of Concord* (Grand Rapids: Eerdmans, 2005), 26–27.

13. *BSELK* 872/873.16–21; *BC* 355.

14. WA 43:458.35–459.6; 43:463.3–17; 43:547.34–548.3; *LW* 5:45–46, 50, 173.

15. WA 18:751.22–24; *LW* 33:239.

wills "whether outside his own realm in his general omnipotence, or inside his own realm by the special power of the Holy Spirit."[16]

This meant that the functioning of the will was totally dependent on the Spirit's empowerment: "Before human creatures are born again as new creatures in the realm of the Spirit, they do nothing and attempt nothing to prepare themselves for this new birth and this realm. When they have been re-created, they do nothing and attempt nothing toward remaining in this realm, but the Spirit alone does both of these things in us, re-creating us without our contribution and preserving us without our help as re-created beings."[17] Indeed, Luther granted that human beings make decisions in the horizontal dimension of their lives that may conform to God's will externally. It is misleading to state that "Luther gives human creatures immeasurably less credit than Erasmus does and God immeasurably more."[18] "Civil righteousness" was not Luther's topic in *On Bound Choice*, but he did affirm that those outside the faith do perform works that externally accomplish God's will for order in society.[19] Nonetheless, he focused on the fact that Paul aptly described the sinner as "ignorant of God, a despiser of God, turned aside from him, and worthless in his sight." "The human creature is ignorant of God and despises God," attitudes that "are the sources of all crimes, the privy of all sins, indeed, the hell of all evils." God's wrath and judgment fall on them. Despising God not only indicates the presence of human mistrust of him but also produces "cruelty and lack of mercy toward our neighbor . . . [and] love of self in all matters in relation both to God and to human creatures."[20] Luther held that sinners are fully responsible for their rejection of God and all its results, yet he also ascribed all human action to the control of God or Satan in his attempt to make clear how powerless and bound the human will is at the core of its being. He used the notorious medieval example of being ridden by God or the devil as someone rides a donkey. If Satan is in the saddle, the sinner moves at Satan's direction. But God comes as the stronger one who overcomes Satan and takes his own as his spoil. Then through his Spirit we are again slaves and captives, though this is a royal freedom, so that we readily will and do what God wills.[21]

Despite this effort to affirm human impotence over against Satan and the captivity of the will to being turned in on itself, Luther went to great lengths to

---

16. WA 18:754.6–7; LW 33:243.
17. WA 18:754.1–12; LW 33:242–43.
18. Heinrich Bornkamm, "Erasmus und Luther," *Lutherjahrbuch* 25 (1958): 16.
19. WA 18:767.40–42; LW 33:264.
20. WA 18:762.30–763.4; LW 33:255–56.
21. WA 18:635.7–22; LW 33:65–66.

dispel the impression that his line of argumentation could leave the almighty God responsible for evil. Two passages from *On Bound Choice* illustrate this:

> When God works in and through evil men, evil things are done, and yet God cannot act evilly although he does evil through evil people, because he who is himself good cannot act evilly. Yet he uses evil instruments that cannot escape the sway and motion of his omnipotence. That evil takes place is the fault, therefore, of the instruments, which God does not allow to be idle even though God himself is the one who keeps all things in motion. It is as if a carpenter were cutting badly with a chipped and jagged ax. Hence it comes about that the ungodly cannot but continually err and sin because they are caught up in the movement of divine power and are not allowed to be idle, but rather they will, desire, and act according to the kind of person they are. All this is settled and certain if we believe that God is omnipotent and also that the ungodly are creatures of God although turned away from God. Left to themselves without God's Spirit, they cannot will or do good. The omnipotence of God makes it impossible for the ungodly to evade the motion and action of God, for they are necessarily subject to it and obey it. But their corruption or aversion from God makes it impossible for them to be moved and carried along with good effect. God cannot lay aside his omnipotence because of human aversion, and the ungodly cannot alter their aversion. It thus comes about that they perpetually and necessarily sin and err until they are put right by God's Spirit.[22]

In a similar vein Luther continues:

> Let no one suppose when God is said to harden or to work evil in us . . . that he does so by creating evil in us *de novo*. You must not imagine God is like an evil-minded innkeeper, full of wickedness himself, who pours or mixes poison into a vessel that is not bad, which itself does nothing but receive or suffer what is bad from the one who is doing the mixing. . . . In us, that is, through us, God is at work when evil takes place, but he is not at fault. The defect lies in us since we are by nature evil and he is good. But as he carries us along by his own activity in accordance with the nature of his omnipotence, good as he is himself, he cannot help but do evil with an evil instrument though he makes good use of this evil in accordance with his wisdom for his own glory and our salvation.[23]

God remains in complete control, but he is not responsible for the evil that has perverted the sinner at the core of being and life. The tension defies logical mastery but preserves both God's responsibility for all things and his creature's responsibility for being the person God created.

22. WA 18:709.28–710.8; *LW* 33:176–77.
23. WA 18:710.31–711.7; *LW* 33:178–79.

Luther on Predestination

Placing God in complete control not only made human impotence clear but also made it clear that God alone is active in restoring sinners from their rebellious and condemned existence. Jesus Christ stands at the center of that restoration, Luther insisted, but the re-creation of the sinner into a child of God rests on God's plan shaped before the creation of the universe (Eph. 1:4). "Predestination" was a word under discussion among scholastic theologians in the 1510s. Two features marked its usage. It designated the whole of God's providing care for his creation, not only his provision of the gift of salvation. Its significance was weakened by scholastic theologians who, when applying it specifically to salvation, diluted its definition to fit in with semi-Pelagian paths to pleasing God. Coupled with that, Luther encountered increasing distress and despair from followers who feared that they had not been predestined for salvation. Even in those passages in *On Bound Choice* that strongly suggest a doctrine of double predestination, Luther was not endeavoring to speak of God's responsibility for sinners' rejection of his Word and lordship.[24] In this work, as in others, he interpreted 1 Timothy 2:4 as an affirmation that Christ died to atone for the sins of all (even though in his translation of this passage in his German Bible he rendered "salvation" as a reference to temporal blessings).[25] Thus, the promise of forgiveness and new life in Christ should be proclaimed to all.

Luther argued that "if grace comes from the purpose or predestination of God, it comes by necessity and not by our effort or endeavor," and thus the doctrine serves as the foundation for the reliability of the promise of salvation in Christ. God's promise to his people in his Word is trustworthy.[26] Luther's understanding of predestination was intended only to reinforce the proclamation of the assurance that comes with God's promise received by believers through the several forms of his Word. Out of concern for troubled consciences that saw their struggles against sinfulness as evidence that they were not elect, Luther largely avoided the term "predestination." In its place he substituted the assurance that God remains ever faithful to the promise he had been giving them from their baptism onward in the various forms of the gospel: written, oral, and sacramental. That did not mean, however, that Luther abandoned resting that promise and the work of Christ on God's plan from before the foundations of the world. In his Galatians commentary of 1535 Luther referred to God's

24. Kolb, *Bound Choice*, 42–43; cf. Martin Doerne, "Gottes Ehre am gebundenen Willen: Evangelische Grundlagen und theologische Spitzensätze in *De servo arbitrio*," *Lutherjahrbuch* 20 (1938): 45–92.

25. Kolb, *Bound Choice*, 40–42.

26. WA 18:772.38–40; LW 33:272.

predestining Paul (1:15)—putting words in the apostle's mouth—"even before
I was born, when I could not think, wish, or do anything good but was a shapeless embryo; . . . this gift came to me by the mere predestination and merciful
grace of God. . . . Then, after I was born, he still supported me even though I
was covered with innumerable and horrible iniquities and evils."[27]

Some of Luther's followers, especially among the nobility, he reported,
were using predestination not as a cause for despair but for presumption.
They reasoned, "If I am predestined, I shall be saved, whether I do good or
evil. If I am not predestined, I shall be condemned regardless of my works."
Luther rejected such "wicked statements" by tying God's choice of his own
inextricably to trust in Christ and his promise received through his Word.
God's inalterable commitment to his promise arose from his faithfulness that
had begun with his choosing his own before creation, according to Ephesians
1:4, for he is the reliable Creator and giver of all good (Mal. 3:6; Rom. 11:29).[28]
In speaking with students and colleagues at their evening gatherings, Luther
placed his hope on God's choosing him before the foundation of the world,
an act he had learned only through God's revealing it in Christ and Scripture.[29]

The distinction of law and gospel governed Luther's use of the concept of
predestination or God's gracious election. This meant that he taught a "broken"
doctrine of predestination.[30] He observed to the students hearing his lectures
on Genesis that "certain ruin" comes "when we soar too high and want to
philosophize about predestination."[31] He expressed his underlying concern in a
letter to an anonymous correspondent who was wrestling with personal doubts
about predestination: "So remember that God the Almighty did not create,
predestine, and choose us to perish but to be saved, as Paul gave witness to the
Ephesians, and had to begin his discussion not with the law or with reason
but with the grace of God and the gospel that is proclaimed to all people."[32]

Luther's Support among Biblical Humanists

Luther was not alone in his rejection of Erasmus's formulation of the
relationship between grace and human action. Many of Erasmus's younger

27. WA 40/1:140.13–24; LW 26:71–72.
28. WA 43:457.33–40; 43:458.31–35; LW 5:42–43; cf. WA TR 5:293–96 §5658a.
29. WA TR 4:642 §5070. This focus on the means of grace instead of God's predestination
can also be found in other *Tischreden*, WA TR 1:427–29 §865; 1:506 §1009; 1:512–13 §1017;
1:514–15 §1019; 1:602 §1208; 2:561–62 §2631a–b; 2:583–84 §2654a–b; 4:420 §4656.
30. Rune Söderlund, *Ex praevisa Fide: Zum Verständnis der Prädestinationslehre in der
lutherischen Orthodoxie* (Hannover: Lutherisches Verlagshaus, 1983), 15–28.
31. WA 42:670.26–28; LW 3:171.
32. Probably written in 1543, WA BR 10:492.128–39 §3956.

humanist supporters also repudiated their older mentor's views.[33] Philip Melanchthon's position on the bondage and freedom of the will has been much disputed by scholars. From the sixteenth century onward, his statements arguing for human responsibility on the basis of the will's ability to choose to perform evil acts have earned him the label "synergist." In fact, his earliest pronouncements supported Luther fully during and following his colleague's debate with Erasmus. Even later, whenever Melanchthon was emphasizing the "freedom of the will," he accompanied the activity of the will that related to God with the drawing power of the Holy Spirit.[34]

Melanchthon summed up the Wittenberg position on "the freedom of the will" in his defense of the biblical faithfulness and catholicity of Luther's teaching in the Augsburg Confession (1530): "A human being has some measure of free will, so as to live an externally honorable life and to choose among the things reason comprehends. However, without the grace, help, and operation of the Holy Spirit a human being cannot become pleasing to God, fear or believe in God with the whole heart, or expel innate evil lusts from the heart. Instead, this happens through the Holy Spirit, who is given through the Word of God" (1 Cor. 2:14).[35] To clarify the implications of this statement for Roman Catholic opponents, he went on to confess the cause of sin: "Although almighty God has created and preserves all of nature, nevertheless the perverted will causes sin in all those who are evil and despise God. This, then, is the will of the devil and of all the ungodly" (John 8:44).[36] His defense of the Confession, the Apology (1531), repeated this position, concluding that "even though we concede to free will the freedom and power to perform external works of the law, nevertheless we do not ascribe to the free will those spiritual capacities, namely, true fear of God, true faith in God, the conviction and knowledge that God cares for us, hears us, and forgives us." Melanchthon's goal was both to preserve outward discipline or human responsibility and to maintain the complete dependence of sinners on the forgiving and regenerating power of the Holy Spirit.[37] However, later in his career his engagement with Roman Catholic accusations of determinism led Melanchthon to avoid ascribing God's election to individuals and to accentuate human responsibility. When he did so, however, his comments about the actions of the will were almost always made within the framework of the

33. Cf. Kolb, *Bound Choice*, 67–70.
34. See Timothy J. Wengert, *Human Freedom, Christian Righteousness: Philip Melanchthon's Exegetical Dispute with Erasmus of Rotterdam* (Oxford: Oxford University Press, 1998).
35. *BSELK* 112.14–21; *BC* 50.
36. *BSELK* 114.21–26; *BC* 52.
37. *BSELK* 548/549.16–552/553.23; *BC* 233–35.

Holy Spirit's drawing the will to faith.[38] This did not prevent his students—suspicious of his stance in the composition of the so-called Leipzig Proposal or Interim of 1548, designed to save Saxon Lutheran pulpits for Lutheran preachers—from charging him with synergism.[39]

Luther's and Melanchthon's students largely followed aspects of the approach of each mentor, avoiding "philosophizing" or speculating about the mechanics of God's unconditional choice of his own and relying on God's Word in oral, written, and sacramental forms of the promise to the faithful to give assurance that their salvation depended on God alone. This was necessary to provide them certainty and thus the comfort of the gospel. At the same time they preached God's law calling believers to daily repentance as they engaged, sometimes less successfully than at other times, in warding off temptations from Satan, the world, and their own inwardly turned desires. The distinction of law and gospel provided the framework for carrying on this "broken" teaching that addressed the reality of some members in the congregation whose lives were slipping back into sinful actions and of others who were repentant and sometimes despairing over their sinfulness but still turning to Christ in faith.

The Strasbourg Dispute

The concern to preserve the proper function of the distinction of law and gospel in preaching and pastoral care moved the head pastor in Strasbourg, Johann Marbach, and his colleagues to challenge the position on the perseverance of the saints advanced by Jerome Zanchi, who was teaching at the Strasbourg Academy. Zanchi believed that the reprobation of those outside the faith was a logical and necessary element of the assurance of salvation that he wished to convey to the elect. Marbach believed that such a teaching brought despair to those who saw in their falling to temptation a sure sign of God's will to damn them and created the presumption in some that since they were elect, their behavior did not matter and they could sin without worry. In early 1563 the Strasbourg city council called on a team

---

38. Cf. Kolb, *Bound Choice*, 70–102; and Timothy J. Wengert, "Philip Melanchthon and the Origins of the 'Three Causes' (1533–1535): An Examination of the Roots of the Controversy over the Freedom of the Will," in *Philip Melanchthon: Theologian in Classroom, Confession, and Controversy*, by Irene Dingel et al. (Göttingen: Vandenhoeck & Ruprecht, 2012), 209–35. The interpretation of Gregory B. Graybill (*Philipp Melanchthon's Doctrinal Journey on the Origins of Faith* [Oxford: Oxford University Press, 2010]) is flawed by its too-frequent failure to take into account the context of specific statements of Melanchthon and the ways in which Melanchthon used the distinction of law and gospel.

39. Kolb, *Bound Choice*, 106–34.

of negotiators from Basel, Württemberg, and Zweibrücken to reconcile the parties.

The "Consensus" this group composed, under the leadership of Jakob Andreae, began by setting a pastoral tone with Romans 15:4: "For whatever was written was written for our instruction, so that by steadfastness and by the consolation of the Scriptures we might have hope." The authors wished to uphold both the apostolic call to repentance and the consolation and hope that troubled Christian consciences are offered in the gospel. They affirmed as axiomatic that God knows all things from eternity (Ps. 139), including the predestination of the elect (Rom. 8–9; Eph. 1). They insisted on avoiding the abyss that thinking about predestination can be apart from Christ, citing Eph. 1:4. Believers must contemplate predestination in such a way that they rely on Christ alone (Matt. 11:25–30), for only he reveals what God has decided in his eternal decree (John 3:16; 6:37–40). On the basis of Ezekiel 18:23, 30, 32 and Matthew 11:28, the "Consensus" affirmed that Christ wants all to find rest in him. Why some reject his call and the saving will of God cannot be explained; believers bow in awe and adoration before this mystery of God (Rom. 11:33; Matt. 11:25). Troubled consciences should not seek God's hidden will but rely on his promise of salvation in Christ. The document affirms that God is not evil but hates sin, which proceeds simply from Satan (John 8:44–47). God forbids sin and is deeply angry over it (Ps. 5:4–5), though he does use it for good in some instances (Rom. 9:17; Exod. 9:16; Rom. 1:18). He is absolutely not responsible for evil in any manner.

Turning to pastoral application, the "Consensus" affirmed that none should judge oneself to be a vessel of wrath (Rom. 9:22–24) but should instead heed the apostolic admonition "All who cleanse themselves will become special utensils, dedicated and useful to the Lord, ready for every good work" (2 Tim. 2:21). Indeed, living according to the flesh brings death (Rom. 8:6; 1 Cor. 6:9–10; Gal. 5:19–21), but those whom the Holy Spirit through the law calls to repentance return through faith to God. Therefore, predestination should be taught in order to eliminate any thought of human contribution or of free will's meriting justification and to assure faithful consciences of God's promise of salvation so that they may battle sin and evil, knowing that no one will tear Christ's sheep out of his hand (John 10:28).[40] Zanchi hesitated, then accepted the "Consensus," but finally broke with the Strasbourg city council and its ministerium and left the city.[41]

40. The "Consensus" is edited in Calvin, *Opera omnia*, CR 47:672–74.
41. Kolb, *Bound Choice*, 173–79.

The Formula of Concord on God's Gracious Election

The issue of the freedom of the will occupied a prominent place in the controversies over the Wittenberg legacy that followed Luther's death. The doctrine of predestination made its appearance within the discussion of the freedom of the will relatively late in the quarter-century-long conflict over defining that legacy. Luther's student Cyriacus Spangenberg published *Seven Sermons on Predestination* in 1567, causing ripples of protest serious enough to place the issue on the agenda of those formulating concord in 1576–77. The Formula of Concord labeled human reason and understanding "blind in spiritual matters"; they "grasp nothing on the basis of their own powers" (1 Cor. 2:14). "The unregenerated human will is not only turned away from God but has also become God's enemy; . . . it has only the desire and will to do evil and whatever is opposed to God" (Gen. 8:21; Rom. 8:7). "As little as a corpse can make itself alive for bodily, earthly life, so little can people who through sin are spiritually dead raise themselves up to a spiritual life" (Eph. 2:5; 2 Cor. 3:5). Indeed, the Holy Spirit works with the human mind and will through the Word, using preaching and hearing of the Word to accomplish conversion, opening hearts as he did Lydia's (Acts 16:14).[42]

The Formula of Concord did use the ancient distinction of foreknowledge and eternal election, contrary to Luther's dismissal of this distinction in *On Bound Choice*. It did so to buttress its rejection of any hint that God might be a cause of evil. It continued Luther's use of the distinction of law and gospel in instructing how the doctrine is to be used. Predestination, or God's eternal election, "extends only to the righteous, God-pleasing children of God." Through his unconditional choosing of his own, God makes clear that he alone is the sole cause of their salvation. God's Word in Christ, who is the book of life (Phil. 4:3; Rev. 3:5), alone reveals that those who have received the promise are elect. The Word, not speculation on the secret counsel of God, is the only source of Christian assurance. Thus, the Formula affirmed Luther's espousal of the universal validity of Christ's death for sin. It did so in order to affirm what believers know from God's election and his promise in the forms of his Word of gospel, that their salvation rests on him not on them.[43]

The Formula of Concord brought a remarkable degree of harmony to Lutheran theology in view of the sharpness of the controversies of the preceding quarter century, but God's election and the preservation of a sense of

---

42. *BSELK* 1226/1227.29/32–1234/1235.14/13; *BC* 491–94; cf. the fuller treatment in the "Solid Declaration" of the Formula of Concord, *BSELK* 1346/1347.1–1386/1387.33/31; *BC* 543–62.

43. *BSELK* 1286/1287.1–1292/1293.14/13; *BC* 517–19; cf. the fuller treatment in the "Solid Declaration" of the Formula of Concord, *BSELK* 1560/1561.4–1596/1597.15/16.

human responsibility did become questions for theologians to answer anew over the next century. The local clergy and the city council of Bern ousted Samuel Huber from his pastorate over his view of "universal election" to grace (even though not all the elect turn in faith to Christ and are saved, in his argument). He became professor in Wittenberg. His position subsequently led to conflict with his Wittenberg colleague Aegidius Hunnius, who formulated a doctrine of election "in view of foreseen faith" (*ex praevisa fide*). With this expression he intended to affirm that God's election created faith in Christ and did not operate apart from such a relationship with the Savior. He did not substantially alter early "orthodox" Lutheran theologians' faithfulness to Luther's commitment to the bondage of the sinner's choice of object of ultimate trust and to God's election of his own before the foundations of the world.[44] However, late in the seventeenth century some of those still regarded as in the mainstream of Lutheran theology taught that God elected the faithful "in view of faith" (*intuitu fidei*), and in at least some cases they affirmed human responsibility by making God's election dependent on their coming to faith. This position was disputed by Lutherans in the United States. In the 1880s many rejected the *intuitu fidei* and supported a return to the position of the Formula of Concord under the leadership of C. F. W. Walther of Concordia Seminary, St. Louis.[45]

Many Lutherans from the late seventeenth century onward have not understood how Luther applied the teaching of Paul in Ephesians 1 and Romans 8 and its basis in the entire Old Testament presentation of God as a choosing God; they have instead found compromises that veer, sometimes sharply, in Erasmus's direction. Their continuing emphasis on God's grace has been undercut by their fear of human licentiousness if people believe that they are elect. Luther's pastoral approach and his careful application of Scripture while using the distinction of law and gospel provide twenty-first-century believers with an effective expression of God's unconditional love as delivered and experienced in Christ.

Election and the Bondage of the Will in the Reformed Tradition

Given the fact that both Lutheran and Reformed share a common commitment to the notion of salvation by grace through faith alone, it is not surprising that they also share considerable common ground on the conceptual foundations of

44. Söderlund, *Ex Praevisa Fide*, 62–132.
45. Ibid., 161–77; Hans Robert Haug, "The Predestination Controversy in the Lutheran Church in North America" (PhD diss., Temple University, 1968).

that doctrine. Although on this issue the Reformed faith has no single classic as famous as Martin Luther's *On the Bondage of the Will*, the same basic anti-Pelagian themes are a vital part of Reformed theology as a whole. If salvation is by grace, then the unilateral action of God and the basic passivity of the human will in the act of justification are points that both communions share.

On this matter, of course, neither Lutheran nor Reformed offer ideas that are particularly innovative. The basic parameters of discussion were set in the anti-Pelagian controversy of the fourth and fifth centuries.[46] Where the Reformers introduced a new dimension to the issue was the connection they made between predestination and assurance, not in the basic substance of the church's specific teaching on the doctrine.[47]

Nevertheless, it is arguable that, from the middle of the sixteenth century, debates about human will and predestination became more and more a characteristic of the Reformed faith in a manner representing a different overall dogmatic emphasis and at points different confessional conclusions from those of later Lutheranism.

Predestination in the Early Reformed Churches

Predestination, with its corollary in the impotence of the human will for salvation, was an unexceptionable doctrine in the early Reformed churches. In 1530, for example, Zwingli submitted his *Ratio Fidei* to the emperor at the Diet of Augsburg, professing both his belief in the absolute predetermining sovereignty of God and the inability of human beings to move toward God in faith because of the depravity of their fallen wills.[48] The doctrine of God as sovereign and therefore determinative of all that happens and the doctrine of the human will as bound by sin after Adam chose to eat the fruit stand side by side.

This is perhaps one point of distinction from the Luther of *On the Bondage of the Will*: the emphasis on the decisive role of the human will in the articulation of the matter of predestination. While Luther arguably roots his understanding of the matter in his doctrine of God, the fall and the subsequent impotence of the human will play an important role in early Reformed formulations. Thus, in the First Helvetic Confession (1536), the writers do not recoil from using the terminology of free will but give it a distinct meaning. Article 9, on free will, reads as follows:

46. An old but still very useful discussion of the doctrine of predestination throughout church history is J. B. Mozley, *A Treatise on the Augustinian Doctrine of Predestination* (London: John Murray, 1855).

47. See *RD* 2:363.

48. Dennison 1:116, 118.

Wherefore we indeed attribute to man free will, as we who experience knowing and wanting to do good and evil; to be sure, we are able to do evil willingly, but we are not able to embrace and follow good (except as we are illuminated by the grace of Christ and moved by His Spirit). For God is the one who works in us both to will and to perform according to His good pleasure. Also our salvation comes from God, but from ourselves comes perdition.[49]

Predestination and election were in fact standard parts of the confessional consensus of the early Reformed churches. Article 17 of the Thirty-Nine Articles of the Church of England offered a brief statement to the effect that predestination to life is the everlasting purpose of God, based on his sovereign choice in Christ.[50] The Belgic Confession advocates a similar position in its article 16, emphasizing this as precluding any notion of good works as the basis for salvation.[51]

A notable exception to this is the Heidelberg Catechism, which has no separate statement on election or predestination, even though its teaching on original sin, the human will, and the role of Christ and the Holy Spirit in salvation seem to require a clear commitment to the Reformed position. This is most likely the result of the specific circumstances of its composition. In the early 1560s in Heidelberg, there had been a major struggle between the Reformed and the Gnesio-Lutherans, which had been exacerbated by the confessional conversion of Elector Frederick III from the Lutheran faith to the Reformed. He commissioned the catechism in part as an attempt to bring together the Reformed and the Philippists in the Palatinate into an alliance against the Gnesio-Lutherans. Given the hesitancy of the Philippists over the matter of predestination, its absence as a separate topic in the catechism is quite plausibly explained as a result of Frederick's ecumenical policy.[52]

With this one exception, however, the basic consensus of the major confessions and catechisms of the Reformed church asserted traditional anti-Pelagian views on predestination. Later in the century, there were significant struggles within the Reformed churches on this issue. In Cambridge in

---

49. Ibid., 1:345.

50. Ibid., 2:759–60.

51. Ibid., 2:433–34.

52. Lyle Bierma comments on the way in which the Heidelberg Catechism is patterned on the language of the Augsburg Confession on this point: "In language that not only respects the boundaries of the AC but echoes its very language, the HC pits in place of the doctrine of predestination a doctrine of the Holy Spirit who works faith in believers." See his *The Theology of the Heidelberg Catechism: A Reformation Synthesis* (Louisville: Westminster John Knox, 2013), 51.

the 1590s, Peter Baro was accused of holding views that contradicted the Reformed consensus and conceded too much to human free agency in a manner compromising predestination and jeopardizing the saints' perseverance, thereby undermining the possibility of assurance. The immediate context was the commission given by Archbishop John Whitgift to William Whitaker, then Regius Professor of Divinity at Cambridge, to compose the so-called Lambeth Articles (1595).[53] These elaborated on various issues such as predestination and perseverance. The nine articles asserted double predestination, denied that this was on the basis of foreseen merits, affirmed perseverance, and emphasized the irresistibility of grace. These articles never achieved official confessional status in the Church of England, but Whitgift regarded them as an accurate explanation of Anglican doctrine as contained in the Thirty-Nine Articles. They were also later incorporated as a whole into the Irish Articles of 1615, a document composed by the Irish bishop James Ussher.[54]

A far greater and more significant revision of the notion of predestination came at the start of the seventeenth century with the advent of Jacobus Arminius and his followers. They came to embody the growing concern with the traditional position in a far more sophisticated way as they launched a theological assault on the position of men like Calvin and his successor, Theodore Beza. Arminius, a Dutchman, was a student of Beza but came to repudiate the predestinarian theology of his teacher. Indeed, he seems to have been particularly repulsed by Beza's supralapsarianism. Instead, he proposed a modified understanding of predestination that, while appearing to rest on only slight theological shifts, effectively overturned the Reformed understanding of grace and predestination. He argued for a modified view of the impact of sin and also for the resistibility of saving grace.[55] The Arminian position was later summarized after his death in the so-called Five Articles of the Remonstrance (1610); these were then answered by the Synod of Dort (1618–19).[56] The synod issued a series of canons asserting human depravity, unconditional election, effectual atonement, the irresistibility of grace, and the perseverance to salvation of the saints.[57]

53. The Lambeth Articles are reproduced in Dennison 3:746.

54. The Irish Articles are reproduced in Dennison 4:88–107.

55. See Richard A. Muller, *God, Creation, and Providence in the Thought of Jacob Arminius: Sources and Directions of Scholastic Protestantism in the Era of Early Orthodoxy* (Grand Rapids: Baker, 1991); also Keith D. Stanglin and Thomas H. McCall, *Jacob Arminius: Theologian of Grace* (New York: Oxford University Press, 2012).

56. On Dort, see Aza Goudriaan and Fred Lieburg, eds., *Revisiting the Synod of Dordt (1618–1619)* (Leiden: Brill, 2010).

57. The Canons of Dort are reprinted in Dennison 4:121–53.

Predestination in Reformed Theology

The notion that Calvin is the theologian of predestination par excellence or that he was morbidly obsessed with the doctrine is a commonplace among those who have never read him (and probably refuse to do so on precisely those grounds). Certainly the issue was of great significance to him. Early in his career the basic elements of his predestinarianism are already present, as is clear in his Catechism of 1537: original sin, the power of human depravity over the will leading to a total moral inability to move toward God,[58] and thus the need for decisive sovereign intervention on God's part. That gracious intervention is rooted in God's predestining will.[59]

The matter also had a certain polemical importance for Calvin. For example, in 1543 he refuted the Catholic theologian Albert Pighius on the bondage of the will. Then, in 1551, Jerome Bolsec was banished from Geneva for criticizing Calvin, particularly on the matter of double predestination. Bolsec believed that such a doctrine made God into the author of evil.[60] In the aftermath, Calvin issued the *Consensus Genevensis* (1552). This was not so much a confessional document as a major treatise on the topic that effectively made the teaching of double predestination a normative requirement for pastors teaching and preaching within Genevan territory.[61] The Bolsec affair was also something that revealed differences within the Reformed tradition itself, with Heinrich Bullinger being concerned that Calvin was pushing the issue beyond the bounds of the Scripture's testimony.[62]

When we turn to the *Institutes*, Calvin's approach is more circumspect than his reputation might suggest. The doctrine is introduced in the 1559 edition after the discussion of Christology and as a means of explaining why the gospel is not preached with equal power to all.[63] In this context,

---

58. Dennison 1:356–57.

59. "The seed of the word of God takes root and brings forth fruit only in those whom the Lord, by his eternal election, has predestined to be children and heirs of the heavenly kingdom" (ibid., 1:366).

60. Bruce Gordon, *Calvin* (New Haven: Yale University Press, 2009), 204–9.

61. The text is reprinted in translation in Dennison 1:693–820.

62. Gordon, *Calvin*, 207; also Cornelis P. Venema, *Heinrich Bullinger and the Doctrine of Predestination: Author of "the Other" Reformed Tradition* (Grand Rapids: Baker Academic, 2002), 58–63.

63. The dogmatic placement of predestination in the *Institutes* did change over time. In 1539, Calvin connected it to providence; in 1559 he moved providence to the doctrine of God. There has been speculation as to whether this represented a shift of theological significance. More recently, Richard A. Muller has argued convincingly that the early position probably reflects the impact of Melanchthon's identification of the topical order in Paul's Letter to the Romans, while the latter indicates a change in the pedagogical structure of the *Institutes*. See Richard A. Muller, "Establishing the *ordo docendi*: The Organization of Calvin's *Institutes*,

Calvin points to Christ himself as the greatest example of election because of the divine freedom and sovereignty demonstrated in his coming as the incarnate Mediator: "In the very head of the Church we have a bright mirror of free election, lest it should give any trouble to us the members, viz., that he did not become the Son of God by living righteously, but was freely presented with this great honor, that he might afterwards make others partakers of his gifts."[64] When reflecting on how individuals become partakers of the salvation that is in Christ, Calvin points to the role of the Holy Spirit and makes it clear that the Spirit only works savingly in those whom God has first chosen for eternal life.[65] This is why the gospel is not preached equally to all: behind the efficacy of the preaching of the Word lies the eternal decision of God to apply that Word to some by the Holy Spirit and not to others.

Election thus provided the foundation for the order of salvation, whereby God's decree in eternity is the causal ground for the salvation of the elect in history. This was most famously articulated by William Perkins in his *A golden chaine: or, the description of theologie: containing the order of the causes of salvation and damnation, according to Gods word* (London, 1600). This work set forth salvation as a scheme based on God's decree to elect some and reprobate others. Most famously, it contained a chart graphically representing salvation from God's decree at the top of the page to eternal life and damnation at the bottom. Based on an original by Theodore Beza, Perkins added a central column, connecting each element of the order of salvation to the life and work of Christ. The diagram has been misread over the years as showing how the whole of Christian salvation is logically deduced from the axiom of the decree and has thus been presented as evidence of an alleged tendency in Reformed theology to make predestination into a central dogmatic principle.[66] In fact, the chart should be read from the bottom upward, thus as an inductive exercise where each step in salvation is only comprehensible in light of what is above it. The chart is, in the

---

1536–1559," in *The Unaccommodated Calvin: Studies in the Foundation of a Theological Tradition* (New York: Oxford University Press, 2000), 118–39; also Muller, "The Placement of Predestination in Reformed Theology: Issue or Non-Issue?," *Calvin Theological Journal* 40 (2005): 184–210.

64. Calvin, *Institutes* III.xxii.1. This christological focus is most dramatically evident in the Scots Confession of 1560, where the whole of chapter 8, on election, is devoted to Christology. See Dennison 2:191–92.

65. Calvin, *Institutes* III.xxi.1.

66. James B. Torrance, "Strengths and Weaknesses of the Westminster Theology," in *The Westminster Confession in the Church Today: Papers Prepared for the Church of Scotland Panel on Doctrine*, ed. A. I. C. Heron (Edinburgh: Saint Andrew Press, 1982), 40–54.

words of Richard Muller, a schematized *ordo salutis*, not an assertion of a deductive predestinarian system.[67]

Given the order of salvation, predestination for the Reformed also undergirds the notion of the perseverance of the saints, the teaching that once an individual is united to Christ through faith by the Holy Spirit, that person cannot fall away from salvation. Those who are elect are those who will be brought to true faith; those who have true faith will therefore persevere in that faith to the end. This was one of the concerns leading to the formulation of the Lambeth Articles, specifically articles 4 and 5, and constituting one of the anti-Remonstrant points at the Synod of Dort (fifth head of doctrine).[68]

The particularity of election and the fact that, as Calvin puts it, the gospel is not preached equally to all, raise two obvious issues for the Reformed tradition: Does this view not undermine the Reformed faith's emphasis on assurance as being, if not strictly of the essence of the Christian life, then certainly something that should normally characterize the Christian life? And is predestination for the Reformed single, in that God positively predestines some to life and merely passes over the rest, leaving them to damnation? Or is it double, with God positively willing both the salvation of some and the damnation of others?

As to the first, the matter of assurance, Calvin (like Luther) sees the sovereignty of God in election as crucial to knowing that God is indeed merciful: "We shall never feel persuaded as we ought that our salvation flows from the free mercy of God as its fountain, until we are made acquainted with his eternal election, the grace of God being illustrated by the contrast, viz., that he does not adopt all promiscuously to the hope of salvation, but gives to some what he denies to others."[69] It is precisely because God does not elect all but only some that those who are elect can truly know how free God's grace is. This might seem somewhat counterintuitive to us, but it does not seem to trouble Calvin at all.[70] The key doctrinal point is that such an election destroys any notion of human merit as a basis for salvation, thus undergirds the idea of

---

67. Richard A. Muller, "Perkins' *A Golden Chaine*: Predestinarian System or Schematized *Ordo Salutis*?," *Sixteenth Century Journal* 9 (1978): 69–81.

68. Dennison 3:746, 4:144–47.

69. Calvin, *Institutes* III.xxi.1.

70. Calvin's thought here is similar to that of Luther in *On the Bondage of the Will*, although Luther expresses it in characteristically more extreme language: "This is the highest degree of faith, to believe him merciful when he saves so few and damns so many, and to believe him righteous when by his own will he makes us necessarily damnable, so that he seems, according to Erasmus, to delight in the torments of the wretched and to be worthy of hatred rather than of love" (*LW* 33:62–63).

justification by grace through faith, and thereby sets assurance on the solid ground of God's action, not on the human response.[71]

For the elect, assurance is to have primarily a christological foundation. According to Calvin, Christ is the mirror in which believers are to contemplate their salvation and thus find certainty of their election.[72] The Second Helvetic Confession echoes this same language, declaring Christ to be a "looking glass, in whom we may behold our predestination."[73] And, in a manner that parallels the emphasis of Luther in *On the Bondage of the Will*, the confession also presses the universality of the gospel promises as a primary source for the believer's assurance.[74] This emphasis was, in fact, a distinctive preoccupation of the confession's author, Bullinger, who maintained that predestination must never be preached in a manner that weakened or compromised the indiscriminate and free call of the gospel to faith in Christ.[75]

On the matter of whether predestination is single or double, there is some variation among the Reformed. As noted above, Calvin held to double predestination and indeed made this normative for Geneva pastors after the conflict with Jerome Bolsec. Bullinger certainly felt that Calvin had gone too far in his treatment of Bolsec; chapter 10 of his Second Helvetic Confession, while speaking of the rejection of those without Christ, is studiedly vague on whether this rejection is based on a positive act of reprobation or simply on the basis that the rejected are not predestined to be united to Christ.[76] Bullinger himself was a careful and cautious advocate of predestination, and it is hard to categorize his thinking in terms of the standard taxonomy of double or single predestination. He affirms double predestination, but in his exposition of the doctrine he tends to identify predestination with election to life.[77] Perhaps Bullinger is best understood as an influential example of an anti-Pelagianism in Reformed theology that is also strongly antispeculative in its concern not to press beyond the plain meaning of Scripture texts.

---

71. This point is made by *RD* 4:227–28. Assurance was nevertheless a constant pastoral issue within the Reformed faith: see Jonathan Master, *A Question of Consensus: The Doctrine of Assurance after the Westminster Confession* (Minneapolis: Fortress, 2015).

72. Calvin, *Institutes* III.xxiv.5.

73. Dennison 2:826.

74. Ibid., 2:827.

75. Venema, *Heinrich Bullinger*, 116.

76. "Therefore, though not for any merit of ours, yet not without a means, but in Christ, and for Christ, did God choose us; and they who are now engrafted into Christ by faith, the same also were elected. But such as are without Christ were rejected, according to that saying of the apostle, 'Prove yourselves, whether ye be in the faith. Know ye not your own selves, how that Jesus Christ is in you, except ye be reprobates?' (2 Cor. 13:5)" (Dennison 2:825).

77. Venema, *Heinrich Bullinger*, 53–54.

The question of double predestination also raises the issue of the difference between supralapsarianism and infralapsarianism, a disagreement over the logical ordering of the decrees of God. In supralapsarianism, the decree of predestination preceded the decree relating to the fall. Therefore God was electing and reprobating human beings without regard to their sinful state. In this system, the fall became an a posteriori justification for damning those whom God had reprobated; it was also necessarily a system of double predestination. In the infralapsarian system, the decree relating to the fall was logically prior to the decree of election and reprobation; thus God elected people from a humanity that was already considered relative to its fallen, sinful state. Both sides of the debate were driven by important and legitimate concerns. Supralapsarians wanted to emphasize the sovereignty and glory of God and to add another safeguard against any notion of human merit. They also wanted to draw out the full implications of the priority of God and his will over creation. Infralapsarians wanted to respect the order of the historical economy as laid out in Scripture and to avoid the notion that God was in any sense directly responsible for sin.[78]

Reformed theologians have disagreed on this issue since it was first mooted at the time of the Reformation. There is no universal consensus on the matter. Figures such as Theodore Beza, Francis Gomarus, and William Perkins held to supralapsarian positions. Others, such as Francis Turretin, were infralapsarians. Still others, such as John Owen, appear to have taken no position on the matter. That diversity in itself indicates that this is an area of doctrine in which breadth and charity are to be exercised.

The position articulated by Herman Bavinck is (in my opinion) the most helpful and judicious in this matter. He regards both supra- and infralapsarianism as reducing the complexity of God's sovereignty over creation and salvation to categories that are too simplistic to do justice to the intricate testimony of Scripture on these matters. The relationship of our sovereign God to his universe is simply too beautiful and elaborate to be reduced to the rather one-dimensional and linear categories involved in the supra/infra debate:

> The counsel of God and the cosmic history that corresponds to it must not be pictured exclusively—as infra- and supralapsarianism did—as a single straight line describing relations only of before and after, cause and effect, means and end; instead, it should also be viewed as a systemic whole in which things occur side by side in coordinate relations and cooperate in the furthering of what always was, is, and will be the deepest ground of all existence: the glorification

---

78. For a clear statement of the supralapsarian and infralapsarian positions, see Louis Berkhof, *Systematic Theology* (Edinburgh: Banner of Truth Trust, 1971), 118–25.

of God. Just as in any organism all the parts are interconnected and reciprocally determine each other, so the world as a whole is a masterpiece of divine art, in which all the parts are organically interconnected. And of that world, in all its dimensions, the counsel of God is the eternal design.[79]

Bavinck's comment is helpful and offers a salutary reminder that divine realities are so much greater than our categories can comprehend. Thankfully, the confessional testimony of the Reformed tradition reflects this. Indeed, it is important to understand that this is not an issue dividing the Reformed at a confessional, ecclesiastical level. It is arguable that the Westminster Confession, for example, is a document with a tendency toward infralapsarianism that nevertheless allows for ministers to hold to a supralapsarian position.[80] Such breadth in a confession is important, because a creedal document should set the bounds of subscription no narrower than those that Scripture itself can be reasonably regarded as establishing.

Providence and the Bondage of the Will

With Lutherans, the Reformed saw predestination as having an anthropological dimension. For all of the emphasis on divine sovereignty in election and predestination, the Reformed were concerned to maintain the fact that human beings were responsible for their own sinful actions and thus justly condemned if they died outside of Christ. Calvin expresses this clearly in the *Institutes*:

> It were here unseasonable to introduce the question concerning the secret predestination of God, because we are not considering what might or might not happen, but what the nature of man truly was. Adam, therefore, might have stood if he chose, since it was only by his own will that he fell; but it was because his will was pliable in either direction, and he had not received constancy to persevere, that he so easily fell.[81]

In considering the fall, Calvin wants to avoid engaging in speculation about the predestining purposes of God and focus rather on the actual events of

79. *RD* 2:392.
80. See the comment of John Murray: "The [Westminster] Confession is non-committal on the debate between the Supralapsarians and the Infralapsarians and intentionally so, as both the terms of the section and the debate at the Assembly clearly show. Surely this is proper reserve in a creedal document" (*Collected Writings of John Murray*, 4 vols. [Edinburgh: Banner of Truth Trust, 1976–82], 4:209). Berkhof (*Systematic Theology*, 125) makes a similar comment with regard to the position of the Christian Reformed Church in his own day.
81. Calvin, *Institutes* I.xv.8.

the day of the fall. Adam, created with a changeable will, freely decided to sin, even though that must be understood against the background of God's absolute sovereignty.[82]

In dealing with the reality of evil, Calvin rejects the notion that God merely permits such to happen. He understands the religious concern underlying this idea—the need to protect God from being morally compromised by having responsibility for evil—but repudiates as a fiction the notion that God only passively permits evil to occur, pointing, for example, to texts such as 2 Kings 22:20; Acts 2:23; 4:28 as proving the contrary.[83] He does not attempt to solve the theodicy problems raised by such texts but rather points to the secret operations and purposes of God in providence.[84]

This position is typical of the Reformed. In his *Commentary on the Heidelberg Catechism*, Ursinus (like Luther in *On the Bondage of the Will*) argues that the very being of God as all-knowing and all-powerful requires that all things happen within the scope of his providential will.[85] Yet Ursinus, unlike Calvin, is also willing to use the language of permission with regard to sin.[86] This does not involve a fundamental deviation from Calvin but represents a careful refinement of the language of permission in order to make it useful for addressing the problem of evil while maintaining the sovereignty of God in providence.

Thus, later Reformed theology also sought to elaborate this position by the use of careful distinctions in a manner that eliminated any notion that God is in some sense morally responsible for evil.

In the *Synopsis Purioris Theologiae*, a collection of theological disputations from the University of Leiden, first published in 1625, disputation 11 is devoted to the theme of providence. Thesis 20 tackles the matter of God's

---

82. Cf. the statement by Bullinger: "[Adam] was once at liberty, and had the Lord to be his friend and favourer; but he did disloyally revolt from God, and got himself another master, the devil, a tyrant as cruel as may be, who for his sin having gotten power over him did, like a merciless lord, miserably handle him like a bond-servant." Heinrich Bullinger, *The Decades*, trans. Thomas Harding, 4 vols. (Cambridge: Cambridge University Press, 1849–52), 2:304.

83. Calvin, *Institutes* I.xviii.1: "Those who have a tolerable acquaintance with the Scriptures see that, with a view to brevity, I am only producing a few out of many passages, from which it is perfectly clear that it is the merest trifling to substitute a bare permission for the providence of God, as if he sat in a watch-tower waiting for fortuitous events, his Judgments meanwhile depending on the will of man."

84. Ibid., I.xviii.2: "The sum of the whole is this,—since the will of God is said to be the cause of all things, all the counsels and actions of men must be held to be governed by his providence; so that he not only exerts his power in the elect, who are guided by the Holy Spirit, but also forces the reprobate to do him service."

85. Zacharias Ursinus, *The Commentary of Dr. Zacharias Ursinus on the Heidelberg Catechism*, trans. G. W. Willard (Cincinnati: Elm Street, 1888), 150.

86. Ibid., 35.

connection to sin by making a twofold distinction. First, sin is seen as an indirect, relative object of divine providence. This means that God uses it as part of a sequence of actions or events proceeding toward a higher end. Second, the thesis distinguishes between various aspects of an evil act.[87] The editors of the critical edition of the text offer a helpful note here:

> For example, the actual taking of a knife, raising one's hand and stabbing the knife into a human body are "positive" actions and can be attributed to God. However, insofar as these actions constitute murder (and are morally defective) they cannot be attributed to God's activity. In terms reminiscent of the Aristotelian duality of matter and form, the act itself is the "matter" of sin, while the sinful character is the "form" that makes it sin. This "form," furthermore, consists of an active deviation . . . from the good intended by God.[88]

This distinction then allows the *Synopsis* to rehabilitate the language of permission as a means of describing God's providential connection to evil. He "permits" sin in that, while he wills the act and permits the form, he uses the evil for a higher, good purpose. This is not a repudiation of Calvin's position. Rather, it is a finely tooled analysis of evil, which refines the terminology of permission in order to avoid the notion that God simply sits in a tower and passively watches evil unfold.

For all of the careful distinctions the Reformed draw on this issue, however, there is an underlying pastoral concern: God's absolute sovereignty over all things is to be a source of comfort to the faithful. The Heidelberg Catechism expresses this beautifully in question 27:

> Q. 27. What do you understand by the providence of God? A. The almighty, everywhere-present power of God whereby, as it were by His hand, He still upholds heaven and earth with all creatures, and so governs them that herbs and grass, rain and drought, fruitful and barren years, meat and drink, health and sickness, riches and poverty, indeed, all things come not by chance, but by His fatherly hand.

The closing words, "by His fatherly hand," indicate the overall framework within which providence, even the evil that it contains, must be understood. God's higher purpose is his fatherly care of his people, and so all things, the good and the bad, are to be seen in that light. This is one of the reasons

---

87. *Synopsis Purioris Theologiae/Synopsis of a Purer Theology: Latin Text and English Translation*, vol. 1, *Dispotations 1–23*, ed. Dolf te Velde, trans. Riemer A. Faber (Leiden: Brill, 2015), p. 277.

88. Ibid., p. 277n22.

why Ursinus declares that the rejection of providence is tantamount to the overthrowing of all true religion, because without trust in God's providence believers would not be patient in adversity, thankful to God for the gifts he bestows on them, or hopeful for the future. All are rooted in God's fatherly providential care.[89]

It is clear from the above that any discussion of the freedom of the will in Reformed theology must be set against the background of God's sovereignty and providence. The Reformed hold that human beings act freely but that their actions are also part of God's providence. Thus in a very real sense human action is determined by God. Freedom exists at the level of secondary causes and is in fact established by God as the first cause, because, if it were not so, it would not exist at all.[90]

We might characterize the Reformed approach to the freedom of the will as a psychological one, in that the will acts freely in accordance with human nature. Though the actions are determined by God as first cause, yet the choices humans make are their own and are not imposed in some external, mechanical way on them. That Adam fell is indicative of the fact that, even before the fall, the human will was in itself changeable and capable of moving toward evil as well as toward good.[91]

The effect of that fall was that Adam and his posterity were plunged into bondage to sin. Because Adam was the federal representative of humanity, a concept typically expressed in Reformed theology by the idea of the covenant of works, all his descendants now stand in a broken covenant relationship with God, which has immediate existential implications for their moral wills. As the Westminster Confession (6.2) expresses it: "By this sin they fell from their original righteousness and communion with God, and so became dead in sin, and wholly defiled in all the parts and faculties of soul and body." The effects of Adam's fall are communicated to his posterity in two ways. There is an imputation of guilt passed on to all; and there is a perversion of the will that is transmitted by natural generation. As the very next paragraph in the Westminster Confession declares: "They [Adam and Eve] being the root of all mankind, the guilt of this sin was imputed; and the same death in sin, and corrupted nature, conveyed to all

89. Ursinus, *Commentary*, 164.

90. "In actions of the free will, a creature endowed with intellect is not exempt from the ordering of the first cause; because it is altogether necessary that every creature and its every action, and even the manner and completion of whatever action it takes are traced back to God, as to the first, most perfect and accordingly most efficient cause" (*Synopsis Purioris Theologiae*, p. 269).

91. Calvin, *Institutes* I.xv.8; *Synopsis Purioris Theologiae*, p. 415.

their posterity descending from them by ordinary generation." This does not mean that everyone is as remorselessly wicked as they can be. The rather dramatic term typically used for this concept—total depravity—is certainly vulnerable to such a misinterpretation, but the caveat of Bavinck is most relevant here: the standard by which human depravity is being judged is the perfect righteousness expressed in the terms of the Decalogue. Therefore, it is entirely correct to acknowledge that fallen human beings are capable of actions that are in themselves good and beautiful.[92] Total depravity does not deny that. It denotes rather that everything that Adam and his posterity do falls below the standard of perfection required by God, and that none are capable in themselves of achieving God's standard, hence the need for Jesus Christ as Mediator.

Given this bondage of the will to sin, the Reformed are still comfortable to an extent in talking about the individual possessing freedom. Again, this needs to be nuanced. To repeat: it is not that the creature stands independent of the Creator, nor that any actions of the creature fall outside of God's decretive will with regard to providence. But human beings still act freely in that their choices and actions are determined at the level of secondary causality by their own wills and not imposed on them in an external, mechanical fashion. Their choices as those who are sinful covenant breakers will always fall short of the exacting standards of the Decalogue, which means that their choices will always be sinful. But nonetheless they are free choices, decided on by the will of the creature. This means that for a sinner to be saved, to be brought to faith and into union with Christ, requires a unilateral, irresistible act of God. That points toward the role of the Spirit in regeneration. Because the will is bound and cannot of itself move toward God, the Spirit needs to free the will to do so.

Conclusion

Despite a common caricature of "Calvinism," the Reformed have no particular obsession with the doctrine of predestination. The Reformed tradition, like Luther, stands within the bounds of Augustinian anti-Pelagianism in its emphasis on the sovereignty of God in creation, providence, and election. It also exhibits some intraconfessional diversity on the matter in terms of double versus single predestination and supra- versus infralapsarianism. Also, as with Luther, the Reformed see this as crucial to assurance: if salvation is not all of God, there can be no assurance.

92. *RD* 3:122–23.

Yet the Reformed do differ from the Lutherans in maintaining the doctrine of the perseverance of the saints through an emphasis on the inseparability of the elements of the order of salvation as grounded in the decree of divine election and as consummated in glory. This point is significant, but perhaps more for the connection between preaching and pastoral practice than for our understanding of God's sovereignty. On the latter point, Lutheran and Reformed are in agreement.

5

Justification and Sanctification

At the very heart of the Reformation lies the doctrine of justification by grace through faith. It shapes the understanding of everything, from the nature of the sacraments to the nature of church authority to the shape of the Christian life. That we are justified by a divine declaration based on the imputed righteousness of Christ is a matter on which both Luther and Calvin, and the Lutheran and the Reformed traditions, agree. This unites us in opposition to the view of Roman Catholicism, as expressed at the Council of Trent, which sees justification as a process involving the impartation of Christ's righteousness. Medieval theologians differed from both Reformation traditions on the matter of grace. Faith as fiducial trust, the foundation of Reformation teaching, stood in strong contrast to the view of Roman Catholic opponents of Luther and Melanchthon, Calvin and Bullinger. The exclusive role of Christ's death and resurrection emphasized by the Reformers made these opponents fearful that public order—society itself—would collapse if human merit played no role in salvation.

Yet the Christian life is more than justification. The New Testament presents a vision of the church as a renewed community and of Christians as those who live lives that are different from those of their non-Christian friends and neighbors. That raises the perennially tricky question of the relation of justification to sanctification, of the connection between God's declaration that we are righteous in Christ and the practicalities of the subsequent Christian life. As the clash between Pelagius and Augustine in the fifth century started as a disagreement over the nature of practical Christianity, so the relationship between justification and sanctification in the Reformation traditions is also one with important practical consequences. In this matter, as will be clear,

117

there are important differences between Lutheran and Reformed. Nevertheless, there is also common ground of a kind that makes fruitful interaction and mutual appreciation a very real possibility.

Justification and Sanctification in the Lutheran Tradition

The young Martin Luther was hounded and haunted by the question of how to attain sufficient merit to win God's approval and finally gain eternal life. When he entered the monastery and later began to study theology formally, his instructors only refined his childhood impression that his contributions were critically necessary to activate and facilitate the grace that God gives to those who do what they can to conform to his law. His reading of Augustine and Scripture finally convinced him that God gives his grace freely, apart from all human merit, thus restoring the integrity and identity of humans as his children through their trust in Christ. Nonetheless, Luther was still driven by the question of how he might find assurance and peace that he would not stray from grace and lose his salvation. Finally, when he came to trust the faithfulness of God and the reliability of God's promise, he sought answers to the question of what it means to be God's righteous child in daily life.

Defining Justification

Luther chose to express his understanding of how he became God's child with one of the medieval terms used for salvation, "justification." To justify means literally, in Latin, "to make righteous or just." To be righteous is to be right, to be and act correctly according to who one is. God is righteous, Luther discovered through his reading of Scripture, because he is faithful, loving, merciful, a giving God who creates unconditionally. God comes to terms with his human creatures, who have abandoned their righteousness or rightness as he created them, by dying and rising in Christ Jesus (Rom. 3:25–26). Human righteousness, or true human identity faithful to God's design, has two aspects, Luther concluded. Human beings are right in God's sight when they are trusting in him and depending on him alone. But God has created his children to love him, one another, and all creation as well and to demonstrate that love in their actions. They act (their "active righteousness") on the basis of their God-given identity as his new creatures, his own children (their "passive righteousness").[1]

---

1. Robert Kolb, "Luther's Hermeneutics of Distinctions," in *The Oxford Handbook of Martin Luther's Theology*, ed. Robert Kolb, Irene Dingel, and L'ubomír Batka (Oxford: Oxford University Press, 2014), 176–78.

Therefore, Luther believed that much of his confusion about his identity as God's child had sprung from conflation of the two kinds of human righteousness and the vertical and horizontal dimensions of life in medieval theology. Scholastic theologies all regarded what makes human beings righteous in God's sight as their performance of his law, not simply his gracious favor. Grace might empower good works, but only the good works themselves render human beings righteous before God. Luther rejected this reading of Scripture. As Martin Chemnitz explained in his *Examination of the Council of Trent*, what separated Trent and its medieval models from the Lutherans was the answer to the question "What is it that makes believers righteous in God's sight?" It is not their grace-wrought works, he answered, echoing Luther: "Faith may be certain that it has a reconciled God and remission of sins not because of the renewal which follows and has been begun, but because of the Mediator, the Son of God." It is the unconditional love and favor that God showed in first bringing them to be his reborn children that causes him to be pleased with them.[2]

This fundamental axiom of Luther's teaching and pastoral care rested on the presupposition that ultimate reality is not to be defined in substantial terms of what an object is, as Aristotle had done, but in relational terms, a presupposition creeping into Luther's perception of the world as early as 1509, well before his turn to Augustine's anti-Pelagian rejection of all human contribution to salvation and his subsequent construction (around 1520) of the complex centered on the distinctions of law and gospel and the two kinds of righteousness.[3] Luther's understanding of the reality of being God's child on the basis of God's justifying action arose in the context of this relational view of reality.

Justification and Atonement

Luther grounded and centered his understanding of this restoration to righteousness in God's sight completely on Jesus Christ and trust in him. Jesus alone has caused and accomplished the abolition of human sin and the restoration of human identity as children of God. Thus, Luther's doctrine

---

2. See chap. 3 above; Martin Chemnitz, *Examen Concilii Tridentini*, ed. Eduard Preuss (Berlin: Schlawitz, 1861), 1:147; Chemnitz, *Examination of the Council of Trent, Part I*, trans. Fred Kramer (St. Louis: Concordia, 1971), 465.

3. Stefano Leoni, "Der Augustinkomplex: Luthers zwei reformtorische Bekehrungen," in *Reformatorische Theologie und Autoritäten: Studien zur Genese des Schriftprinzips beim jungen Luther*, ed. Volker Leippin (Tübingen: Mohr Siebeck, 2015), 190–94. On this dating of the completion of Luther's evangelical maturation, see Reinhard Schwarz, *Martin Luther: Lehrer der christlichen Religion* (Tübingen: Mohr Siebeck, 2015), 1–3.

of justification through faith rests on his understanding of Christ's atoning work. Luther believed that Christ achieved the salvation of sinners by being born as a fully human creature even as he is true, eternal God, the Second Person of the Holy Trinity. Jesus lived the perfect human life in total obedience to the Father and the law, laying down the design for proper, good human living. Accounts of the atonement must take his suffering into account, and his ascension into heaven and his coming to liberate his people on the last day round out the picture of his atoning work. But Luther's proclamation of forgiveness and salvation centered on the substitutional sacrifice of the Lamb of God on the cross and on his return to life, leaving his tomb empty. Romans 4:25, John 1:29, and the description of the Suffering Servant, especially in Isaiah 53, formed the basis for Luther's relating Christ's atoning work to the gift of righteousness to himself and other believers throughout human history.[4]

As is usually the case with those who treat these subjects, Luther could not separate Christ's atoning death and resurrection in the first century from the Holy Spirit's delivery of its benefits in the sixteenth. The verbs of the atonement—forgive, satisfy, substitute, liberate, redeem, re-create—flow back and forth between the centuries, binding the justification of sinners today with the atoning work in Pontius Pilate's time. In his pioneering study of the historical unfolding of atonement theory, *Christus Victor*, Gustaf Aulén claimed Luther as the one later advocate of the ancient church's interpretation of Christ's atoning work as victory over all the believer's enemies. Aulén admitted that Luther also occasionally used the "vicarious satisfaction" language of the medieval period, for which he found Anselm a prime example.[5] Ian Siggins is more accurate in observing, "Luther has no theory of the atonement," meaning that he does not offer a "coherent explanatory discourse about how the atonement works." Instead Luther's works "abound" with various depictions of how Christ came to terms with sin and claimed new life for his chosen people. He does not try to search the mind of God for explanations.[6] On the basis of Romans 4:25, Luther viewed the justification of sinners as the burial of their sins in Christ's tomb and their resurrection with him, which restored their righteousness (Rom. 6:4; Col. 2:12).

Luther believed that justification takes place through the Word of promise, for instance, the baptismal promise, which raises those whose sins now reside

---

4. E.g., in the Smalcald Articles, *BSELK* 726/727.25–728/729.14; *BC* 300–301. Cf. Robert Kolb, "Resurrection and Justification: Luther's Use of Romans 4,25," *Lutherjahrbuch* 78 (2011): 39–60.

5. *Christus Victor: An Historical Study of the Three Main Types of the Idea of Atonement*, trans. A. Hebert (New York: Macmillan, 1961).

6. Ian D. K. Siggins, *Martin Luther's Doctrine of Christ* (New Haven: Yale University Press, 1970), 108–43 (quote on 109).

in Christ's tomb to a new life through faith in the power of God (Rom. 6:4; Col. 2:12). In this way Luther proclaimed that the law's just claim on sinners had been met, sin's wages had been paid (Rom. 6:23) through Christ's vicarious death, and new life had been created through the new birth in baptism (John 3:5–8) or some other vehicle—oral or written—of the promise of new life in Christ. He had struck this theme as early as his Romans lectures in 1515:

> The death of Christ is the death of sin, and his resurrection is the life of righteousness, for through his death he made satisfaction for sin and through his resurrection he delivers righteousness to us. Thus, his death does not merely signify but also accomplishes the remission of sins as an all-sufficient satisfaction. His resurrection is not only the sacrament of our justification, but it effects this righteousness in us, if we believe in it. The resurrection is its cause.[7]

A few months later Luther used this passage to assert, "God's proper work, however, is the resurrection of Christ, justification in the Spirit, and the vivification of the new creature."[8]

Luther depicted the atonement in dramatic ways. One of his central interpretations he labeled "the joyous exchange," in which Christ gives his righteousness to the sinner, whose sins become Christ's possession. Christ died and rose "for you," Luther repeatedly emphasized, transferring the sinners' sins to himself. In 1529 he told students: "You must say, 'I see my sin in Christ. Therefore, my sin is not mine but belongs to another person. I see it in Christ.'"[9] Early on, the reformer employed the image of Christ as bridegroom uniting himself with the sinful bride, in a union that, according to the analogy, enhances the individuality of each without confusing their identities. Christ remains who he is, and sinners remain fully human, enjoying their humanity in a fullness unknown when they were dominated by sin. In keeping with German common law's definition of the full sharing of the property of both marriage partners, Luther proclaimed that Jesus assumed for himself the sins of his bride, while the believer, as bride, received possession of his righteousness and innocence.[10]

By the 1530s Luther had devised an even more vivid picture of Christ's substituting himself under the wrath of the Father. His exposition of Galatians 3:13 before his students in 1531 portrays Jesus's taking on the sinful identity of all sinners in order to abolish their sinfulness and re-create them

---

7. WA 56:296.17–23; *LW* 25:284.
8. WA 21:352; 41:587.20–33; *LW* 77:221; WA 1:112.24–113.10; *LW* 51:19.
9. WA 31/2:434.3–6; *LW* 17:223.
10. E.g., in *Freedom of a Christian*, WA 7:54.31–55.36; *LW* 31:351–52.

as God's children. Luther asserted that Jesus is "the greatest thief, murderer, adulterer, robber, desecrator, blasphemer, etc. there has ever been anywhere in the world," although, he added, in this role Christ "is not acting in his own person. Now he is not the Son of God born of the Virgin but a sinner, who possesses and bears the sins of Paul, the former blasphemer, persecutor, and assaulter; of Peter, who denied Christ; of David, who was an adulterer and a murderer, and who caused the Gentiles to blaspheme the name of the Lord."[11] Luther fashioned a dialogue in which the Father tells Christ, "Be Peter the denier; Paul the persecutor, blasphemer, and assaulter; David the adulterer; the sinner who ate the apple in Paradise; the thief on the cross. . . . The one who has committed the sins of all people. . . . See to it that you pay and make satisfaction for these sins." Thus, he assumed for himself the condemnation of the law, which brought death.[12] "He has and bears all the sins of all people in his body—not in the sense that he has committed them but in the sense that he took these sins, committed by us, on his own body, in order to make satisfaction for them with his own blood."[13]

This imagery continued to appear in Luther's preaching and instruction until the end of his life. Lecturing on Isaiah 53 in 1544, he wrote:

> The one who is regarded as a criminal, a sinner, carries all iniquities. It is true. But Isaiah says that this is a remarkable sinner in that he is a sinner who carries not his own sins, but the sins of others. . . . God's only Son is sinner, criminal, condemned to death, under the power of the devil and hell. . . . We know that he bore our sins but not only that: he rose from the dead, ascended into heaven, sits at the right hand of the Father, and pours out the Holy Spirit to make everyone holy, righteous, to give life and righteousness. In the living person you see nothing of sin. Our sins were laid to his account, and he rose for us.[14]

Nonetheless, these images were not the only ones in the Wittenberg arsenal of proclamation on the benefits of Christ's atoning work. Luther interpreted the justification of the sinner as *Erlösung*, which embraces a spectrum of meaning from ransoming the kidnapped to loosing the bonds of the prisoner and bringing the person into new relationships, such as those of a family. His preaching proclaimed Christ's saving work as parallel to both God's original creative work and his leading Israel out of Egypt, triumphing gloriously by

11. WA 40/1:433.26–31; *LW* 26:277. Cf. Siggins, *Christ*, 144–56.
12. WA 40/1:437.23–27; 40/1:438.12–13; *LW* 26:280.
13. WA 40/1:433.33; 40/1:434.12; *LW* 26:277.
14. WA 40/3:744.36–745.10.

throwing Satan and death into depths far deeper than those of the Red Sea. He also employed the metaphor of the "magnificent duel" between Satan and Jesus, the protector of his people and the conqueror of their foes.[15]

Like many Christian preachers, Luther presented the parallels between God's liberation of Israel from Egypt and Christ's victory over sin, death, and Satan in his resurrection. In preaching on Exodus 14 in 1525, he compared the exodus with the delivery from captivity to sin under Satan's rule through Christ's saving work, and he likened Moses's staff to the Word of God as it pronounces forgiveness on Christ's people.[16] The proclamation of Christ's "rising for our righteousness" elicits trust in what that resurrection has effected: the serpent's enmity, the curse, sin, death, and the devil have all been snatched away and trampled into the dust. The gospel is God's liberating word as it is proclaimed, and through faith it overcomes death, the devil, sin, and every adversity and claims believers' hearts. It turns them to Christ, "who has taken my sins on himself, trampled on the serpent's head, and has become the blessing that lifts sin from my conscience and placed it on himself, whom my sins wanted to kill. . . . God came and tore Christ away from those sins, made him alive, and not just alive, but placed him in the heavens and has him ruling over everything." The result, Luther said, is "that I have a good conscience, am filled with joy, blessed, without fear of this tyrant since Christ took my sin from me and placed it upon himself."[17]

Luther's Large Catechism presents his motif of justification as liberation most clearly. Jesus Christ is Lord "because he has redeemed and released me from sin, from the devil, from death, and from all misfortune. Before this I had no lord or king but was captive under the power of the devil. I was condemned to death and entangled in sin and blindness." Satan had led human beings into sin and death, and therefore they lay under the wrath of God, without the resources or means to find help and comfort. "Those tyrants and jailers have now been routed, and their place has been taken by Jesus Christ, the Lord of life, righteousness, and every good and blessing. He has snatched us, poor lost creatures, from the jaws of hell, won us, liberated us, and restored us to the Father's favor and grace." Luther did not separate this theme of victory from that of satisfaction. He also wrote that Christ suffered, died, and was buried, "so that he might make satisfaction for me and pay what I owed, not with silver and gold but with his own precious blood . . . so that

---

15. Robert Kolb, "Bound, Freed, Freed to be Bound: The Wittenberg Understanding of Justification," *Unio cum Christo* 4 (2016): 43–54.

16. WA 16:264.2–274.20; cf. 16:237.9–20.

17. WA 10/1.2:220.19–221.30. Cf. Uwe Rieske-Braun, *Duellum mirabile: Studien zum Kampfmotiv in Martin Luthers Theologie* (Göttingen: Vandenhoeck & Ruprecht, 1999).

he might become my Lord. . . . He rose again from the dead, swallowed up and devoured death."[18]

God's Re-creative Word

The motif of new creation depends in part on an understanding of the sixteenth-century term *rechtfertigen*, "to justify," which, as Martin Chemnitz wrote, had three shades of interpretation. Some Lutherans viewed the literal translation of the Latin *justificare*, "to make righteous," as a term associated with medieval views of justifying faith made complete or perfect by love, or good works, and thus they avoided it. Chemnitz only briefly mentioned an early modern German definition that Luther presumed more often: to justify means "to do justice to a criminal," or "to execute justice." Luther saw in the forgiveness of sins precisely such an act abolishing the identity of the sinner as guilty before God while restoring the believer's status as child of God.[19] Chemnitz more prominently argued that the Greek δικαιοῦν means "to judge or to pronounce something righteous" but also "to inflict punishment not by a private penalty but chiefly when someone is, so to say, 'judicially' punished after the case has been judged."[20]

Chemnitz's contemporaries and successors favored this definition, based on both Hebrew and Greek usage, which used what is generally labeled a "forensic" interpretation, "to pronounce innocent," as in the courtroom. Some, from the sixteenth century to the twenty-first, have accused the Wittenberg theologians of making justification into a legal fiction with this definition: those whom God merely pronounces righteous still obviously remain sinners. Such critics ignore the fact that in another sense of the word "forensic," God's justification of sinners takes place just as his creation of the reality of his entire universe took place, by virtue of—that is, by the power of—his Word. His re-creation happens, Luther asserted, when God gives his promise of new life in Christ to his chosen people. They become in God's regard, by his reckoning, his children, forgiven of sin, innocent through the death and resurrection of Christ. This promise, God's regard or reckoning (imputation), creates and determines reality, including the reality of the new state of the sinner forgiven and given new birth (John 3:5–8).

---

18. *BSELK* 1054–57; *BC* 434–35.
19. Werner Elert, "Deutschrechtliche Züge in Luthers Rechtfertigungslehre," in *Ein Lehrer der Kirche: Kirchlich-theologische Aufsätze und Vorträge von Werner Elert*, ed. Max Keller-Hüschemenger (Berlin: Lutherisches Verlagshaus, 1967), 23–31. Cf. Henry George Liddell and Robert Scott, *A Greek-English Lexicon*, rev. ed. (Oxford: Clarendon, 1958), 429.
20. Chemnitz, *Examen*, 149; Chemnitz, *Examination*, 1:470–71.

Luther regarded the verbs "impute" (*imputare*) and "repute" (*reputare*) as words designating the creation of reality. Relatively seldom used by medieval theologians (Ockham used the latter at times),[21] these two verbs were transformed by Luther into key expressions of God's way of restoring the righteousness or integrity of sinners on the basis of his view of God's almighty power and ability to meet the demands of the law through Christ's substitutionary death and to bring those pardoned from their sin to a new and restored life in trust toward himself.

Jonathan Trigg argues that Luther's understanding of justification is "intimately related to—indeed even predicated upon—Luther's understanding of the abiding covenant of Baptism."[22] The definition of justification as the execution of justice on the sinner also fits into Paul's description of baptism. Baptism bestows both the gift of the end of sinful identity through burial in Christ's tomb and the gift of new life in the identity of God's child in the resurrected Christ (Rom. 6:3–11; Col. 2:11–15). Preaching on John 1:12, Luther noted that believers are indeed children of God, because despite being old sacks of worms as sinners in this world, they have been made children of the heavenly Father, siblings of Christ, and as his fellow heirs will enjoy all the blessings of his family.[23]

In his *On Bound Choice*, Luther affirmed that God completely controls the salvation of sinners and has their rescue from sin totally in his own hands. Luther's explanation labeled conversion an act of creation ex nihilo (out of nothing) and the believers' remaining in the faith a continuing act of divine preservation, citing James 1:18, "Of his own will he brought us forth by the word of his power that we might be the beginning of his creation," adding, "that is a renewed creation."[24] Lecturing on Isaiah 61 in 1529, he declared: "Justification is the work of God alone, just as creation was God's work alone. Because we are born sinners, it is necessary that we be reborn. We became righteous as Christ says in John 3[:3] and the righteous person is called by Paul a new creature or the new human being."[25] Nearly a decade later, the Wittenberg congregation heard the same, this time from John 3:16: Justification creates children of God out of the nothingness of sinners. When the gift of Jesus Christ is grasped by faith with the heart,

---

21. Cf. Joannes Altenstaig and Joannes Tytz, *Lexicon Theologicum* (repr., Hildesheim: Olms, 1974), where these words do not appear where they would if included (see pages designated Ggg1a [p. 417] and Ggggg2b [p. 788]); cf. *Dictionary of Medieval Latin from British Sources*, ed. D. R. Howlett (Oxford: Oxford University Press, 1989), 1275, 2783–84.

22. Jonathan D. Trigg, *Baptism in the Theology of Martin Luther* (Leiden: Brill, 1994), 2.

23. WA 46:611.23–26; LW 22:88.

24. WA 18:753.36–754.17; LW 18:242–43.

25. WA 25:373.1–4.

the former self does not remain; "You become a new person, for the light dwells in your heart."[26]

Justification also gave the sinner a new birth as child of God, a theme Luther developed early in his Reformation thinking. In sermons on the Decalogue from 1518, he wrote that God gives birth to his people, fashions them, creates them anew through his Word of truth (James 1:18).[27] A year later, he referred again to James 1:18, along with 1 Corinthians 4:15 (Paul's words, "I have given birth to you through the gospel"), and added Isaiah 46:3 ("who have been carried in my womb"), to which the Reformer added, "for this reason the Word is called the uterus and womb of God . . . because we are indeed born of God and have been carried by the Word of his power."[28] Titus 3:4–7 frequently provided Luther opportunity for associating justification with the new birth that God's promise effects in baptism, where sign is joined to Word to actualize God's saving will.[29]

An important element of Luther's understanding of what trust in God's justification of the sinner means for believers on a daily basis is summarized in his relatively seldom-used but often paraphrased concept of the status of his people on earth as *simul justus et peccator*, righteous and yet sinners at the very same time. This concept expressed the mysterious truth that in God's sight his people are fully forgiven and re-created as his beloved children while continuing to experience the infection of sin in every aspect of their lives. In 1539 he noted that "we are happy today, sad tomorrow, but in the view of the Father and the gospel we have been made perfect, and not with the law which changes, but with the remission of sins which remains eternally."[30] Believers experience this *simul* in the midst of the battle between Christ and Satan, which takes place in their lives each day, Luther stated in 1526. In that battle, however, they remain under Christ's rule, and he draws them back to himself when they stray into sin,[31] for God's justifying promise has secured the victory. Thus, in the midst of oppression and temptation, "the Christian is completely invincible, a most powerful king, a glorious victor, who conquers reason, heresies, wisdom, assertions, pronouncements [of scholastic instructors], argument, Satan himself with his angels, the flesh, and sin."[32]

---

26. WA 47:97.26–27; LW 22:374.
27. WA 1:477.3–5.
28. WA 2:430.7–11; cf. a similar expression in his 1522 sermon on John 1:1–14, WA 10/1.1:232.13–14.
29. Small Catechism, BSELK 854/855.1–11; BC 359; but also in his lectures on Titus, 1527, WA 25:62.26–67.6; LW 29:80–86; and in sermons, e.g., WA 10/1.1:1125–1127.10; 45:171.1–175.26.
30. WA 47:747.6–8.
31. WA 20:560.3–9.
32. WA 20:772.9–12.

The re-creative power of the justifying promise creates faith in those who hear it and whom the Holy Spirit moves to trust it as an expression of the new reality God has fashioned for Christ's sake. God's Word is his instrument for this new creation. "Our Lord God has placed forgiveness of sins not in any work that we do, but solely in this work alone: that Christ has suffered and is risen. But he has placed that same work in the mouths of the apostles and ministers of his church—yes, when necessary, in the mouths of all Christians—that they may distribute the forgiveness of sins and proclaim it to all who desire it. . . . Apart from the Word there is no forgiveness of sins."[33]

Justified to Be Sanctified

Faith saves, because faith responds to God's promise with trust, confident that the one who promises is totally reliable. Faith recognizes and accepts the reality of God's saying, "You are my righteous child." Faith recognizes the veracity and reliability of what God believes about his chosen people, that they belong to him and are living under his rule.

Luther could bring together both the substitutionary role of Christ and his liberating action against Satan and at the same time move from this restoration of righteousness and identity as God's child into the impact of this justification on the believer's way of life. He explained that Christ helps sinners in two ways. First, he takes our part against God and serves as "the cloak that is thrown over our shame—ours, I say, the cloak over our shame because he has taken our sin and shame upon himself—but in God's sight he is the mercy seat, without sin and shame, pure virtue and honor. Like a brooding hen he spreads his wings over us to protect us from the hawk, that is, the devil with the sin and death that he causes. God has forgiven this sin for Christ's sake."[34] But the gospel does not only speak of the forgiveness of sins. It also provides the power and strength to live as the children of God. God bestowed this new identity on sinners by means of that forgiveness. "He not only covers and protects us, but he also wants to nourish and feed us as the hen nourishes and feeds her chicks. That is, he wants to give us the Holy Spirit and the strength to begin to love God and keep his commandments." When Christ demanded that the man give up everything to follow him (Matt. 19:16–25), he was saying that keeping God's commandments involves knowing and having Christ.[35] Luther's formulation of these dimensions of the gospel's activities also illustrates his

33. WA 52:273.29–37; LW 69:397.
34. WA 45:153.33–154.14.
35. WA 45:153.15–154.36.

efforts to hold together God's justification of sinners and their practice of the sanctified life as distinct but inseparable.

Later Lutherans emphasized the distinction of justification and sanctification to make sure that the good works of the sanctified life did not become a partial basis for the believer's understanding of salvation. Luther spoke of the relationship between God's justifying action and his people's sanctified action in a different way. The explanation of the first article of the Apostles' Creed in his Small Catechism declared that God created human beings out of the dust of the earth and his breath and that the existence of every human creature is due to "his fatherly, divine goodness and mercy without any merit or worthiness in me." God's gift of life and all his other gifts make it the duty of his people "to thank and praise, serve and obey him." In Luther's explanation of the creed's second article, Christ's redemption "acquired" the sinner "that I might be his own, live under his rule, and serve him in everlasting righteousness, innocence, and blessedness."[36] In presenting the Holy Spirit's sanctifying action, the catechism's emphasis fell on the work of the Spirit through the Word to establish and maintain faith in Christ. The catechism's structure then led into the life that proceeds from this sanctifying activity of the Holy Spirit. It first gives a pattern for the use of prayer to respond to God's address to believers and then in their entire life of listening to the Word and responding (the section on morning, mealtime, and evening prayer). Then it sets down instructions from Scripture for the daily activities to which God calls believers to meet their neighbor's need (the household chart of Christian callings).[37]

This household chart is organized according to the three "estates" or "walks of life" that had shaped medieval social theory: the *ecclesia*, which taught the people the truth; the *politia*, which provided social order and governance; and the *oeconomia*, which embraced the majority of the people, the location of family and economic life. Luther distinguished family and economic roles and functions as he laid out his plan for human living, and he expanded the concept of these life situations so that each person was given roles and responsibilities in all four spheres of life. Service in these spheres marks the life of all human creatures. Christians recognize them as callings from God. Within the structures of the callings that God has established for use in providing earthly benefits and, through the church and the family, the gifts of his Word, Luther taught that believers are to carry out God's commands, using wisdom and freedom to apply them properly but always within God's definition of

36. *BSELK* 870/871.9–872/873.10; *BC* 354–55.
37. *BSELK* 890/891.25–898/899.30; *BC* 363–67.

what human living should be. Believers learn this definition from their own hearts (in the natural law written there) and in biblical commands, which do not specify proper action in every detail of life but give definite direction for the new obedience that faith makes possible and motivates.

In his instructions for confessing sins, the reformer outlined how the framework of decision making functions for believers: "Here reflect on your place in life (walk of life) in light of the Ten Commandments: whether you are father, mother, son, daughter, master, mistress, servant; whether you have been disobedient, unfaithful, lazy, ill-tempered, unruly, quarrelsome, whether you have harmed anyone by word or deed; whether you have stolen, neglected, wasted, or injured anything."[38] In his Large Catechism, Luther used the Ten Commandments as the framework with which to outline what God wills his human creatures to be doing to reflect his love.[39] Reinhard Schwarz observes that the *love* of neighbor is produced by *faith*, as it experiences the *crosses* of daily life that accompany discipleship. Love for the neighbor becomes concrete in the context of loving the neighbor in the callings of each person's life situation. Love is not restrained by the boundaries of these spheres of life but goes beyond their normal boundaries of responsibility to meet human need wherever it can.[40]

Luther's Followers on Justification

Although some scholars have accepted the argument of Albrecht Ritschl that Luther and Melanchthon disagreed on the doctrine of justification and its relationship to the sanctified Christian life, this contention does not hold up under closer scrutiny.[41] Melanchthon's simple statement in the Augsburg Confession laid the foundation for all later Lutheran expressions explicating God's way of restoring sinners to himself:

> We cannot obtain forgiveness of sins and righteousness before God through our own merit, work, or satisfactions, but we receive forgiveness of sin and become righteous before God out of grace for Christ's sake through faith when we believe that Christ has suffered for us and that for his sake our sin is forgiven and righteousness and eternal life are given to us. For God will regard and reckon this faith as righteousness in his sight.[42]

38. *BSELK* 886/887.5–10; *BC* 360.
39. *BSELK* 930/931.10–1048/1049.3; *BC* 386–431.
40. Schwarz, *Martin Luther*, 407–42.
41. Rainer Flogaus, "Luther versus Melanchthon? Zur Frage der Einheit der Wittenberger Reformation in der Rechtfertigungslehre," *Archiv für Reformationsgeschichte* 91 (2000): 6–46.
42. *BSELK* 98/99.5–32; *BC* 38–41.

The following two articles formed the completion of his definition, affirming that God creates this faith through his Word, the means by which the Holy Spirit elicits trust in Christ, and that faith yields good fruit, good works, as God has commanded.[43] This definition echoes through Melanchthon's entire oeuvre. In his 1556 commentary on Romans, he defined justification as "the forgiveness of sins, reconciliation, imputation of righteousness, that is the reception of eternal life in connection with the gift of the Holy Spirit."[44] His commitment to a "forensic" understanding of God's justifying Word of promise, in oral, written, and sacramental forms, is clear throughout his life. God's Word is the instrument, the power of God to save.[45]

It is true that Melanchthon emphasized the satisfaction paid for sin through the ransom of Christ's blood more than Luther and the re-creation through his resurrection less, but Melanchthon did highlight the mediating role of Christ on behalf of his people that is the result of the resurrection.[46] In the Apology of the Augsburg Confession, he used Colossians 2:11–12 to speak of baptismal justification in terms of dying as sinner and rising as one made alive by the Holy Spirit to serve God in faith.[47] His exposition of justification and its inextricable relationship to sanctification is seen particularly clearly in his defense of the Augsburg Confession. His treatment of articles IV to VI, on justification, the means of grace, and new obedience, is the longest section of the Apology of the Confession.[48]

In the early 1550s, the challenge to the Wittenberg understanding of justification from Andreas Osiander, an early and steadfast advocate of Wittenberg reform, initially in Nuremberg and later as professor in Königsberg, led to further discussion and reiteration of Luther's and Melanchthon's teaching on justification in the 1550s–70s. From all sides the disciples of Luther and Melanchthon attacked Osiander's teaching that saving righteousness consists in the indwelling divine nature of Christ, which enters believers through faith. Osiander's university studies had immersed him in the kabbalistic hermeneutic of medieval Jewish interpretation, with its Neoplatonic presuppositions and framework. He thus regarded any "merely" word-based or forensic pronouncement of righteousness as only a legal fiction. He sought a "substance" that would make real the righteous nature of the believer; the divine nature

---

43. *BSELK* 100/101.1–102/103.4; *BC* 40/41.

44. *CR* 15:810.

45. *Loci communes* 1535, *MSA* 2/2:360.31–33; cf. *MSA* 2/2:8–10; Romans commentary, 1532, *CR* 15:501, 510–11; Romans commentary, 1556, *CR* 15:807, 815. Cf. Robert Kolb, "Melanchthons Rechtfertigungslehre," in *Melanchthon Handbuch*, ed. Günter Frank (Berlin: de Gruyter, 2016).

46. Romans commentary, 1532, *CR* 15:610.

47. *BSELK* 449.28–451.25; *BC* 194.

48. *BSELK* 266–397; *BC* 120–73.

of Christ was the most righteous "substance" possible.[49] The Wittenberg critics attacked Osiander's understanding of the two natures of Christ; his concept of the Word of God that, according to the Königsberg professor, did not have the power to determine reality; his downplaying of the sacrificial suffering and death of Christ; and his concept of trust and its restoration of relationship with God.[50]

The Formula of Concord rejected Osiander's teaching and its criticism by his colleague Francesco Stancaro, who argued that only Christ's human nature is at work in the salvation of sinners. Jakob Andreae wrote a summary of the Formula's response:

> Christ is our righteousness neither according to his divine nature alone nor according to his human nature alone. On the contrary, the whole Christ, according to both natures, is our righteousness, solely in his obedience that he rendered his Father as both God and a human being, an obedience unto death. Through this obedience he earned the forgiveness of sins and eternal life for us. . . . Our righteousness before God consists in this, that God forgives us our sins by sheer grace, without any works, merit, or worthiness of our own, in the past, at present or in the future, that he gives us and reckons to us the righteousness of Christ's obedience and that, because of this righteousness, we are accepted by God into grace and regarded as righteous. . . . Faith alone is the means and instrument through which we lay hold of Christ and thus in Christ lay hold of this righteousness which avails before God [Rom. 4:5].

"Justify" means, Andreae continued, "to absolve, that is to pronounce free from sin," citing Proverbs 17:15 and Romans 8:33. He noted that "new birth" and "making alive" are synonyms for justification.[51] The Formula agreed with Luther that Christ's indwelling in believers results from God's re-creative Word of promise and the faith it produces but is not a cause of justification or the means by which justification takes place.[52]

Seventeenth-century Lutheran theologians may have narrowed the focus of the definition of justification to the metaphor of the courtroom and the pronouncement of righteousness on the person in whom the Holy Spirit works faith, yet they did understand that word of absolution to be efficacious,

---

49. Theodor Mahlmann, *Das neue Dogma der lutherischen Christologie: Problem und Geschichte seiner Begründung* (Gütersloh: Gütersloher Verlagshaus, 1969), 93–124; Martin Stupperich, *Osiander in Preussen, 1549–1552* (Berlin: de Gruyter, 1973).

50. Timothy J. Wengert, *Defending Faith: Lutheran Responses to Andreas Osiander's Doctrine of Justification, 1551–1559* (Tübingen: Mohr Siebeck, 2012).

51. BSELK 1236/1237.27–36; BC 495–96.

52. BSELK 1410/1411.10–22; BC 571–72.

creating a new reality through the forgiveness of sins.[53] Their insistence on the distinction of justification and sanctification did not hold the "orthodox" back from insisting likewise on the leading of a life filled with the fruits of faith.[54]

In his engagement with Scripture, Luther encountered a God sorely displeased with his sins, who took the initiative through his incarnation to alter the identity of his rebellious creatures, thereby restoring them to being his children. The Wittenberg Reformer regarded Christ's death and resurrection, which buries sinful identities and raises up this identity as God's own child to be the central event of human history and the fundamental event of the life of each believer. God alone acts in delivering that renewed righteousness, that new identity. In so doing he restores the sinner to being a functioning human being, who from the newborn nature as God's child demonstrates this new identity or righteousness to the world under the power of the Holy Spirit. In this way Luther acknowledged and affirmed both the Creator's full responsibility for the re-creation of the fallen human being and the justified person's full responsibility for being all that God has remade his people to be.

Justification and Sanctification in the Reformed Tradition

For Protestants, the issue of justification and its connection to sanctification is of supreme importance in the dispute with Rome, because it connects to so many points of fundamental disagreement: authority, clarity of Scripture, the nature of God's grace, and the sacraments, to name but the most obvious. It is also, from the Roman perspective, an obvious point at which to press the Protestants in polemic. If justification is by grace through faith on the basis of Christ's imputed righteousness, then what is the place for good works? Is Protestantism not simply a license for antinomianism, for acting as one pleases without care for the consequences—precisely because there are no consequences? Thus the issue of justification and sanctification also lies at the heart of the practical theology of Protestantism.

Having said this, justification is a matter on which there is substantial agreement between the Lutherans and the Reformed. Luther is the watershed figure for the Reformed in this matter, as for Lutherans. Without Luther, the Reformed would not have developed their understanding of salvation as they

53. Kenneth G. Appold, *Abraham Calov's Doctrine of* Vocatio *in Its Systematic Context* (Tübingen: Mohr Siebeck, 1998).

54. Jonathan Strom, *Orthodoxy and Reform: The Clergy in Seventeenth-Century Rostock* (Tübingen: Mohr Siebeck, 1999).

did. Nevertheless, dependence does not mean identity on all matters, and there are some differences on the matter of sanctification.

We can see the importance of Luther on justification for the Reformed by glancing at his reputation among their foremost theologians. Thus, in the seventeenth century, the English congregational divine and Puritan John Owen makes numerous references to Luther in his writings. He cites him as an authority on the imputation of Christ's righteousness,[55] on faith as the sovereign gift of God,[56] on justification by faith as central to the existence of the church,[57] and on the limited authority of church councils and synods.[58] At a number of points, Owen cites him as the great inceptor of the Reformation or as one of a number of illustrious leaders of a previous generation.[59] At no point does Owen offer any direct criticism or make any pejorative comment about Luther. This diplomatic immunity that Owen grants is rooted in the facts that Luther is a hero of the Reformation as a whole for the Reformed and that this heroic stature connects doctrinally to his stand on justification.

Such is a commonplace among the Reformed. Direct criticism of Luther among the Reformed is muted and frequently nonexistent because of his heroic status as the man who confronted the Roman Catholic Church over its errors regarding salvation. Owen's Reformed contemporary Thomas Goodwin refers to Luther repeatedly as the one who made the key breakthroughs on justification, both in terms of imputation of Christ's righteousness and the instrumentality of faith.[60] Such is Luther's historical significance on this point that the question of the historical integrity of the doctrine is often posed by Owen and others in terms of where his church was before Luther, Luther being acknowledged as the historical watershed on the matter.[61] Such was in fact a fairly typical periodization of church history; fundamental disagreements on sacraments and Christology were by and large passed over by the later Reformed, for whom Luther was simply too positive and impressive a figure on justification to be removed from their own narrative.

Setting aside the hagiography and hero worship, however, it is clear that the basics of Luther's approach to justification—the centrality of union with Christ and of Christ's work; and the notions of the instrumentality of faith, the gift of faith, and of the imputation of Christ's righteousness—are

55. John Owen, *The Works of John Owen, D.D.*, ed. William H. Goold, 17 vols. (Edinburgh: T&T Clark, 1862), 2:320.
56. Ibid., 4:462.
57. Ibid., 5:67.
58. Ibid., 8:61.
59. Ibid., 13:38, 219.
60. Ibid., 5:128; 8:475.
61. Ibid., 13:10.

foundational to both Lutheran and Reformed theology. As demonstrated by Calvin's subscribing the Augsburg Confession *variata*, the fundamentals of Lutheran soteriology, with the exception of the status of the sacraments vis-à-vis the ungodly and the related christological underpinnings, are shared by both Lutheran and Reformed.[62]

Union with Christ and Imputation

Calvin opens book III of the *Institutes*, which deals with how the believer obtains grace, with a justly famous statement:

> We must now see in what way we become possessed of the blessings which God has bestowed on his only-begotten Son, not for private use, but to enrich the poor and needy. And the first thing to be attended to is, that so long as we are without Christ and separated from him, nothing which he suffered and did for the salvation of the human race is of the least benefit to us.[63]

This statement is consonant with the position of Martin Luther in *The Freedom of the Christian Man* whereby the context for the "joyful exchange" of sins and righteousness is the union, analogous to a marriage, between the Christian and Christ.[64] What Calvin is doing, of course, is prefacing his discussion of faith by laying a foundation precluding any notion that faith itself might be meritorious or a constitutive part of the believer's righteousness. Part of what prevents faith from being a "work" is that it is Christ and his righteousness that is the basis of justification. Herman Bavinck expresses it perhaps even more powerfully:

> All the benefits of grace therefore lie prepared and ready for the church in the person of Christ. All is finished: God has been reconciled; nothing remains to be added from the side of humans. Atonement, forgiveness, justification, the mystical union, sanctification, glorification, and so on—they do not come into being after and as a result of faith but are objectively, actively present in Christ.[65]

The christological foundation of salvation is clear: salvation in all its glorious aspects is accomplished fully and perfectly in Christ.

We examined the person and work of Christ in chapter 3. Christ is the counterpoint to Adam. As Adam was disobedient, so Christ was obedient.

---

62. Calvin signed the Augsburg Confession *variata* in 1540, though it appears that in the long term he overestimated the influence of Melanchthon and underestimated that of the Gnesio-Lutherans such as Westphal. See Bruce Gordon, *Calvin* (New Haven: Yale University Press, 2009), 246.

63. Calvin, *Institutes* III.i.1.

64. WA 7:54.32–38.

65. *RD* 3:423.

As Adam was the first great representative of all human beings, and as his failure thus implicated all of us, so Christ, the second and last Adam, is the representative of all those given to him by God the Father, and so his work has relevance for all of them.

All that remains is for individuals to be united with Christ in order for all of this work to be true of them too. This then points us toward another area of common ground between the Lutherans and the Reformed: the basis of justification in the imputation of Christ's righteousness. The Westminster Larger Catechism (1648) summarizes justification as follows:

> Q. 70. What is justification? A. Justification is an act of God's free grace unto sinners, in which he pardoneth all their sins, accepteth and accounteth their persons righteous in his sight; not for anything wrought in them, or done by them, but only for the perfect obedience and full satisfaction of Christ, by God imputed to them, and received by faith alone.

This bears comparison with the Lutheran definition as provided by the Apology to the Augsburg Confession: "Because the righteousness of Christ is given to us through faith, therefore faith is righteousness in us by imputation. That is, by it we are made acceptable to God because of God's imputation and ordinances, as Paul says (Rom. 4:5), "Faith is reckoned as righteousness."[66] The important point to note in both of these definitions is the precise role of faith. Faith does not consist in the righteousness that is the basis for the divine declaration that we are justified. Rather, it is what binds us to Christ, by whose righteousness we are justified. Justification is thus a declaration of God based on a righteousness that is, strictly speaking, extrinsic to us but made ours by the way in which faith unites us to Christ. Faith, in short, is the instrumental cause of our justification. This raises the question of the definition of faith.[67]

The Instrumentality of Faith

In the Reformed tradition, faith is always closely connected to the Word of God. It is never contentless nor a mere sentiment. But there are nuances

---

66. Apology III, *BC* 154.

67. In the seventeenth century, a debate arose within Reformed theology concerning the nature of Christ's imputed righteousness. Was it that of his whole obedience, active and passive (his positive fulfillment of the law and his submitting himself to suffering and death), or simply his passive obedience? The debate connected to wider concerns about the role of the law and the need for good works. The consensus position is that both Christ's active and passive righteousness are imputed to the believer. For a summary of the debate and its significance, see Carl R. Trueman, *John Owen: Reformed Catholic, Renaissance Man* (Aldershot, UK: Ashgate, 2007), 102–13.

of definition. Calvin famously defines faith this way: "We shall now have a full definition of faith if we say that it is a firm and sure knowledge of the divine favor toward us, founded on the truth of a free promise in Christ, and revealed to our minds, and sealed on our hearts, by the Holy Spirit."[68] This definition captures something very important, faith's trusting certainty, but taken by itself it seems to make assurance the essence of faith, something that Reformed pastors know is not always true of their congregants. Indeed, wider studies of the Reformed tradition show that it is more nuanced on this point, and even Calvin allowed for time of doubt for the genuine believer.[69] Thus, the Westminster Confession of Faith (18.3) allows that true faith and assurance are not so inseparably joined that the former cannot exist without the latter.[70]

The issue of faith and assurance is not the primary concern of this chapter. More important is the content of faith. Calvin defines it as the knowledge of the divine favor toward us, and thus it is inextricably bound to God's revelation of himself in Christ through Scripture. It is not a vague, contentless trust of the kind that seems to be the case in so many contemporary references to the "need for faith." There the idea seems little more than a hopeful desire that all will turn out for the best. By contrast, true, saving faith for the Christian has objective content: the revelation of God in Christ. Faith is trusting in who God has revealed himself to be. It thus involves an intellectual content and an existential attitude. To use the technical terminology of Reformed orthodoxy, it requires *notitia*, or knowledge; *assensus*, or assent to the truth of that knowledge; and *fiducia*, or trust in that knowledge. By making this threefold distinction in the definition of faith, the Reformed were not indulging in idle pedantry. What they were doing was ensuring that faith could be reduced neither to intellectual assent nor to an emotion or a sentiment. On this point, there is really no difference between the Reformed and Luther, a point made with great clarity by Bavinck.[71]

---

68. Calvin, *Institutes* III.ii.7.

69. See Joel R. Beeke, *Assurance of Faith: Calvin, English Puritanism, and the Dutch Second Reformation* (New York: Peter Lang, 1994); also Jonathan Master, *A Question of Consensus: The Doctrine of Assurance after the Westminster Confession* (Minneapolis: Fortress, 2015).

70. It is important to remember that the Reformation was a pastoral work in progress throughout the sixteenth and seventeenth centuries. New doctrinal insights and definitions created new pastoral questions and problems. These in turn then required revisions and nuancing of those insights. A movement of reaction against the medieval denial of the general possibility of assurance (such as the Protestant Reformation) inevitably overstated its case at points. A century of Protestant pastoral experience produced the more nuanced and variegated approach of the mid-seventeenth century and beyond.

71. *RD* 4:110–11.

When it comes to justification, it is the function of that faith that is important. Here is how the Larger Catechism expresses the idea:

> Q. 72. What is justifying faith? A. Justifying faith is a saving grace, wrought in the heart of a sinner by the Spirit and Word of God, whereby he, being convinced of his sin and misery, and of the disability in himself and all other creatures to recover him out of his lost condition, not only assenteth to the truth of the promise of the gospel, but receiveth and resteth upon Christ and his righteousness, therein held forth, for pardon of sin, and for the accepting and accounting of his person righteous in the sight of God for salvation.
>
> Q. 73. How doth faith justify a sinner in the sight of God? A. Faith justifies a sinner in the sight of God, not because of those other graces which do always accompany it, or of good works that are the fruits of it, nor as if the grace of faith, or any act thereof, were imputed to him for his justification; but only as it is an instrument by which he receiveth and applieth Christ and his righteousness.

Faith is thus the instrument by which the believer receives Christ, and this is identified with the person and work of Christ in the sight of God.

The Gift of Faith

If Christology provides one basic foundation for excluding the idea that faith is itself a constitutive part of the believer's justifying righteousness, this is reinforced by the Reformed insistence that faith is the gift of God and a sovereign work of God by the Holy Spirit. As noted in the chapter on predestination, this is a function both of the sovereignty of God and of the sinful impotence of humanity. Dead in trespasses and sins, the individual cannot turn to God without God's aid any more than a corpse can rise unaided from the grave.

The work of the Spirit in bringing the individual into a saving union with Christ is regeneration. The application of salvation to the individual is analyzed by the Reformed in terms of the order of salvation (as opposed to the history of salvation, which deals with God's redemptive historical acts as they culminate in Jesus Christ), something they see summarized in Scripture in Romans 8:30. In the order of salvation, calling is followed by regeneration.[72] Calling itself is partly external and partly internal. Externally,

---

72. Louis Berkhof notes that a number of Reformed theologians—among whom he names Johannes Maccovius, Alexander Comrie, Abraham Kuyper Sr., and Abraham Kuyper Jr.—place justification before regeneration in the order of salvation, a point that he connects to their tendency toward a doctrine of eternal justification (the idea that the righteousness of Christ is imputed to the elect in the eternal counsels of God). See Louis Berkhof, *Systematic Theology* (Edinburgh: Banner of Truth Trust, 1971), 418.

it involves the confrontation of the individual by the Word of God, typically through preaching. Internally, it involves the application of that Word to the believer by the Spirit. Of course, the individual is dead in sin and so cannot respond to this calling unless God himself intervenes directly to bring about true faith. When that happens, the Reformed refer to it as effectual calling, a work whereby the Spirit uses the Word in a manner that savingly enlightens the mind, renewing and powerfully determining the will so that the individual is made willing and free to answer the call and embrace the grace offered in the Word.[73] Regeneration is this work of the Spirit causing the individual to grasp the Word by faith and thus to become savingly united to Christ.

In the early years of the Reformation, regeneration was used in a broad sense to speak of the renewal of human beings after the image of God. As such, it subsumed both the beginning of the Christian life and continued sanctification under the same term.[74] Later generations of Reformed theologians, however, came to use the word in a more restricted sense, as referring to the origin or genesis of the renewed life. Bavinck notes that this restricted sense is both helpful in giving precision to the term and narrower in meaning than that implied by the language of regeneration in Scripture, a point he counsels Christians to bear in mind in order to avoid reading the restricted sense into biblical texts that do not contain it.[75] The technical term is thus used not to cover all that the Bible might imply by the language of renewal but rather to emphasize the anti-Pelagian genesis of the Christian life in the subjective work of the Holy Spirit.

Faith and Repentance

On the matter of repentance, Reformed and Lutheran are agreed on its basic content. It involves a sorrow for, and turning from, sin and thus a despair in one's own moral abilities to please God. Talking of repentance at the moment of conversion, Bavinck characterizes it in the following terms: "Conversion always consists in an internal change of mind that prompts persons to look at their sinful past in the light of God's face; leads to sorrow, regret, humiliation, and confession of sin; and is, both inwardly and outwardly, the beginning of a new religious-moral life."[76] Repentance is thus theological, in that it involves knowledge of God; existential, in that it impacts individuals in

---

73. Paraphrasing the answer to question 67 of the Larger Catechism.
74. Calvin, *Institutes* III.iii.1–2.
75. *RD* 4:76–77.
76. Ibid., 4:139.

terms that we might describe as psychological or emotional; and practical, in that it manifests itself in action. It is not simply feeling sorry for sin. It grips individuals in their whole being, because it forces on them a basic redefinition of who they are in relation to God.

The phrase Bavinck uses here, "in the light of God's face," points to a matter of some dispute even among the Reformed, that of the relationship of repentance and faith. Whatever the intention, Luther's basic law-gospel structure (which was followed in its essentials by the Reformed) lends itself naturally to a construction of justification that places repentance before faith. Individuals are first confronted by the demands of God's holiness as expressed in his law; then, convicted of their sin, they turn to place their trust in Christ as their righteousness. But where does faith enter the picture?

The Augsburg Confession, article XII, makes the two simultaneous.[77] In the Smalcald Articles, Luther himself emphasizes that law and gospel are to be inseparably connected.[78] Nevertheless, the tendency of the law-gospel dialectic as popularly presented (and as exemplified in Luther's own experience) in both Luther and Reformed circles seems to give logical, and perhaps chronological, priority to repentance over faith. One must first be terrified before one can have any hope of forgiveness.

There are, however, two potential weaknesses in this. First, conviction of sin, which comes prior to any perception of God's grace in Christ, is always vulnerable to becoming merely a form of despair. Second (and while Luther would certainly have repudiated this idea), such repentance might also become a kind of meritorious condition of salvation, whereby individuals are denied any warrant of turning to Christ until such time as they have repented enough to meet the condition.

Reformed theology has itself exhibited a variety of opinions on the matter. The standard definition of repentance is provided by question 76 of the Larger Catechism:

77. "Properly speaking, true repentance is nothing else than to have contrition and sorrow, or terror, on account of sin, and yet at the same time to believe the Gospel and absolution (namely, that sin has been forgiven and grace has been obtained through Christ), and this faith will comfort the heart and again set it at rest" (*BSELK* 106/107.6–11).

78. "This is what the beginning of true repentance is like. Here man must hear such a judgment as this: 'You are all of no account. Whether you are manifest sinners or saints, you must all become other than you now are and do otherwise than you now do, no matter who you are and no matter how great, wise, mighty, and holy you may think yourselves. Here no one is godly,' etc. To this office of the law the New Testament immediately adds the consoling promise of grace in the Gospel. This is to be believed, as Christ says in Mark 1:15, 'Repent and believe in the Gospel,' which is to say, 'Become different, do otherwise, and believe my promise'" (*BSELK* 752/753.1–16).

Q. 76. What is repentance unto life? A. Repentance unto life is a saving grace, wrought in the heart of a sinner by the Spirit and Word of God, whereby, out of the sight and sense, not only of the danger, but also of the filthiness and odiousness of his sins, and upon the apprehension of God's mercy in Christ to such as are penitent, he so grieves for and hates his sins, as that he turns from them all to God, purposing and endeavoring constantly to walk with him in all the ways of new obedience.

The catechism's answer is well-balanced, pointing both to the terror involved in the believers realizing that they can never achieve the standard of righteousness that God demands and to the fact that an apprehension of God's mercy is crucial in true repentance.

Most famously, the question of the ordering of faith and repentance became the center of a major controversy in the Church of Scotland at the start of the eighteenth century, focused around the rediscovery and subsequent republication of a book, *The Marrow of Modern Divinity*, published by Edward Fisher in the 1640s. The work, a dialogue between Nomista, Antinomista, and Evangelista, argued that faith preceded repentance in the order of salvation.[79] The work was endorsed by members of the Westminster Assembly and so should have been uncontroversial. However, in early eighteenth-century Scotland, its teaching became very contentious, particularly on the matter of the order of repentance and faith. Championed by leading churchmen James Hog and Thomas Boston (who wrote a set of influential notes on the book), it was yet condemned by the General Assembly.[80] This so-called Marrow Controversy indicates the extent to which a legalistic tendency had infiltrated certain strands of Reformed church life by this time.[81]

Of course, as the names of the parties in Fisher's work indicate, the matter is part of the much bigger question of the role of works in the Christian life, to which we will turn below. That issue has been a source of perennial vexation for Protestant theologians. Yet it is quite clear that Calvin himself understood faith to come before repentance. In fact, he expresses his position on this matter in fairly strong terms: "Those who think that repentance

79. The three characters represent three ideal types within the Reformed world. Nomista is a legalist who places a high premium on obedience to the law in the Christian life. Antinomista is an antinomian who dramatically downplays to the point of irrelevance the moral imperatives of the Christian life. Evangelista is the one who has the appropriate balance of law and gospel.

80. The text of the *Marrow*, with Boston's notes, is still in print: Edward Fisher, *The Marrow of Modern Divinity* (Fearn, UK: Christian Focus, 2009).

81. On the controversy and its significance, see William VanDoodewaard, *The Marrow Controversy and Seceder Tradition* (Grand Rapids: Reformation Heritage Books, 2011); Sinclair B. Ferguson, *The Whole Christ: Legalism, Antinomianism, and Gospel Assurance—Why the Marrow Controversy Still Matters* (Wheaton: Crossway, 2016).

precedes faith instead of flowing from, or being produced by it, as the fruit by the tree, have never understood its nature, and are moved to adopt that view on very insufficient grounds."[82] Calvin's argument is straightforward. It is that "no man will ever reverence God who does not trust that God is propitious to him."[83] It is only as individuals see that God is merciful and gracious, one who will be kind toward them, that they can turn to God in faith and then repent of their sins. There can be no true repentance without faith.[84]

To this we must also add one final comment. Repentance is not to be identified with a crisis experience, although it may involve such. There could well be a moment in an individual's life when the person is first brought to see sin and rebellion in the light of the grace of Christ and the holiness of God and then to turn to God in repentance and faith. But repentance cannot be exclusively reduced to such. Strictly speaking, repentance for the Reformed—as for the Lutherans—involves a constant turning away from sin, just as faith involves a constant turning toward God through faith in Christ. Both are wrought by the Holy Spirit, both are inseparable, and both are constant. Christian repentance is thus not so much simply a moment of decision as it is an ongoing pattern of life.

Justification and Sanctification

This brings us to the vexed issue of sanctification. I say "vexed" because the nature and status of good works in Protestant theology were points of polemical contention from the start of the Reformation, first with Roman accusations of antinomianism against Luther and then later within Lutheran and Reformed communions themselves. Inevitably, the move from medieval perspectives, in which justification came about by some form of imparted righteousness, to a belief in its happening by imputation raised serious questions about the status and purpose of intrinsic righteousness.

A good place to start the discussion is with the basic distinction that the Westminster Larger Catechism makes between sanctification and justification. In defining the two, the catechism uses precise and important terminology. Justification is characterized as "an act of God's free grace" (Q. 70), while sanctification is "a work of God's grace." The difference between "act" and "work" is deliberate and significant. The former is punctiliar and refers to the fact that justification is declarative. The latter carries connotations of a

---

82. Calvin, *Institutes* III.iii.1.
83. Ibid., III.iii.2.
84. Ibid., III.iii.5.

process and is something that is ongoing and incremental over a period of time. This is brought out clearly in question 77:

> Q. 77. Wherein do justification and sanctification differ? A. Although sancti-
> fication be inseparably joined with justification, yet they differ, in that God in
> justification imputeth the righteousness of Christ; in sanctification his Spirit
> infuseth grace, and enableth to the exercise thereof; in the former, sin is par-
> doned; in the other, it is subdued: the one doth equally free all believers from
> the revenging wrath of God, and that perfectly in this life, that they never fall
> into condemnation; the other is neither equal in all, nor in this life perfect in
> any, but growing up to perfection.

Here the difference is clear. Justification is a declaration built on imputation. Sanctification is a process whereby the individual is slowly but surely conformed to the image of God by the subjective work of the Holy Spirit. In this context it is indeed interesting to see the language of infusion of grace being used. Clearly, it is different from what we find in the Middle Ages, whereby infusion of grace is intimately connected to the sacramental system of the church, and justification is built on the actual righteousness for which this infusion of grace is the basis.

Though distinct, the catechism makes clear that the two, justification and sanctification, are "inseparably joined." One cannot have one without the other. Calvin makes this point by locating both in the believer's union with Christ:

> Christ given to us by the kindness of God is apprehended and possessed by
> faith, by means of which we obtain in particular a twofold benefit; first, being
> reconciled by the righteousness of Christ, God becomes, instead of a judge,
> an indulgent Father; and, secondly, being sanctified by his Spirit, we aspire to
> integrity and purity of life.[85]

Believers, united to Christ, thus enjoy a twofold blessing or benefit: they are justified and reconciled to God, and they are given a desire to move toward actual holiness embodied in thought and action.

The precise nature of this sanctification has proved contentious even within Reformed circles, since the grounding of both justification and sanc-tification in union with Christ might be seen as giving to both an equal ultimacy. Luther, of course, guarded against this by seeing any intrinsic righteousness as grounded firmly in the extrinsic, imputed righteousness of

---

85. Ibid., III.xi.1.

Christ, and good works as flowing in a grateful response to God's justifying action in Christ.[86]

For the Reformed, this construction was vulnerable to making sanctification simply an optional extra. By connecting it to union with Christ, the indispensability of both justification and sanctification could be maintained. Bavinck explains, "To understand the benefit of sanctification correctly, we must proceed from the idea that Christ is our holiness in the same sense in which he is our righteousness. He is a complete and sufficient Savior." In other words, the righteousness of sanctification is the righteousness of Christ, but it is also a righteousness imparted to us by the regenerating and renewing work of the Holy Spirit. This continues until we have been wholly conformed to the image of the Son—something that happens in the fullest sense only after death.[87] Thus, growth in actual holiness is to be the aim and expectation of the normal Christian life, even if this might vary dramatically between believers.

Sanctification in Reformed theology has a dual reference. In terms of its more narrow biblical usage, it refers to believers being set apart and placed in a special relationship with God. This is why the New Testament calls believers "saints" (e.g., Acts 26:10; Rom. 1:7; 1 Cor. 1:2; 2 Cor. 1:1) and also a "holy nation" (1 Pet. 2:9). This positional sanctification is the context for ethical sanctification. In this there are two components: the work of the Holy Spirit and the actions of the believers. In a deep, mysterious sense, sanctification is thus the work of both the Holy Spirit and believers, as they put to death their sinful nature and strive toward the good. The Reformed build on the Pauline construction of the Christian life: Christians have an identity given to them in Christ whereby they are dead to sin, and sin can have no dominion over them; they must therefore strive to live consistently with that identity; and God through his Spirit gives them the resources to do so. Sometimes this is expressed in terms of the imperatives of the Christian life being grounded in the indicatives: what the believer must do is determined by what the believer already is.

Central to this is the so-called third use of the law—which makes the Decalogue a guide to the kind of behavior that is to characterize the sanctification of the Christian. This is discussed in chapter 2. Suffice it to say here that this represents a significant difference from the typical Lutheran emphasis on love as the guiding principle. Clearly, love needs an ethical shape. Despite

---

86. See his sermon "On Two Kinds of Righteousness," WA 2:145–52; and "On the Freedom of the Christian Man," WA 7:49–73.

87. *RD* 4:428. The Reformed do believe in infused righteousness, but this is to be distinguished from the position of Roman Catholics in that this is not the basis for the declaration of justification. For the Reformed, justification is based on righteousness imputed, received by faith.

what modern society tells us, love for the Christian is not an empty sentiment whose ethical content can be invented to suit circumstances and tastes. Of course, the Reformed would see no opposition between love and striving to shape one's life by the principles of the Decalogue. Yet it remains at least a difference in emphasis between the two traditions.

Mortification and Vivification

The most elaborate discussion of sanctification in the Christian life from a Reformed perspective is found in the work of John Owen, the English Puritan Congregationalist. In the 1650s, while vice-chancellor at the University of Oxford, he wrote treatises *On the Mortification of Sin* and *On the Power of Indwelling Sin*, in both of which he wrestled with the problems raised by the fact that justified believers were still in themselves sinners and yet, while justified by Christ's righteousness, were still commanded to strive after personal holiness.[88]

Owen's basic text is Romans 8:13, as he cites it: "If ye through the Spirit do mortify the deeds of the body ye shall live."[89] He comments that this verse contains a duty, a person obligated to that duty, a promise, a cause, and a condition. The ensuing text elaborates on these significantly. The foundation of mortification is union with Christ, and the principal agent is the Spirit, by whom alone Christ works.[90] The Spirit works to make grace and its fruits abound in the believer's life.[91] He also brings the cross of Christ into the heart of the believer both as a motivation to mortification, given the cross's revelation of the depth of God's love of the sinner and hatred of sin;[92] and as a paradigm of the agonizing struggle against sin.[93] Yet the Spirit does more than this. He also implants habits of grace within the lives of believers, habits that both empower individuals to put to death their sinful deeds and desires and to live in newness of life.[94] But even with all of this mortifying and vivifying work of the Spirit, rooted in the believer's union with Christ, mortification remains a duty commanded to the believer—not a legalistic duty driven by craven fear and the need for self-justification, but a filial duty based in our relationship with God through Christ and our Spirit-transformed hearts and minds.[95]

88. Both treatises are found in Owen, *Works*, vol. 6.
89. Ibid., 6:5.
90. Ibid., 6:18.
91. Ibid., 6:19.
92. Ibid., 6:41, 72.
93. Ibid., 6:30.
94. Ibid., 6:19.
95. Ibid., 6:20.

Owen, of course, is not a perfectionist. The process of mortification and vivification is never completed in this life. Indeed, it is to be a continual struggle such that, to use Owen's famous summary phrase, if the believer is not killing sin, then sin will be killing the believer.[96] What he does is draw out the theological framework and the psychological structure of the Reformed understanding of sanctification.

Conclusion

The doctrine of justification is perhaps the central Protestant insight into the gospel, impacting as it does not only the existential shape of the Christian life but also how we understand authority and sacraments. It tracks back to the person and work of Christ and forward to the expectations of the Christian life. It is therefore a doctrine that is important to understand correctly. Further, given the numerous imperatives in the New Testament and, at least in Paul's Letters, the position of these imperatives after his declaration of the gospel of Jesus Christ, the question of sanctification and its connection to justification is also of vital importance.

The Lutherans and the Reformed are in basic agreement on justification: it comes by grace alone through faith alone by the imputed righteousness of Christ. This distinguishes them from Roman Catholics. Yet there are important differences. What the Reformed do, at which the Lutherans perhaps balk, is move from this to an understanding of the Christian life that does place emphasis on growth in sanctification and the Spirit-led fight against sin. This is a tricky issue: the dangers of legalism on the one side and antinomianism on the other are never far away. But it does represent a serious attempt to emphasize both the glories of the Protestant understanding of justification and the role of New Testament imperatives and to address Roman Catholic accusations that Protestantism does not take ethics seriously. In the current climate of moral chaos in our culture, there is surely no more important and practical lesson for the church to teach.

---

96. "Do you mortify; do you make it your daily work; be always at it whilst you live; cease not a day from this work; be killing sin or it will be killing you. Your being dead with Christ virtually, your being quickened with him, will not excuse you from this work" (ibid., 6:9).

6

Baptism

Baptism is the basic rite of initiation into the Christian church. Christ was baptized. The book of Acts contains numerous accounts of baptisms. In the *Didache*, a late-first-century Christian text, instructions are given for preparing for and administering baptism. Throughout the Middle Ages, there was extensive theological reflection on the issue of baptism and its practice, but no orthodox theologian ever questioned the importance of the practice itself.

On the basic point that baptism is the rite of Christian initiation, all who profess Christianity are agreed, even though they might differ over the subjects of baptism (believers or believers and their children) and the mode (immersion, affusion, sprinkling). It is also a point on which both Lutherans and Reformed agree in terms of outward practice: at the Reformation both communions continued the practice of baptizing infants and opposed the Anabaptists, who wanted to restrict baptism to those who professed faith. Indeed, they shared this position even with their Roman Catholic opponents.

Both Lutherans and Reformed also accept the validity of baptism in other churches outside of their own communion if administered in the correct fashion: with water and in the name of the trinitarian God: Father, Son, and Holy Spirit. The infant baptized in a Lutheran church would not later in life need to be rebaptized to join a Reformed church, or vice versa.

This basic identity of practice, however, hides some significant differences in underlying theology. The question of the connection of the act of baptism to the faith of the recipient is a vital one. Does baptism create faith? Is the sign (the water) therefore inextricably connected to the thing signified (Christ)

147

such that the two are simultaneous? Or are the sign and the thing signified chronologically separable? Is God acting directly in the words of baptism and actually making his promise effective? And baptism also connects to other Christian doctrines, raising yet more questions. How do our understandings of original sin and baptism correlate with each other? How does the reality of postbaptismal sin influence our understanding of the sacrament? How does baptism function within the ongoing Christian life?

All these are important and basic questions for the Christian, ones where Lutherans and Reformed share some common ground yet also have significant differences. Understanding baptism within the broader history and theological contours of the two traditions on the most basic element of Christian discipleship is therefore foundational to promoting the mutual understanding, enrichment, and respect that should characterize truly ecumenical Christian fellowship.

Baptism in the Lutheran Tradition

Martin Luther's Small Catechism used four questions to guide children to a proper understanding of the sacrament of baptism as a tool that God uses to deliver his promise of salvation. These questions offer an outline summarizing Luther's view of this form of God's re-creative promise, which establishes and helps sustain his relationship with his reborn children. What is baptism? What does it do? How is that possible? And, crudely paraphrased, so what? Although Luther's earliest writings (apart from direct catechetical treatments of the sacrament) mention baptism relatively seldom, baptism came to occupy an ever more important place in his application of the biblical message to daily life. With reference particularly to Luther's lectures on Genesis (delivered 1535–45), Anglican church historian Jonathan Trigg comments: "Luther's appreciation of baptism continued to grow; it is in the writings of the last years of his life that it assumes the highest profile of all. It is also in the years from the mid 1530's onwards that his praise of it is loudest."[1]

---

1. Jonathan D. Trigg, *Baptism in the Theology of Martin Luther* (Leiden: Brill, 1994), 1. This essay reflects the author's earlier research, reported in Robert Kolb, "'What Benefit Does the Soul Receive from a Handful of Water?': Luther's Preaching on Baptism, 1528–1539," *Concordia Journal* 25 (1999): 346–63; Kolb, "Lutheran View: God's Baptismal Act as Regenerative," in *Understanding Four Views on Baptism*, with Thomas J. Nettles, Richard L. Pratt Jr., and John D. Castelein, ed. John H. Armstrong (Grand Rapids: Zondervan, 2007), 91–109; Kolb, "The Lutheran Theology of Baptism," in *Baptism: Historical, Theological, and Pastoral Perspectives* (Eugene, OR: Pickwick, 2011), 53–75.

What Is Baptism?

Luther presumed that baptism is not simply plain water. Instead it is "water enclosed in God's command and connected with God's Word."[2] He expanded this definition in his Large Catechism: "These two, the Word and the water, may by no means be separated from each other. For where the Word is separated from the water, the water is no different from the water that the maid uses for cooking and could indeed be called a bathkeeper's baptism. But when the Word is with it according to God's ordinance, baptism is a sacrament [that is, a gift from God], and it is called Christ's baptism."[3] "Baptism is a very different thing from all other water, not by virtue of the natural substance but because here something nobler is added, for God himself stakes his honor, his power, and his might on it. Therefore it is not simply a natural water, but a divine, heavenly, holy, and blessed water—praise it in any other terms you can—all by virtue of the Word, which is a heavenly, holy Word that no one can sufficiently extol, for it contains and conveys all that is God's."[4]

Luther believed that God communicates in multimedia fashion. Luther creatively put his appreciation for God's repertoire for communicating his message in an exchange between a peasant and his priest. After receiving absolution from the priest, the peasant requested the Lord's Supper, only to be challenged by the priest: did he regard the absolution as an insufficient forgiveness? Luther's peasant replied no, but "to receive God's Word in many ways is so much better."[5]

God acts in baptism; he gives and the one being baptized receives. This tool of the Holy Spirit restores sinners to God's family. In 1539 Luther reminded the Wittenberg congregation, "Baptism is the water of regeneration through the Holy Spirit in this life for life eternal. This is the proper definition of baptism."[6] Some months earlier he told his hearers, "The [baptismal] word may not look like much, and the water either, but let nothing else sway you. Look instead to him who is giving the command."[7] The validity and performance of the sacrament depended on God's command. Luther told the Wittenberg congregation that whores may live with men, but apart from the institution of marriage as God commanded, there is no marriage. Criminals and magistrates both use the sword, but only the latter, who do their work according to God's institution, are God-pleasing. Thieves possess property, but having

---

2. *BSELK* 882/883.10–12; *BC* 359.
3. *BSELK* 116/117.5–9; *BC* 459.
4. *BSELK* 1114/1115.13–19; *BC* 458.
5. *WA* 30/1:345.9–12; *LW* 53:118.
6. *WA* 47:653.21–22.
7. *WA* 46:168.5–6. On this association, see Trigg, *Baptism*, 67–75.

acquired it against God's plan and institution for economic life, they are in violation of God's ordained structure for life. So with baptism: apart from God's command to deliver his promise of forgiveness of sins, life, and salvation, the use of water, even in religious ceremonies, has no beneficial impact.[8]

Luther viewed the human agent as well as the water and the human words simply as instruments of God's re-creative speaking. "All these instruments ought to be placed before our eyes, and we are to grasp only the Word, which God gives through his means. It is God himself who is speaking when it is God's Word that someone uses to comfort you, and if it is God's Word, then God is acting here, so remember that God himself is doing it."[9] In 1538 the congregation heard, "Christ ordained this baptism. God and the Holy Spirit confirmed it. God gave his testimony with his voice, the Holy Spirit his with his presence. Those who want to be saved shall hold to it, to him who here was baptized (Christ) [by John the Baptist at the Jordan, the text of the sermon] and confirmed by the Father's voice."[10] Thus, the one "who baptizes is an instrument which carries out the baptism. He lends God his hands and tongue, but the words are God's, not the person's. 'I baptize you' is not said by the one who is performing the baptism but by the Trinity. The Trinity is baptizing through this tool."[11]

A part of Luther's legacy from Augustine was the bishop of Hippo's definition of "sacrament" as the joining of God's Word with some created material.[12] To the promise of salvation in the Word and the material element, Luther added a third criterion for a sacrament: the specific institution and command of Christ.[13] In his earlier years the Wittenberg Reformer frequently used Augustine's concept of *signum*, a sign that conveyed or delivered what it signified, not merely a symbol. His colleague Philip Melanchthon continued to use this term, but Luther's use of it diminished significantly by the late 1520s when he came into conflict with Anabaptists, who regarded the sacrament as "a mere sign." In his lectures on the Old Testament, Luther explained that God had always used physical signs of various kinds, including the form of a dove and of fire to bestow his presence in the midst of his people. His Ockhamist training had taught him that God created and ordained the laws governing life within his creation, and so he concluded

8. WA 47:646.31–647.32.

9. WA 46:150.20–26, 33–38.

10. WA 46:185.12–29. Luther repeated these ideas at the beginning of the next sermon, 46:194.15–196.31. He had treated the baptism of Jesus perhaps most extensively in the third of the 1534 sermons, WA 37:270–73.

11. WA 46:148.36–149.27. Luther repeated the point in 1539, WA 47:648.2–3, 23–25.

12. WA 37:260.1–22; 37:261.14–15.

13. WA 37:259.7–10.

that God could certainly place Word together with water in presenting and effecting his promise in dramatic form.[14]

Luther insisted that God approaches sinners through "external means," including the human language encountered in Christian conversation, in sermons and absolution, in hymns and catechisms, and authoritatively in Holy Scripture, as well as in sacramental forms of his promise.[15] He regarded this way of approaching sinners as most assuring. God had ordained these audible, readable, graspable tools as his instruments for effecting his will in the world. For when Luther had searched for God and his assurance through his inner spirit under the influence of the monastic-mystical piety of the cloister, he had found no solid ground for trusting Christ. When the Word came from outside himself, it brought assurance from the Holy Spirit.

God has always worked through signs, Luther asserted. Thus he could conclude, as had Peter (1 Pet. 3:20), that God delivers the promise of salvation just as, mutatis mutandis, God had saved Noah and his family in the ark (both the apostle and the professor seem to have missed the lack of parallel in the changing role of water as foe and friend).[16] God revealed his will to Gideon through a fleece (Judg. 6:37), placed kings in office by anointing them with oil, and guided David through the rustling of the breeze under the pear tree (2 Sam. 5:24). The Holy Spirit continued this kind of conversation in the New Testament. "Christ gave all such signs not only for the sake of love but also to confirm people in the faith, that they might believe in him and through him in God. The whole of salvation history unfolds through the external signs: Mary's virginity, Pilate's administration, the church, the Word."[17] In good scholastic fashion, Luther asked for counterproof: "You cannot give me a single example of a person who was made a Christian or received the Holy Spirit apart from something external. Where did these Christians get the information that Christ is their Savior? Was it not from reading or from hearing? It did not drop down from heaven. It came from Scripture and the Word. . . . He always grasps something physical as a means by which he deals with you, something that is beneficial."[18]

The Wittenberg Reformer joyfully embraced this divine reaching out to human creatures with sensitivity to all five senses as a special indication of God's gracious nature. He works through the hand and the tongue of the

14. WA 27:60.9–21.
15. Smalcald Articles III.v, *BSELK* 764/765.34–766/777.5; *BC* 319.
16. WA 27:59.10–12.
17. WA 27:57.6–29.
18. WA 27:60.20–23.

minister of the gospel.[19] "In baptism there is an oral word and a pourer, in the sacrament [the Lord's Supper] an oral word and a feeder, in preaching an oral word and a speaker, as in absolution." If God had sent our justification through an angel instead of through those who pour, feed, and speak, the angel too would have had to pour, feed, and speak. For God himself is pouring, feeding, and absolving. The angel would be no more than his instrument.[20]

In addition to the sacramental sign pointing to salvation, Luther also viewed the sacrament as a "sign" among Christians, uniting them in love as the family of God.[21] Through the elements of human language accompanied in this case by water, God had entered into the earthly conversation with his human creatures and conveyed to them the promise that brings forgiveness of sins, life, and salvation.

What Does Baptism Do?

Luther's simple answer to his second question for children in his Small Catechism is that baptism "brings about forgiveness of sins, redeems from death and the devil, and gives eternal salvation to all who believe it, as the words and promise of God declare."[22] Luther marshaled the variety of images used by the evangelists and apostles to describe baptism, but already in 1520 he admitted his preference for the words of Paul in Romans 6:3–11 (with its parallel in Col. 2:11–15), which set forth baptism as burying the sinful identity with Christ and being raised from the death of sinfulness to walk in Christ's footsteps. For Luther, that description conveyed what God accomplishes in baptism more clearly than the weaker image of cleansing.[23] In his first treatise on this sacrament, in 1519, Luther associated the word "baptism" (*Taufe*) with immersion, his favorite mode of administering the sacrament (although he did not object to pouring the water over the head of the child), because it demonstrated that baptism is "a blessed dying unto sin and a resurrection in the grace of God, so that the old person, conceived and born in sin, is there drowned, and a new person, born in grace, comes forth and rises."[24]

Luther's use of Romans 4:25, specifically its concept of the atonement as Christ's being handed over to death for the sins of his human creatures and being raised to restore them to righteousness, informed his use of Romans

---

19. WA 46:148.16–21.
20. WA 46:149.23–150.30.
21. WA 27:57.30–58.1.
22. *BSELK* 882/883.18–21; *BC* 359.
23. *The Babylonian Captivity of the Church*, WA 6:534.3–20; *LW* 34:67–68.
24. WA 2:727.1–728.9; *LW* 35:29–30. This treatise reflects Luther's position before his understanding of the re-creative power of God's Word, also in sacramental form, had developed.

6:3–11.[25] Trigg postulated that Luther's "doctrine of justification by faith is intimately related to—indeed even predicated upon—[his] understanding of the abiding covenant of baptism."[26] Thus, the themes that Luther emphasized in treating justification emerge in his discussion of baptism: forgiveness of sins and also God's liberation of his people from captivity to Satan and sin as well as the new creation involved in raising people dead in sin to life in Christ. Baptism deals death to the sinful identity, effecting forgiveness of sins and promising continuing pardon in the life of the faithful. Luther sometimes associated God's sacramental promise directly with the blood of the Savior. It was a kind of chrism: as recorded by one student notetaker, Johann Stoltz, the baptized are "anointed and seasoned with the blood of the innocent Christ." For being washed in Christ's blood means "the presence of the mortification of sin and death as well as the gift of righteousness and life." All this is effected by the Trinity, as was confirmed at Christ's own baptism.[27] "The Word of Christ brings the power of Christ's suffering into baptism. No other water is designed to make atonement with this kind of power. For it effects the remission and washing away of sins, the drowning of death, and the putting on of the garment of eternal life because of the one who instituted baptism, who is the Great One."[28]

Furthermore, baptism involves resurrection with Christ, new life through re-creation or rebirth. In 1519 Luther wrote, "The significance of baptism is a blessed dying unto sin and a resurrection in the grace of God, so that the old person, conceived and born in sin, is there drowned, and a new person born in grace emerges and rises." Citing Titus 3:5 and John 3:3–5, Luther made the comparison of natural birth and new birth in Christ. "Just as a child is drawn out of his mother's womb and is born, and through this fleshly birth is a sinful person and a child of wrath [Eph. 2:3], so one is drawn out of baptism and born spiritually. Through this spiritual birth he is a child of grace, a justified person. Sins are drowned in baptism, and in place of sin righteousness emerges."[29] This baptismal new birth is, in accord with Titus 3 and John 3, the beginning of a new existence as if "from another mother."[30] Through baptism God releases his chosen people from their boundness to sin and Satan, freeing them and extricating them "from the old generation,

25. Cf. Robert Kolb, "Resurrection and Justification: Luther's Use of Romans 4,25," *Lutherjahrbuch* 78 (2011): 39–60.

26. Trigg, *Baptism*, 2.

27. WA 46:176.1–12. Stoltz's observation is found in 46:176.36–37.

28. WA 46:195.4–7.

29. WA 2:727.33–728.8; LW 35:30.

30. WA 46:176.4–8.

from their corrupt and diabolical skin, and transplant[ing them] into original innocence. Is not this a significant blessing from God that the human creature is freed from the old filth and received into grace, so that God's wrath, sin, death, and eternal damnation may be destroyed? These are works of God, not human works."[31] This act of liberation is the act of new creation, creating out of the chaos of sin a child of God, who is freed from the power of the devil, sin, death, and the law, from God's wrath and judgment, through the forgiveness of sins.[32]

How Is That Possible?

Luther had children explain how baptism could do "such great things": "Clearly the water does not do it, but the Word of God, which is with and alongside the water, and faith, which trusts this Word of God in the water. For without the Word of God the water is plain water and not a baptism, but with the Word of God it is a baptism, that is, a grace-filled water of life and a 'bath of the new birth in the Holy Spirit, as St. Paul says to Titus in chapter 3 [vv. 5–8].'"[33] God's promise did not magically convey a ticket to heaven but rather established a relationship paralleling that of earthly parents with their children. Long before the ability of the child to express anything regarding the relationship, parental care surrounds and sustains the child. So with the baptismal promise: God assumes the role of heavenly Father in his pledge in the words of baptism and commits himself to exercising divine parental care. Because God is the one acting in baptism, he is able to establish the relationship apart from human reaction—but always with the expectation of the response of trust in the promise when that becomes psychologically possible.

In 1520 Luther could say that baptism does not save but faith in what it does saves, in order to emphasize that trust in the promise is the necessary side of the relationship when the human being is able to trust.[34] Later he most often concluded that baptism, as the Holy Spirit's instrument of delivery, does indeed bestow forgiveness, life, and salvation.[35] For those who can exercise the psychological characteristics of trusting, it does so by creating the relationship that consists, on the human side, of faith or confidence in the reliability of God's promise that through Christ's death and resurrection this forgiveness,

---

31. WA 46:175.25–29.
32. WA 47:650.18–652.21. This section was repeated in summary form in the following sermon, 47:654.17–20, 37–655.21.
33. *BSELK* 884/885.2–11; *BC* 259.
34. WA 6:532.29; *LW* 36:66.
35. E.g., in the Small Catechism, *BSELK* 882/883.18–21; *BC* 359.

life, and salvation are given to the baptized. Indeed, Luther posited defenses of "infant faith," but with the disclaimer that precisely how the relationship is established with infants through God's baptismal promise lies beyond human grasping. He argued that because God's action in baptism is primary and its promise creates and elicits faith through the power of the Holy Spirit, and because original sin is present in the child born to mortality, the church's ancient practice of baptizing infants has proved itself through its creation of believers throughout the centuries.[36] Also when adults are baptized, Luther wrote, they do not boast that their faith is the reason for receiving baptism. Instead, God's command suffices; with its gift of God's covenant and on the basis of God's Word, faith will grow, not of itself.[37]

Nonetheless, Luther insisted that the baptismal promise cannot be enjoyed apart from the faith that throws itself in trust upon the one who has delivered the promise. He labeled it foolish to "separate faith from the object to which faith is attached and secured, all on the grounds that the object is something external. Yes, it must be external so that it can be perceived and grasped by the senses and thus brought into the heart, just as the entire gospel is an external, oral proclamation. In short, whatever God does and effects in us he desires to accomplish through such an external ordinance." Faith arises from God's address, God's promise, as it comes in the sacrament as well as the oral conveying of the Word, Luther presumed.[38]

Perhaps because the Ockhamists had used the word "covenant" to describe the process by which human beings did their best and thus qualified themselves for grace sufficient to win them eternal life, Luther largely avoided the term. He most often translated διαθήκη as "testament." One exception is his labeling of baptism as a "covenant" (*Bund*) probably because it is clear that the infants are contributing nothing to the new birth effected in the sacrament. "No one can say [of baptism], 'I did this myself.' This covenant proceeds from God without our input."[39] Christ serves as chief priest of the new covenant just as Abraham did of the old. But this covenant is given to the faithful throughout the nations of the earth. "God has established a covenant not just with one people but with the whole world."[40] "Baptism is an eternal covenant which does not lapse when we fall but raises us up again. If we fall out of the ship,

36. *BSELK* 1122/1123.15–1132/1133.16; *BC* 462–67. See also Jaroslav Pelikan, "Luther's Defense of Infant Baptism," *Luther for an Ecumenical Age*, ed. Carl S. Meyer (St. Louis: Concordia, 1967), 200–218.

37. *WA* 26:164.39–169.5; *LW* 40:252–58.

38. *BSELK* 118/119.4–8; *BC* 460.

39. *WA* 27:33.27–29.

40. *WA* 27:50.16–52.25.

God helps us on board once again. When Christians fall, they always remain in their baptisms, and God binds himself to them so that he will help them when the baptized call upon him."[41] Shortly after this sermon, in 1538, Luther also reminded his Wittenberg listeners,

> You see! we make an eternal covenant with the Son in baptism, that he wants to be our God and Savior, whom God has given us as his only Son that we may dwell in his wonderful heaven. . . . He is eternal. Therefore, this covenant is also eternal. Even though I fall away and break the covenant, he does not break it but accepts me again into his grace as soon as we come before his throne of grace. He will not be unfaithful even though we fall. Therefore, we should look to baptism and find comfort in it for our lives. . . . Do not accept the error that baptism only takes away original sin and that thereafter a person must make satisfaction. No! no! baptism dare not be squeezed so tight! It is supposed to be our comfort our whole life long, that we may be restored and revived through it.[42]

The parallel between baptism and circumcision, drawn by Paul in Colossians 2:11–12, won Luther's attention, especially in his Genesis lectures.[43] In the midst of them he preached a series of sermons on baptism in 1538, in which he stated that the sacrament is "a new circumcision, or birth, and it fashions true children of Abraham and God, who are not to be called children or servants but God's children, who have another essence and are holier than the holiness of all the Jews, to say nothing of the contrived holiness of all the papists."[44]

Luther rejected several false views of baptism that he had encountered in his youth and university studies. His own attempts at seeking peace in his monastic vows brought him to react with lively disgust to the monastic conviction that the monks' or nuns' vows brought them onto a steeper but more direct and more certain path to godliness and heavenly bliss than had their baptism. He singled out with horror and mockery Carthusian claims that entering the monastery was a second baptism.[45] For his congregation in 1538 he repeated his critique of the baptismal theology of two leading medieval theologians, which he had recorded in the Smalcald Articles a little over a year earlier. Thomas Aquinas had associated baptism's saving quality with a "secret divine power, which the Holy Spirit had placed in the water, which

41. WA 46:172.29–35.
42. WA 46:196.35–198.40; the concept of the baptismal covenant is treated throughout much of the sermon, 46:195–99.
43. Trigg, *Baptism*, 39–47.
44. WA 36:107.11–14, 22–30.
45. WA 36:99.13–101.27. Cf. WA 46:146.7–16; 47:640.12–13.

bathes the soul." "That is an obscure way of speaking," Georg Rörer records Luther commenting, for he strove to avoid any lingering medieval attribution of power to the material elements apart from their being tied to God's promise. He also rejected Duns Scotus's view that baptism's power to convey grace sprang from God's will alone, apart from his Word. Luther admonished the congregation to rely simply on God's Word. Its power purifies sinners from all sins and death and bestows new birth, through the power of the Father, Son, and Holy Spirit.[46] Throughout his career Luther also rejected the common medieval belief, based on a famous citation of Jerome, that penance provides the plank of salvation after the shipwreck of postbaptismal sins. The nature of baptism as God's promise and covenant called for sharp rejection of this view,[47] which Luther found blasphemous.[48]

Anabaptist preaching in Saxony rose to prominence in 1528 and thus informed much of Luther's later teaching and preaching on this sacrament.[49] He emphasized the objective nature of God's Word and argued that God uses selected elements of his created order to work his saving will. He had heard that Anabaptists were contending that children cannot believe, because they do not exercise reason and therefore cannot say, "I believe." He responded in 1539, largely repeating an argument he had used while preaching eleven years earlier: "Christ did not die only for older people but for all of humankind. When a child is brought to baptism, the gospel says, 'do not forbid this,' 'for of such is the kingdom of heaven'" (Matt. 19:14). The interpretation of the word "child" here as a large child is false, Luther concluded, because according to the text their mothers had to carry them. "God is acting here, not the human creature. Father, Son, and Holy Spirit baptize. Baptism is true. If it is possible that children do not have faith—and that they cannot demonstrate—, nevertheless, we should piously believe that God himself baptizes children and gives them faith and the Holy Spirit. That follows from the text. Therefore, regard baptism as a divine word, for God himself does it." There would be no church at all on earth if God did not assemble it through baptism, Luther added.[50]

46. WA 46:168.8–24, 30–169.29. Cf. *BSELK* 766.9–15; *BC* 320.
47. WA 46:172.18, 199.5–17; see also 46:198.39–199.26.
48. WA 47:643.19.
49. E.g., he dedicated the entire fourth sermon of the series of 1534 to a critique of their arguments, WA 37:278–84.
50. WA 47:655.1–657.3. Luther had made similar comments in 1528, WA 27:44.29–45.14; 27:50.4–52.25. Cf. Trigg's treatment of "baptism and ecclesiology" in *Baptism*, 174–203.

So What?

Luther's 1520 programmatic critique of medieval sacramental practice, *On the Babylonian Captivity of the Church*, included the observation that while the medieval church had not been able to erase the fundamental understanding of the sacrament as God's gift of grace, it had banished baptism to the beginning of the Christian life and substituted the sacrament of penance for baptism's ongoing significance and role in daily living.[51] In fact, Luther viewed daily repentance as the Holy Spirit's repetition of his action of killing and making alive, ending sinful identities and renewing identity as a child of God. That occurs because of the mystery of the continuation of sin and evil in the lives of Christ's faithful people. Johannes Brenz, Luther's ardent adherent, who led the Wittenberg-style reform in southwestern German lands, structured his popular catechism on baptism as the foundational point from which the entire Christian life proceeds. Like Luther, Brenz taught that baptism is an expression of God's word of promise in Christ, a sign through which he bestows the salvation he had planned for his people in election before the creation of the world. Baptism ratifies and delivers that salvation in the same way that a wedding ceremony confirms a relationship that God has already established.[52]

Luther maintained that baptism initiates and remains an integral part of the eschatological battle between God's truth and Satan's lie (John 8:44) in the Christian's life. Because baptism has transformed the identity of the sinner and rendered the baptized person a child of God, Satan attacks in a host of ways. Therefore, the "Christian life is nothing else than a daily baptism. . . . For we must keep at it without ceasing, always purging whatever pertains to the old Adam so that whatever belongs to the new creature may come forth."[53] Luther took seriously the need for believers to be "mortified"—that is, to work on eliminating sinful practices and attitudes—and to cultivate godly practices and attitudes that serve others and embody the righteousness that God has freely bestowed on them. "This is the right use of baptism. . . . Where this does not take place but rather the old creature is given free rein and continually grows stronger, baptism is not being used but resisted."[54] Hence the faith that produces fruits is absolutely necessary in those psychologically capable of conscious assessment of the world and decisions for proper living. That requires continuing engagement with all forms of God's Word, so that his baptismal promise can continue to "snatch us from the jaws of the devil and

---

51. WA 6:527.9–528.19; LW 36:57–59.
52. *Catechismus* (1535; Wittenberg: Schwenck, 1563), A7b–A8a, D6a.
53. *BSELK* 1128/1129.3–19; *BC* 465.
54. *BSELK* 1128/1129.20–1130/1131.7; *BC* 465.

[to] make us God's own, overcome and take away sin and daily strengthen the new person." Thus, baptism serves as "the daily garment" (Gal. 3:27) that Christians wear continually as they produce the fruits of faith.[55]

The faith that baptism generates clings to the gift of death to the sinful identity and of new life through resurrection that baptism bestows. It sets the believer following the path of Christ's footsteps. "In Baptism, therefore, every Christian has enough to study and practice all his or her life. Christians always have enough to do to believe firmly what Baptism promises and brings—victory over death and the devil, forgiveness of sin, God's grace, the entire Christ, and the Holy Spirit with his gifts."[56]

Luther's German baptismal liturgy of 1523 reminded those who were bringing their children to be baptized that "it is no joke to take sides against the devil and not only to drive him away from the little child but to burden the child with such a mighty and lifelong enemy."[57] This liturgy retained the minor exorcism (a formal renunciation of the devil's works and ways), which later in the sixteenth century became an issue dividing Lutherans and Calvinists. For Calvinists, the exorcism was a remnant of medieval superstition;[58] Luther and his followers regarded it as a tool to combat the devil.

Luther's students echoed this emphasis on the importance of baptism for daily Christian life in conflict with Satan. In the city of Braunschweig, Martin Chemnitz impressed on his fellow pastors that baptism delivered the forgiveness of sins and salvation, arguing, against certain streams of Roman Catholic theology, that this liberation covered both original and actual sins.[59] He reiterated Luther's emphasis on the continuing validity of God's baptismal promise. God remains faithful even when his children are unfaithful (2 Tim. 2:13) and seeks to return to his family those who leave his household. God's Word, as it comes in remembrance of baptism and in other forms, creates repentance and faith in believers' hearts throughout their lives. The person who has received the gift of righteousness in baptism practices that righteousness, Chemnitz insisted, in obedience to God's

---

55. *BSELK* 1130/1131.23–1132/1133.19; *BC* 466–67.

56. *BSELK* 1120/1121.19–24; *BC* 461.

57. *WA* 12:47.11–20; *LW* 53:102; the order is found in *WA* 12:42–48; *LW* 53:96–103; the 1526 revision, *WA* 19:537–41; 53:107–9. It was republished in many versions of the Small Catechism, *BSELK* 906.3–12; *BC* 372.

58. Bodo Nischan, "The Exorcism Controversy and Baptism in the Late Reformation," *Sixteenth Century Journal* 18 (1989): 31–51.

59. Martin Chemnitz, *Loci theologici . . . quibus et Loci communes d. Philippi Melancthonis perspicue explicantur . . .* (Frankfurt am Main: Spies, 1591–92), Yyb.

commands.[60] Chemnitz defended infant baptism as God's way of delivering the promise; yet he repeated arguments against a ritualistic, "superstitious" use of baptism, because God's promise produces trust in Christ's saving work.[61] He defended the use of the formula for exorcism in the baptismal rite, because to set it aside would diminish the recognition of Satan's power, the hold of original sin that continues to affect believers, and the liberating grace of God.[62]

Not only instructors of theology continued this baptismal emphasis in the following generations, but hymn writers also taught the importance of baptism. Paul Gerhardt (1607–76) composed a hymn based on Titus 3, in which he celebrated baptism as God's tool for liberation from Satan's prison, the curse of sinful nature, and death itself. In baptism God's chosen people put on Christ and become holy, pious, and good through God's pronouncement in the sacrament.[63] Erdmann Neumeister (1671–1756) recorded the blessing of becoming God's own child in baptism; into the mouths of those who sang his hymn, he put notes of thanksgiving for Christ's bestowing the benefits of his suffering and death through baptism's cleansing waters, making the baptized heirs of his victory over death and of the paradise he had won for them.[64] Neumeister's contemporary Emilie (Ämilie) Juliane von Schwarzburg-Rudolstadt (1637–1706) confessed her faith that her baptism had dressed her in Christ and made her a member of God's family (Gal. 3:27), which prepared her for death.[65] Danish bishop Thomas Hansen Kingo (1634–1703) used Mark 16:16 as the basis of a hymn accenting the role that baptism plays in the Christian's daily life and the assurance it gives believers that they will live eternally with Christ.[66]

Despite such examples, to a large extent Lutherans returned to the medieval model Luther had criticized in 1520, that of relegating baptism to a memory of God's beginning of a relationship, without much use of its promise as a factor in daily life, a weapon against the devil's reassertion of the sinner's identity

---

60. Martin Chemnitz, *Examen Concilii Tridentini*, ed. Eduard Preuss (Berlin: Schlawitz, 1861), 273, 277, 274; Martin Chemnitz, *Examination of the Council of Trent*, trans. Fred Kramer (St. Louis: Concordia, 1971–86), 1:145, 157, 149.

61. *Loci theologici*, Yya–Yy2b; cf. *Examen*, 284, *Examination*, 1:175.

62. *Loci theologici*, Yy2a–Yy3b.

63. *Paul Gerhardts Lieder und Gedichte*, ed. Wilhelm Nelle (Hamburg: Schloessmann, 1907), 101–3.

64. *Lutheran Service Book* (St. Louis: Concordia, 2006), 594.

65. Ibid., 598.

66. Ibid., 601.

as one who is not a child of God.[67] In the twentieth century, however, a revival of earlier emphases in Lutheran baptismal thinking took place. For example, Dietrich Bonhoeffer (1906–45) described baptismal dying in the rhythm of daily repentance with his oft-cited "When Christ calls a man, he bids him come and die" (literally, "every call of Christ leads into death"); that meant for Bonhoeffer that "the call to follow Jesus, baptism in the name of Jesus Christ, is death and life. The call of Christ and baptism lead Christians into a daily struggle against sin and Satan."[68] Edmund Schlink also accentuated the rhythm of death and resurrection that baptism initiates in the believer's life, which gives assurance of God's faithfulness to his promise and leads people to follow the Holy Spirit's guidance in the footsteps of Christ,[69] a position affirmed by Werner Elert, who anchored the Christian life in the baptismal promise.[70]

For Luther himself, baptism provided daily comfort and the impetus to give thanks to God for his promise that life and salvation come through the death and resurrection of Jesus Christ. He was confident that God had established the relationship between the Creator and Martin through the re-creative power of the baptismal form of his Word, and he was committed to living out the life that God had thus bestowed, renewed, and re-created for him through baptism.

Baptism in the Reformed Tradition

The subject of baptism was contentious at the Reformation and remains so now, even though the personal stakes are not as great today. Protestants are divided on the subjects and mode of baptism. Is it for believers and their children, or for believers only? Is it by sprinkling, affusion, or immersion?

On these matters, there is no major difference between the Lutherans and the Reformed. Both traditions baptize infants prior to a personal profession of faith; both traditions allow that sprinkling is legitimate, while seeing the

---

67. Cf. Mark D. Tranvik, "The Other Sacrament: The Doctrine of Baptism in the Late Lutheran Reformation" (ThD diss., Luther Northwestern Theological Seminary, 1992).

68. *Discipleship*, trans. Barbara Green and Reinhard Krauss (1937; repr., Minneapolis: Fortress, 2001), 87–88. Cf. his chapter (205–12) treating baptismal death as God's act of justification of sinners and thus, for them, a decisive break from sin.

69. *The Doctrine of Baptism*, trans. Herbert J. A. Bouman (1969; St. Louis: Concordia, 1972), 9–41; Schlink, *Ökumenische Dogmatik: Grundzüge* (Göttingen: Vandenhoeck & Ruprecht, 1983), 479–83.

70. *The Christian Ethos*, trans. Carl. J. Schindler (1949; Philadelphia: Muhlenberg, 1957), esp. 221.

mode as a matter of relative indifference.[71] The difference between Lutheran and Reformed positions thus lies in the meaning of baptism, not in its outward administration.

In the Reformation, the Anabaptist practice—repeating baptism on profession of faith or withholding baptism from individuals prior to such—was condemned by both Lutherans and Reformed. In part this was no doubt sociological. Medieval Christendom assumed that all members of civic society were also members of the church. Therefore those who did not fit into this paradigm—Jews and Anabaptists—appeared to be subversive of good social order and were vulnerable to persecution. But there was more to it than that. Both Lutheran and Reformed believed that God is the agent in baptism, that it is something God does rather than a sign of human response to God's action. To use the terminology favored by the Reformed, baptism is a means of grace, not a reaction or response to grace.

Baptism in Zwingli

Of all the magisterial Reformers, Zwingli was the one who dallied, albeit only briefly, with the idea of abandoning infant baptism and connecting the rite to public profession of faith. We must remember, of course, that the political and social framework for Zwingli's Reformation was distinctly different from that of Luther. With a town council rather than a prince and elector of the Holy Roman Empire in charge, there was far more scope for radical innovation and independence in Zurich than in Wittenberg. Power was not the monopoly of an established nobility but was more closely aligned with the rising urban class. This gave Zurich society in general, and thus its Reformation, a more radical ethos.[72]

Indeed, early in the Reformation, various radical figures were part of Zwingli's inner circle, men such as Conrad Grebel, who was later to repudiate Zwingli and suffer for his commitment to believer's baptism before his death in 1526. From its inception, the Zurich Reformation attracted such radicals and for good reason. The hallmark of the Zurich Reformation—a strict emphasis on Scripture as the regulative guide for all aspects of life—meant

71. "The mode of the application of the water is not the important thing. God's Word with the water is" (Robert Kolb, *The Christian Faith: A Lutheran Exposition* [St. Louis: Concordia, 1993], 223). "Immersion is a proper mode of baptism, but so is baptism by effusion or by sprinkling, since they all symbolize purification" (Louis Berkhof, *Systematic Theology* [Edinburgh: Banner of Truth Trust, 1971], 631).

72. On Zwingli, see G. R. Potter, *Zwingli* (Cambridge: Cambridge University Press, 1984). On the general social and political context of the Swiss Reformation, see Bruce Gordon, *The Swiss Reformation* (Manchester: Manchester University Press, 2002).

that all matters pertaining to the church came under rigorous scrutiny. We might perhaps summarize the situation by saying that far more was initially negotiable in Zurich than was ever the case in Wittenberg.

Given Zwingli's emphasis on sacraments as symbols akin to military oaths, it is not surprising that he would be attracted to credobaptism. A symbol reflects something that is already the case, as a wedding ring indicates that someone is married. A military oath is something that the participant does. In each case, the sacramental action is not vertical, a gift coming from heaven to earth, but horizontal, a sign to each other and to those around. For Zwingli, the sacraments found their most important meaning in the public profession of faith that they involved, a position clearly placing him at odds with Luther's approach.

Yet Zwingli's short-lived dalliance with credobaptism ended with his ferocious support for paedobaptism. The breach in the understanding of society that Anabaptism posited between church and state was simply too radical and potentially destabilizing. Then, having broken with Anabaptism, Zwingli's later work served to lay the foundations for the Reformed covenantal view of baptism. In his *Commentary on True and False Religion*, his case for infant baptism was quite simple, based in part on an inconsistency he found within Anabaptist arguments. He argued that because his opponents did not consider infants to be damned, they were making a concession that was fatal to their overall case; they were in effect acknowledging that infants were under grace. Further, in an anticipation of later arguments regarding the expansion of the bounds and terms of grace under the New Testament, he pointed out that if the children of Christians were not under grace, then they were actually in a worse position than the children of the Old Testament Jews. Granted, his argument may not be compelling today, but in a culture where infant baptism was the default position and credobaptism the novelty requiring rigorous justification, it had considerable persuasive power. Most important for later developments, it points toward a more covenantal understanding of baptism.[73]

This covenantal aspect of Zwingli's thought is clear at numerous points where he draws close parallels between circumcision and baptism. This is not a novelty with Zwingli, since many patristic and medieval writers, even Luther himself, had drawn the same parallel. But Zwingli is careful to develop it in a covenantal direction. In a letter to fellow Reformer Urbanus Rhegius, Zwingli makes it clear that neither circumcision in the Old Testament nor

---

73. See his *Commentary on True and False Religion* in *The Latin Works of Huldreich Zwingli*, vol. 3, ed. C. N. Heller (Philadelphia: Heidelberg, 1929), 197.

baptism in the New saves in and of itself. Rather, both connected to the covenant community, the membership of which was not identical with those who would eventually prove to be true Christians. However, because infant Jews belonged to visible Israel and received the covenant sign, infant Christians who belong to the visible church should also receive the covenant sign.[74] This, of course, is the critical move in a covenantal understanding of infant baptism, bringing circumcision and the Abrahamic covenant into a position of foundational importance.

Zwingli did not believe that baptism conveyed grace, any more than circumcision had. Rather, it set infants within the visible church and was a tangible expression of the grace available in and through the visible church. It marked the children off and put them in a context of Christian nurture. It was also a public witness that allowed all to see the unconditional action of God in graciously building his church. Baptism was therefore a matter of great *corporate* significance. If Roman Catholics, Lutherans, and Baptists in their different ways emphasize the significance and benefits of baptism specifically for the recipient of the rite, Zwingli emphasized its benefits for the corporate body. It was an action of the community for the community.[75]

Baptism in Calvin

Any treatment of the views of the Reformed on baptism needs to give Calvin a central place. Before addressing his views in detail, however, it is important to set his overall sacramental theology within the broader contours of Reformation debates. On the sacraments in general, we might characterize Calvin as standing somewhere between Luther and Zwingli. Herman Bavinck describes his views this way: "The Reformed definition of the sacraments is special, in the third place, in that it unites the action of God with the confession of believers taking place in them. In that way Calvin reconciled Luther and Zwingli. Calvin agreed with Luther in saying that God's action in the sacrament is primary, but Calvin with Zwingli judged that in the sacrament believers made confession of their faith and love before God, angels, and humans."[76]

---

74. See *The Latin Works of Huldrych Zwingli*, vol. 2, ed. W. J. Hinke (Philadelphia: Heidelberg, 1922), 42–43.

75. On this point, see the helpful exposition of Zwingli on baptism in J. V. Fesko, *Word, Water, and Spirit: A Reformed Perspective on Baptism* (Grand Rapids: Reformation Heritage, 2010), 60–65.

76. *RD* 4:475.

Sacraments are therefore not simply matters of divine action, nor are they to be reduced to mere symbols or outward testimonies of faith before others. They involve God's action (action that has priority) and a human response. This is evident in his general definition of a sacrament: "[A sacrament is] an external sign, by which the Lord seals on our consciences his promises of good-will toward us, in order to sustain the weakness of our faith, and we in our turn testify our piety towards him, both before himself, and before angels as well as men."[77]

At first glance, this seems to be a standard view of the sacraments, similar to what we might find in Augustine, treating the sacraments as visible signs of invisible grace. The reference to promise, however, adds that important generic Reformation Protestant insight: the sacrament is to be understood in connection with the Word of God. God works through his Word, even in the sacrament. But God does not do this ex opere operato as in the Roman Mass, whereby the sacramental action itself is efficacious. For Protestants, the attachment of the sign to the Word is crucial. It is the Word that makes the sign potent. We might even say that the sacraments function as a kind of visible or tangible Word, to borrow Augustine's term. By physical elements and liturgical action, the sacraments represent to us what the Word brings when read and preached: Jesus Christ and his grace. Therefore the sign speaks to us precisely because it is placed in the context of proclamation. The sacraments are thus not equal to the Word nor independent of it. While there can be proclamation without administration of the sacraments, there can be no sacraments without proclamation of the Word. Indeed, for Calvin as for Luther, the Word must be proclaimed *before* the sacraments, because otherwise they are just meaningless, dead symbols. The Reformation priority of the Word is evident.

Calvin also develops the idea of baptism within the general context of his understanding of the sacraments as seals, analogous to those placed on official documents. My will was drawn up by my lawyer and contains specific verbal instructions on how my property is to be disposed of after my death. Yet it is also notarized. An official stamp, which authenticates the document and gives it authority, has been placed on the paper on which it is written. This is similar to how Calvin sees the sacraments functioning with regard to the Word preached. The Word of God preached is what contains the promise of God's grace. The Word proclaims salvation in Christ and calls on the hearer to put faith in Christ. It is a purely verbal communication. The sacraments, however, then seal that grace on the hearer's heart in a very tangible manner. This is

---

77. Calvin, *Institutes* IV.xiv.1.

why preaching is important, for without preaching the seals are meaningless. But it is also why the sacraments/seals are important, for the seals themselves press home the authority of the preaching.[78] I hear the Word and grasp its truth by faith, but that truth is sealed on my heart by the sacraments. The content, strictly speaking, is the same: Jesus Christ. But the mode of impact is different. The sacraments supplement the Word in a way that makes the Word somehow more real and immediate.

One final comment on Calvin is that he (as is typical of the Reformed tradition) makes the two sacraments (baptism and the Lord's Supper) marks of the true church, along with the preaching of the Word. As Calvin points out, Christ gave the sacraments to the apostles and thence to the properly called officers of the church.[79] This is an important point since it makes clear that these rites are churchly activities, to be performed within the context of a properly ordered church and not to be done by those who are not called to the office of minister or in private when the congregation is not present. The former would lead to anarchy; the latter is vulnerable to superstition. Thus, the Reformed did not allow the medieval Roman Catholic practice of baptism by midwives when the infant's life was in danger and no priest was available. Such emergency measures implied that baptism was essential to salvation.[80]

Calvin and the Reformed Tradition

When Calvin discusses baptism, he describes it as consisting in three specific actions: that our sins are forgiven in Christ; that we are united to Christ for the mortification of indwelling sin and for newness of life; and that we are united to Christ so as to be partakers in all his benefits.[81] These basic points become standard in the Reformed tradition. Here, for example, is what the Westminster Confession says of baptism in chapter 28:

> Baptism is a sacrament of the new testament, ordained by Jesus Christ, not only for the solemn admission of the party baptized into the visible church; but also, to be unto him a sign and seal of the covenant of grace, of his ingrafting into Christ, of regeneration, of remission of sins, and of his giving up unto God,

78. Ibid., IV.xiv.5.
79. Ibid., IV.xv.20.
80. Women, and sometimes midwives, are singled out as not allowed to baptize in a number of Reformed confessions: Scots Confession 22; Second Helvetic Confession 20; cf. Calvin, *Institutes* IV.xv.20. Given that a general ban on nonordained people administering the sacrament should have been sufficient, it is reasonable to suppose that the specific references to women should be understood against the background of Roman Catholic practice and the theology it assumed.
81. Calvin, *Institutes* IV.xv.1, 5, 6.

through Jesus Christ, to walk in newness of life. Which sacrament is, by Christ's own appointment, to be continued in his church until the end of the world.

What is striking is that all the gifts of baptism are deeply connected to God's grace as it is manifested in Christ. Union with Christ, the remission of sins, mortification, and newness of life are all actions of the sovereign God in which he is the agent. God is the agent of baptism. Baptism is a means of grace, not a response to God's grace. Thus, far from being a means of testifying to one's faith before the world, let alone an opportunity for giving thanks for a new child, baptism encapsulates what it means to be a Christian—to be one on whom the grace of God has acted in a powerful fashion. Thus, Bavinck lists the benefits of baptism as justification, regeneration, and fellowship (both with Christ and with his body the church), all three of which he roots in the communion of the one baptized with the Triune God.[82] The Zwinglian accent on the horizontal witness of the act is thus eclipsed by the fact that baptism is God's work performed by God. Thus, for Calvin and the Reformed confessional tradition, as for Luther, baptism is primarily about what God does, and only secondarily about our response. It is a means of grace, because it is an act of grace.

This, of course, tracks back to the rooting of baptism in the covenant of grace, a point increasingly accented in the Reformed tradition after Calvin. The promise made to Abraham is critical to the Reformed tradition, because it provides both a basis for the unity of the redemptive history of the Old and New Testaments and, as we will see below, the application of the sign of baptism to the children of believers. All of the promises given to Abraham in the covenant of grace are also offered to the recipients of baptism.

All of this helps to explain another Reformed notion, that of improving one's baptism. This is stated at some length in the Westminster Larger Catechism:

Q. 167. How is baptism to be improved by us? A. The needful but much neglected duty of improving our baptism, is to be performed by us all our life long, especially in the time of temptation, and when we are present at the administration of it to others; by serious and thankful consideration of the nature of it, and of the ends for which Christ instituted it, the privileges and benefits conferred and sealed thereby, and our solemn vow made therein; by being humbled for our sinful defilement, our falling short of, and walking contrary to, the grace of baptism, and our engagements; by growing up to assurance of pardon of sin, and of all other blessings sealed to us in that sacrament; by drawing strength

82. *RD* 4:519–21.

from the death and resurrection of Christ, into whom we are baptized, for the mortifying of sin, and quickening of grace; and by endeavoring to live by faith, to have our conversation in holiness and righteousness, as those that have therein given up their names to Christ; and to walk in brotherly love, as being baptized by the same Spirit into one body.

The language may well be unfamiliar to Lutherans, since it seems to imply that baptism is somehow lacking or can be "improved" in the common sense of "being made better," but that is not what the catechism means to convey. To improve baptism means to take the reality of baptism seriously and to bring to fruition what it represents.

The structure here is clear. In Pauline fashion, the Reformed see the great indicatives of baptism as placing imperatives on the one baptized. Identity drives behavior. The person who receives the sign of the covenant is a member of the covenant community. That is who they are. As God's grace brings the person into Christ, so this new identity is to be the foundation for the Christian life. Christians are to strive to be in reality what they already are publicly through baptism.

Luther, of course, famously cited his baptism as a means of assurance when tempted by the devil.[83] For the Reformed, this existential note is more muted, with the objectivity of baptism connecting not simply to the promise of the gospel but also to the consequent obligations of membership in the covenant community: to believe and to live out the Christian life. We might say that, for the Reformed, baptism more typically places the challenge of God's covenant before his people, something that finds its sharpest theological formulation in the work of the twentieth-century Reformed biblical scholar Meredith G. Kline, for whom baptism represented both the covenant cure and the covenant blessing to the one baptized.[84] That is why in the baptismal liturgies of many Reformed denominations there are challenges issued to both the parents and the congregation, reminding them of their obligations to pray for the children and to work together to raise them in the fear and knowledge of the Lord.

---

83. Carl R. Trueman, *Luther on the Christian Life: Cross and Freedom* (Wheaton: Crossway, 2015), 142–44.

84. Meredith G. Kline, *By Oath Consigned: A Reinterpretation of the Covenant Signs of Circumcision and Baptism* (Grand Rapids: Eerdmans, 1968). For a recent Reformed assessment of the history of debates about baptism both outside and within the Reformed tradition, see Fesko, *Word*.

Baptism, Roman Catholic Baptism, and the Spirit

We noted above that sacraments are powerful not in themselves in some kind of mechanistic way but because they are attached to God's Word. In baptism, this is the trinitarian formula: "In the name of the Father, and of the Son, and of the Holy Spirit." It is this that gives the sacrament its objectivity. Thus, Calvin and his Reformed contemporaries did not see any need to rebaptize somebody who had been baptized by a Roman Catholic priest. It is not the moral character of the baptizer that makes a baptism valid but rather the Word that is attached to it. The Reformed were mindful of the Donatist controversy of the fourth/fifth centuries, which established the objective validity of the sacraments as a church rite regardless of the personal morality of the officiant.[85]

Elaborating on the validity of Roman Catholic baptism, Francis Turretin distinguished the essence of the rite from various particulars. The Roman Catholic Church had added all manner of extraneous aspects, such as the use of oil and the sign of the cross, but the basic essence of the rite—the words of institution and the visible element used—was true; therefore, baptism was not to be repeated for those who join a Reformed church after being baptized in the Roman Catholic Church as infants.[86]

Yet the mere enunciation of the trinitarian formula is not in itself effective for salvation. The Reformed do not believe in baptismal regeneration, because they do not see the sign and the thing signified as necessarily simultaneous. Certainly, God is sovereign and all-powerful, and so the one baptized might be spiritually united to Christ at the moment of baptism, but not necessarily so. The substance of baptism is a spiritual reality, but not in the vague sense of having no real connection to the sacramental elements or action. This is not some ethereal, mystical thing. No, baptism is spiritual because it is the Holy Spirit who makes effective those things that baptism signifies. We shall see in the Lord's Supper that the role of the Spirit is vital in overcoming what the Reformed see as the basic dilemma presented by Luther's objective realism and Zwingli's memorialism. Here, in baptism, the Spirit fulfills a similar function. Those things that baptism indicates—union with Christ, forgiveness, regeneration—are matters that only the subjective work of the Holy Spirit on the believer can bring into existence.

---

85. Calvin, *Institutes* IV.xv.15. Later Reformed theologians did disagree about this point. In the nineteenth century, for example, the Southern Presbyterian theologian James Henley Thornwell argued that Roman Catholic baptism was invalid on the grounds that the Roman Catholic Church was not a true church, while his contemporary, Charles Hodge of Princeton, maintained the more traditional approach. The Reformed remain divided on this point, but the majority historical position is that of Hodge.

86. Turretin, *Institutes* XIX.xviii.

First, the Reformed do understand that the action of the Spirit and the performance of the sacramental rite are not so attached that the two necessarily coincide chronologically. In other words, one can truly receive the benefits of baptism sometime after being baptized. The sign and the thing signified are not to be so identified that one cannot have the former without necessarily having the latter.[87]

Second, baptism nevertheless truly exhibits and offers something to the subject of the rite. It offers Christ; it is a seal of the gospel. It does not save in itself any more than a wedding ring guarantees that a marriage will be happy and fruitful. Nevertheless, baptism does represent something real: the gospel and the entry of the recipient into the visible covenant community. This, of course, points to the most contentious aspect of the Reformed position, that of infant baptism.[88]

The Baptism of Infants

Of all the questions surrounding baptism, the issue of the appropriate subjects of baptism is the most contentious of all among Protestants. As with the clash between Zwingli and the Anabaptists, this debate has generated much heat over the years. Yet when narrowly considered, this is not a point at issue between Lutherans and Reformed, both of whom maintain the practice of baptizing infants prior to and independent of any profession of faith. Where they differ is in the rationale for so doing.

We should note that the typical Reformed understanding of baptism draws on the cumulative force of biblical texts rather than pointing to only one verse or passage. Key elements are the continuity of the covenant of grace between the Testaments, the analogy of baptism to circumcision, the practice of household baptisms, and the way in which some biblical texts are addressed to little children.[89] As such it would be true to say that the Reformed view of baptism

---

87. The Westminster Confession expresses this point well in 28.6: "The efficacy of baptism is not tied to that moment of time wherein it is administered; yet, notwithstanding, by the right use of this ordinance, the grace promised is not only offered, but really exhibited, and conferred, by the Holy Ghost, to such (whether of age or infants) as that grace belongeth unto, according to the counsel of God's own will, in his appointed time" (*The Westminster Confession of Faith and Larger and Shorter Catechisms with Proof Texts* [Willow Grove, PA: Orthodox Presbyterian Church, 2005]).

88. As noted at the start of the chapter, this is not of course historically contentious, as the baptism of infants has been the practice of the overwhelming number of churches—Roman Catholic, Eastern Orthodox, Protestant—over the centuries. It is contentious in Reformed circles, however, because of the proximity of the Reformed to other Protestant Baptist groups on issues of soteriology.

89. E.g., Gen. 17; Col. 2:11–12; Acts 2:39; 16:33; 1 John 2:12.

is not simply a question of whom we understand its subjects to be. Rather, it actually connects to how the Bible as a whole is understood. It is really a fundamentally hermeneutical matter. This is reflected in the Westminster Confession (1.6), which declares that the whole counsel of God is therein set down in Scripture "or by good and necessary consequence may be deduced" therefrom. That this clause is omitted from the 1677 Baptist Confession of Faith, which is heavily dependent on the text of the Westminster Standards, indicates that this was a crucial methodological point dividing Presbyterian paedobaptists from credobaptists.

For the Reformed, the analogy between circumcision in the Old Testament and baptism in the new is vital. Calvin develops his argument for this in book 4 of the *Institutes*. First, he points to the basic identity of the promise attached to circumcision in the Old Testament and baptism in the New Testament. For example, circumcision represents God's promise to Abraham that he will be his God (Gen. 17) and a fount of every blessing toward him. This, Calvin says, is what baptism also means in the New.[90] In the history of redemption, it is clear that baptism has come to replace circumcision: "For just as circumcision, which was a kind of badge to the Jews, assuring them that they were adopted as the people and family of God, was their first entrance into the Church, while they, in their turn, professed their allegiance to God, so now we are initiated by baptism, so as to be enrolled among his people, and at the same time swear unto his name. Hence it is incontrovertible, that baptism has been substituted for circumcision, and performs the same office."[91] This circumcision-baptism connection is the linchpin of the Reformed argument for baptizing infants because it connects the New Testament rite to the covenant of grace and allows for the inclusion within that covenant of the children of believers. The covenant with Abraham is not simply, or even primarily, understood as a covenant about land. It is about the spiritual relationship of God with his chosen people as it culminates in the life and work of Jesus Christ. Thus its provisions, while transformed with the coming of Christ, are not substantially modified. The promise to believers and their children remains in place.[92]

90. Calvin, *Institutes* IV.xvi.3. Cf. Calvin's comment on Col. 2:12: "Christ, says he, accomplishes in us spiritual circumcision, not through means of that ancient sign, which was in force under Moses, but by baptism. Baptism, therefore, is a sign of the thing that is presented to us, which while absent was prefigured by circumcision." *Commentaries on the Epistles of Paul the Apostle to the Philippians, Colossians, and Thessalonians*, trans. John Pringle (Edinburgh: Calvin Translation Society, 1851), 185.

91. Calvin, *Institutes* IV.xvi.4.

92. "We condemn the Anabaptists, who deny that young infants, born of faithful parents, are to be baptized. For according to the doctrine of the gospel 'theirs is the kingdom of God'

This argument is developed further within the Reformed tradition. Thus, Herman Bavinck points to the death and resurrection of Christ as the fulfillment of what circumcision signified and the dawn of the new era of baptism as presented in Colossians 2:11–12. This makes baptism more than circumcision but not more in terms of its essence—for that is the fulfillment of God's covenant purposes in Christ. Rather, it is more in terms of degree, because it looks back to Christ just as circumcision looked forward to Christ; therefore, it represents a much fuller revelation of God's purposes.[93] Because of this essential continuity, the sign applies to children under the New Testament as it does under the Old; to do otherwise would be to run counter to the increasing scope of grace in redemptive history.[94] This remains the redemptive-historical foundation of Reformed paedobaptism to this day.[95]

One typical objection, of course, might be that the New Testament clearly changes the scope of the covenant and that the mark of the covenant people is now identification with Christ by public profession of faith. This would be the Reformed Baptist claim, as I understand it.

Of course, no Christian theologian would want to argue that the coming of Christ and then Pentecost make no difference. The question is what difference they make. Baptists argue that they make membership of the church, of God's people, something restricted to those who profess faith and that therefore baptism, as a sign of covenant or church membership, is to be restricted to professed believers. The covenant is thus broader, in that it no longer generally respects the ethnic boundary of the Israelites, but narrower in that it does not automatically embrace the children of members of the covenant.[96]

The Reformed, however, traditionally argue the opposite, that the covenant has become broader in scope and that this offers a powerful reason for

---

(Luke 18:16); and they are written in the covenant of God (Acts 3:25). Why then should not the sign of the covenant be given to them?" (Second Helvetic Confession [Dennison 63]).

93. *RD* 4:256.

94. A modern defense of the circumcision-baptism analogy in Colossians is David Gibson, "Sacramental Supersessionism Revisited: A Response to Martin Salter on the Relationship between Circumcision and Baptism," *Themelios* 37 (2012): 191–208.

95. E.g., David Gibson, "'Fathers of Faith, My Fathers Now!': On Abraham, Covenant, and the Theology of Paedobaptism," *Themelios* 40 (2015): 14–34.

96. Thus, the London Baptist Confession of 1677 (chap. 26.6) specifically restricts membership of the church community to believers: "6. The members of these churches are saints by calling, visibly manifesting and evidencing (in and by their profession and walking) their obedience unto that call of Christ (Rom. 1:7; 1 Cor. 1:2); and do willingly consent to walk together, according to the appointment of Christ; giving up themselves to the Lord, and one to another, by the will of God, in professed subjection to the ordinances of the gospel (Acts 2:41–42; 5:13–14; 2 Cor. 9:13)" (Dennison 4:562).

including children within the covenant community. Calvin explicitly points to Christ's mission to enlarge rather than to limit the grace of the Father and to do so by reaching out to little children.[97] Bavinck too makes the point that the placing of the covenant sign on females is another indication of the expansion of the riches of grace in the church age.[98]

Finally, in the face of Baptist objections, the Reformed also make a crucial distinction between the scope of election and the scope of the covenant, arguing that the New Testament clearly indicates the existence of a category of people who have been covered by the blessing of the covenant in Christ and yet who choose to rebel against such and, as a result, face more severe judgment. As modern Reformed theologian David Gibson comments:

> To baptize an infant is to elevate the seriousness of baptism and to highlight the importance of faith as part of the covenant of grace. For without faith it is impossible to please God (Heb. 11:6). With faith, baptism becomes an effectual means of grace. Without faith, with grace spurned, the sign of covenant blessings becomes the promise of covenant curses, and the baptized in their unbelief live continually as a marked man or woman. Once baptized, always baptized. From baptism onwards, a child bears the family name of the triune God and he or she either brings shame on the household of God and judgment on themselves, or lives within the Father's care and show themselves to be inheritors of the kingdom of light.[99]

Baptism as objectively placing blessings and curses on a child, as putting the child under the responsive obligations of the covenant promise, has a powerful meaning and allows those of us who believe in irresistible grace and perseverance of the saints to make sense of the existentially urgent warnings against apostasy in the New Testament, as found, for example, in Hebrews 6.

Conclusion

A high view of baptism, especially infant baptism, marks off the confessional traditions of Lutheranism and the Reformed from many other strands of Protestant church life, particularly the Baptists, who repudiate the practice, and the Evangelicals, who are often at best indifferent to it. For those with a high view of God's grace, there is no more dramatic representation of it than infant baptism. The helpless child is brought to the font, and the minister administers the rite in the context of the proclamation of what God

---

97. Calvin, *Institutes* IV.xvi.6.
98. *RD* 4:526–27.
99. Gibson, "Fathers of Faith," 33.

has done. It is a beautiful analogy of the way God works, for it denies the idea that baptism is in any sense something that we do in response to God or to publish abroad that we have professed faith. It is rather a sign that the child is a member of the visible covenant community, with all of the privileges of regular exposure to the Word and to the fellowship of the church, in addition to the imperatives it brings for the child to grasp Christ by faith as he is offered.

For the Reformed, infant baptism also sets the stage for a specific view of Christian discipleship. First, it connects the ritual life of the church today with that of the people of God back through the centuries to Abraham and the covenant of circumcision. It is thus a beautiful redemptive-historical act, full of rich theological meaning and setting the child into the ongoing history of God's dealings with his covenant people.

A second aspect of this is that it sets Christian discipleship from birth within a covenant context. Some Reformed believers may well have a testimony of conversion as a crisis experience or at least as a dramatic process that turned their lives around at some point. But not all will. To be set within a covenant context means to understand discipleship as something connected to the ordinary means of God's grace and the routine work of the church: hearing the Word read and preached, partaking in the sacraments, being prayed for (and praying with) the family and the congregation, and being catechized. In short, it means growing as a Christian within the household of faith into which one was received as an infant. This is not exciting or dramatic. But the Reformed believe that it is the way God has gloriously chosen to build his church and his kingdom. Infant baptism is thus a vital part of both the theology and the theological practice of the church, and one for which we should give thanks to our gracious God.

7

The Lord's Supper

Along with baptism, the Lord's Supper, or Eucharist, is one of the two sacraments maintained by Lutheran and Reformed Christians. It was instituted by Christ at the Last Supper before his betrayal to the authorities, and Christians are commanded by him to repeat it until he comes again. The earliest extant liturgical text, the *Didache* (probably late first century) contains a eucharistic liturgy, which underlines the fact that the Lord's Supper has always been a vital part of Christian piety and practice. The Supper has fed and nourished Christians from the very birth of the church. Sadly, it has also divided them.

In the Middle Ages, the Mass was the central focus of Christian worship, the place where God came to his people as the bread and the wine at consecration became the very body and blood of Christ. The Mass was also linked to notions of church authority, since the ability to withhold the Eucharist became a means of coercive power, allowing the possibility that a channel of God's grace might actually be used as a weapon with which to control people. In addition, the late medieval practice of withholding the cup from the laity and giving them communion only in one kind, that of the bread, served to reinforce priestly power and hierarchy.

It was therefore inevitable that the Mass would be a major focus of controversy at the Reformation, for it touched on so many important issues: the nature of Christ's presence with his people, the means by which grace was received, and the structure of ecclesiastical authority. In addition, it also required significant reflection on the nature of the incarnation itself, for how should the key words "This is my body" and "This is my blood" be understood? This in turn had an impact on how the power of the promise in the second part of the words of institution—"shed *for you*" should be understood. Lutheran and Reformed shared no consensus on these important matters. In the story of the Reformation, this meant that not only did Protestants break with Rome but they also fell out acrimoniously among themselves. Lutherans and Reformed differed in serious ways on the matter of the Eucharist, ways that divided the two communions.

The simplicity of the basic actions of the Lord's Supper—the congregational sharing of bread and wine—belies the complexity of the theological debates that have surrounded it over the years. Indeed, there is surely a deep irony in the fact that this sacrament of Christian unity has become one of the primary sources of Christian division. The Lord's Table is the place where Christians come together to be most obviously united, yet it is in practice the place where our divisions are most obvious.

Divisions in Christ's body are deeply problematic and not something with which any Christian should be ultimately comfortable; however, the reasons for the divisions should not be dismissed as of only minor importance. Particularly in the matter of the Lord's Supper, the division between Lutheran and Reformed rests on very important doctrinal differences. If unity is ever to be achieved between the two, it is therefore important first of all for both sides in the eucharistic debate to understand not only their own position but also that of the other side.

The Lord's Supper in the Lutheran Tradition

Luther looked back to his baptism to hear God's promise of forgiveness of sins, life, and salvation as God established the relationship of love and trust between them. The Wittenberg professor looked to the Lord's Supper as a second expression of God's promise, linking the oral Word with the sacramental elements of bread and wine, through which Christ gives his body and blood with all the benefits of their being given into death and poured out "for us."

Much of the discussion of Luther's understanding of the Lord's Supper from his own time until today has focused on the question of how Jesus Christ is present in the sacrament. However, what separated him from many other Christians was and remains, in addition, the equally fundamental issue of what the Lord's Supper does and how it does what it does. Thus, while devotional writings and sermons often applied his sacramental teaching to the lives of readers and hearers, general perceptions of his views look most often to his controversial writings against those who attacked his treatises and against the medieval practices he wished to deconstruct so that a biblical use of the sacramental form of God's Word might replace them.

Luther's criticism of medieval sacramental practice did not ignore the question of Christ's presence. Initially, however, he was chiefly concerned with the Mass, the liturgy of the sacrament. He addressed the medieval failure to recognize that in the Supper God was pronouncing his promise by giving Christ's body and blood and that he was thus creating and sustaining the relationship of trust in him through this embodied presentation of his gift of the forgiveness of sins. That is a more general foundational aspect of the debate. Later, when attacked by critics such as Ulrich Zwingli—who could not believe that the material elements of bread and wine could convey Christ's body and blood and, with them, forgiveness of sins, life, and salvation—Luther concentrated on the question of Christ's presence.

God is present when the Lord's Supper is observed, most agreed, but in what form? How literally should one understand Christ's words instituting the sacrament? That led implicitly to the question of the purpose of Christ's presence: what did it accomplish? Luther's Small Catechism posed four questions regarding the Lord's Supper as the guide for instructing children in the nature and use of this sacrament. The first three are identical with those that guided the teaching on baptism. The fourth—Who, then, receives this sacrament worthily?—appears to be quite different from the fourth question on baptism, which asks about the significance of that sacrament for daily life. Yet in this question the affirmation of the impact of the Lord's Supper on those who receive it only through trust in its promise places the Supper squarely in the middle of daily life, where God's baptismal covenant also directs and determines the believer's sense of identity as child of God.

What Is the Lord's Supper?

"It is the true body and blood of our Lord Jesus Christ under the bread and wine, instituted by Christ himself for us Christians to eat and to drink,"[1] Luther had children learning his catechism answer.

By 1529 the question of how to define Christ's presence in the Lord's Supper had come to claim center place in public discussion of the sacrament for sixteenth-century believers. Its delivery of forgiveness, life, and salvation was for Luther the most important issue, but this depended on a proper understanding of what Jesus meant when he said, "This is my body." The Wittenberg Reformer's search for the best expression to preserve the biblical truth

---

1. *BSELK* 888/889.13–15/14–19; *BC* 362.

in Christ's words, while setting limits to human reason's intrusion into what must remain God's mysterious action, resulted in his describing this presence as the "true presence" of Christ's body and blood, or their "sacramental presence." His view is not halfway between a medieval interpretation using Aristotle's concept of substance—transubstantiation—and the symbolic or spiritual interpretations of Zwingli, Karlstadt, and Oecolampadius.[2] Luther instead proceeded from a different set of presuppositions. On the basis of his Ockhamist training, he presumed that God structured his world as he saw fit and was indeed able to place his body and blood in the bread and wine. He rejected any use of Aristotle's concept of substance, since it placed the mystery of God's sacramental action under human rational analysis. Luther presumed that the Lord's Supper is one form of God's promise that does not magically or automatically bestow its benefits but rather creates and sustains trust in God and what God says. In the Lord's Supper, God's Word of promise in Christ and the response of the believer in trust and confidence in that presence also claimed priority in Luther's thinking.

Luther's scholastic instructors had refined his childhood impressions of Christ's substantial presence on the altar, produced by the priest's use of the words of institution. In July 1520 Luther's *A Treatise on the New Testament, That Is, The Holy Mass* gives evidence that he was abandoning the theory rooted in Aristotle's physics; in October his *Babylonian Captivity of the Church* rejected and deconstructed the use of the Aristotelian concept of substance, setting aside transubstantiation and consubstantiation as well as other aspects of medieval sacramental teaching.[3] He rejected transubstantiation with ever more vigor as he came to view this materializing of Christ's body and blood as a support for superstitious use of the elements of bread and wine that made faith in its promise of forgiveness incidental to its benefits in the minds of many of the faithful.

Luther's Ockhamistic principle that God is sovereign or almighty and as such had the power and ability to create the world according to his own will led to his rejection of the realist acceptance of the principle that the finite cannot convey or deliver the infinite. Instead, Luther held that God wrote the rules for all creation. If he decided to offer his body and blood, and with

---

2. In 1529 Luther and several of his supporters met with Zwingli and Oecolampadius in Marburg and reached agreement on most points of doctrine but not on the nature of Christ's presence in the Lord's Supper (cf. WA 30/3:160–71; LW 38:15–89). In his *Brief Confession concerning the Holy Sacrament* (1544), Luther expressed bitter disappointment that Zwingli had remained steadfast in his rejection of the presence of Christ's body and blood in the sacrament (WA 54:141–67; LW 38:287–319).

3. WA 6:508.1–512.6; LW 36:28–35.

them forgiveness, life, and salvation, with or under the bread and wine of the Supper that Christ instituted, that was indeed possible and actually was the way Christ was operating. "Let go of reason and intellect, for they strive in vain to understand how flesh and blood can be present. Because they do not grasp it, they refuse to believe it. Lay hold of the word which Christ speaks, 'Take, this is my body, this is my blood.' One must not do such violence to the words of God as to give to any word a meaning other than its natural meaning, unless there is a clear and definite Scripture [passage] to require this."[4]

Luther developed other supporting arguments that ventured possible explanations for how Christ's body and blood might be present in the Supper by arguing christologically[5] and posing alternative forms of presence that could be established metaphysically.[6] But he relied chiefly on his conviction that there is no reason not to interpret what Christ says in instituting the Supper literally. "Impossible" was not a possible argument for someone trained in the Ockhamist tradition when speaking of what God might institute. Among Luther's adherents were those who relied more on christological argumentation, such as Johannes Brenz, to defend the Wittenberg understanding of Christ's presence, while others—for example, Martin Chemnitz—hewed more to Luther's approach on the basis of a literal interpretation of Christ's words.[7] As part of God's economy of salvation, that the Lord's Supper remained a mystery defying human reason seemed quite reasonable to the Lutherans.[8]

The proper definition of the nature of Christ's presence in the Supper became an issue when other Reformers rejected Luther's views. Two concerns drove his defense. First was his belief that the words of Christ in instituting the Supper, as part of Scripture, which is the voice of the Holy Spirit addressing his people,[9] should be believed because the Lord said them. The second

---

4. *The Adoration of the Sacrament* (1523), WA 11:434.17–22; LW 36:279; cf. in *On the Lord's Supper, Confession* (1528), WA 26:297.27–298.23; LW 37:194.

5. See the Lutheran section of chap. 3 above; cf. WA 26:326.29–338.17; LW 37:214–26.

6. WA 26:326.29–327.20; LW 37:214; quoted in Formula of Concord, Solid Declaration VII, BSELK 1492/1493.16–1494/1495.3; BC 609.

7. Cf. Martin Chemnitz, *Repetitio sanae doctrinae de vera praesentiae corporis et sanguinis Domini in coena* (Leipzig: Ernst Vögelin, 1561); translated as *The Lord's Supper*, trans. J. A. O. Preus (St. Louis: Concordia, 1979); and Theodor Mahlmann, *Das neue Dogma der lutherischen Christologie: Problem und Geschichte seiner Begründung* (Gütersloh: Gütersloher Verlagshaus, 1969).

8. Cf. Luther's *The Sacrament of the Body and Blood of Christ—Against the Ravers* (1526), WA 19:482.15–499.38; LW 36:335–46.

9. The controversy over the Lord's Supper was for Luther first of all a controversy over the authority of the biblical text, even though he responded to the arguments of his opponents that employed citations from the church fathers; cf. WA 23:208/209.28–244/245.34; LW 37:104–26. The patristic battleground remained very significant as the controversy continued; cf. Esther Chung-Kim, *Inventing Authority: The Use of the Church Fathers in Reformation Debates*

concern was his fear that another view of the nature of the sacrament and Christ's presence in it would deprive believers of the comfort gained from Christ's coming in this unique way to deliver forgiveness and life. His colleague Andreas Bodenstein von Karlstadt first aroused these concerns. Luther's three sermons preached in Wittenberg in early 1526 against deviations from his teaching on the sacrament of the altar[10] preceded other treatises.[11] Then came a burst of attacks on Luther's understanding of Christ's sacramental presence from Ulrich Zwingli, Johannes Oecolampadius, and others, who were moved by fear of reliance on material objects instead of on faith in Christ and whose philosophical presuppositions did not permit the kind of presence that brought Christ's body and blood into bread and wine in a mysterious fashion that defied rational definition.[12] These opposing views provoked Luther's *That These Words of Christ, "This Is My Body," etc. Still Stand Firm against the Schwärmer* (1527) and *Concerning Christ's Supper, Confession* (1528). Both works reflect his failure to understand how his opponents would limit God's power and cut off the comfort provided by receiving Christ's body and blood for the assurance of salvation and comfort in the face of Satan's attacks. If the two sides talked past each other, it was due to the two different theological grammars provided by their metaphysical presuppositions.

As Luther solidified the way he expressed his understanding of Christ's presence in the Supper, he and his followers found three key phrases that helped clarify his definition. First, Christ's body and blood were "sacramentally present"— that is, in some form that makes them truly present but does not submit itself to rational human investigation, proof, or elucidation. Second, Christ's body and blood are received through the mouth (oral partaking, *manducatio oralis*).[13] Third, because God's Word, not human faith, establishes this presence, false believers—those who do not look to Christ for salvation in faith—also receive

---

over the Eucharist (Waco: Baylor University Press, 2011); and Irene Dingel, "Das Streben nach einem 'Consensus Orthodoxus' mit den Vätern in der Abendmahlsdiskussion des späten 16. Jahrhunderts," in *Die Patristik in der Bibelexegese des 16. Jahrhunderts*, ed. David Steinmetz (Wiesbaden: Harrassowitz, 1999), 181–204.

    10. WA 19:482–523; *LW* 36:335–61.

    11. *Was sich D. A. Bodenstein von Karlstadt mit . . . Luther beredet zu Jena* (1524), WA 15:334–47; *Erklärung, wie Karlstadt seine Lehre vom hochwürdigen Sakrament . . . achtet und geachtet haben will* (1525), WA 18:453–66; *Entschuldigung D. A. Karlstadts des falschen Namens des Aufruhrs*, WA 18:436–45; *Wider die himmlischen Propheten . . .* (1525), WA 18:62–125, 134–214; *LW* 40:79–143, 144–223. See Amy Nelson Burnett, *Karlstadt and the Origins of the Eucharistic Controversy: A Study in the Circulation of Ideas* (New York: Oxford University Press, 2011); and Mark U. Edwards Jr., *Luther and the False Brethren* (Stanford: Stanford University Press, 1975), 34–59.

    12. Some twenty-five are listed in *LW* 37:8–11; cf. Edwards, *False Brethren*, 82–111.

    13. Cf. Formula of Concord, Solid Declaration VII, *BSELK* 1480/1481.32–1483/1484.12; *BC* 604.

Christ's body and blood, albeit to their condemnation (1 Cor. 11:29) (partaking by the ungodly, *manducatio impiorum*). The promise that the body and blood deliver the promised blessings is effective only for those who trust Christ's pledge that the sacrament is "for you." Likewise, Luther rejected the Donatist belief that the validity of the sacraments depends on the holiness of the priest; rather, it is the Word that determines the validity of the sacraments.[14]

Luther recognized that those who were attacking him did not themselves have a common interpretation of the word "is" in the words of institution, yet their fundamental position was the same. His opponents argued that it is simply not possible for Christ's body and blood to be present in, with, or under the bread and wine, and so an alternative interpretation must be found.[15] Luther's linguistic interests led him into an extensive exploration of how literal and metaphorical modes of interpretation function. Never doubting the presence of metaphor in Scripture, he argued that in the case of Christ's words instituting the Supper, there is no reason (apart from false philosophical presuppositions) not to believe that Christ has here given the precious gift of his body and blood to his church.[16]

Among other arguments, Zwingli had found it impossible for the human nature of Christ to be present on earth when it is sitting at the right hand of God the Father in heaven. This reasoning provoked two responses from Luther, expressed as sharply as the attacks against his position from his Swiss opponents. "The right hand of God" is a Hebrew expression for sharing the majesty, power, and dominion of the monarch, not a physical place somewhere "above" the earth, Luther wrote.[17] Second, he relied on a strong definition of the hypostatic or personal union of the human and divine natures of Christ, as he understood biblical teaching and its interpretation by the Council of Chalcedon (451). He believed that while the two natures retain their own characteristics and never acquire the attributes of the other, thereby preserving the integrity of their own natures, they do share those characteristics fully with each other. In this way he maintained the ancient doctrine of the communication of attributes (*communicatio idiomatum*). Therefore, the one person of Christ could exercise his ability to be present where and in what form he wishes with his human body and blood.[18]

14. E.g., Large Catechism, *BSELK* 1136/1137.22–27; *BC* 468.
15. WA 23:88/89.32–98/99.2; *LW* 37:30–35; cf. WA 26:262.26–282.9; *LW* 37:163–80.
16. WA 23:96/97.10–114/115.13; *LW* 37:34–46; cf. WA 26:282.10–292.23; *LW* 37:180–90; and WA 26:437.30–445.17; *LW* 37:294–303, where Luther explores several linguistic aspects of the argument.
17. WA 23:128/129.13–144/145.11; *LW* 37:55–64; cf. WA 26:314.17–32; *LW* 37:203–4.
18. WA 23:144/145.32–160/161.17; *LW* 37:65–74.

Luther also dismissed the argument that believing Christ's body and blood are truly present in the sacrament is simply too difficult and burdensome for the common people. He insisted that the manner in which human beings engage biblical teaching with their rational analysis does not determine the truth of God's Word.[19] Against his opponents' use of John 6:63, "The flesh is of no avail," Luther maintained the interpretation of the passage that he had held, in line with one medieval strain of interpretation, before the controversy broke out. He argued that "flesh" here—the text does not say "my flesh," he noted—has the same meaning as in Paul's writings, where it includes all that is apart from the activity of the Holy Spirit and does not refer to the Lord's Supper at all.[20]

The rejection of Zwingli's and others' dismissal of his understanding of Christ's bodily sacramental presence in the Supper did not mean that Luther did not also recognize Christ's spiritual presence alongside his sacramental presence and beyond it. "We Christians are the spiritual body of Christ and collectively one loaf, one drink, one spirit. All this is achieved by Christ, who through his own body makes us all to be one spiritual body, so that all of us take part alike in this body and are therefore equal and united with one another" (1 Cor. 10:17).[21]

The interpretation of 1 Corinthians 10:16, "The bread that we break is a sharing [κοινωνία, participation] in the body of Christ," became an increasingly important issue in the course of the sacramental controversies of the sixteenth century. Melanchthon abandoned his earlier application of the passage as a definition of the presence of Christ's body in the bread and the wine used in the sacrament; toward the end of his life he related the passage to the communion of Christians with one another. Luther's position is well represented in the judgment of the Formula of Concord that "the bread would not be a sharing of the body of Christ but of the Spirit of Christ if Christ's body were not truly present but only the Holy Spirit."[22] This passage also demonstrated the necessity of the laity's receiving both elements in the celebration of the sacrament[23] and rendered an interpretation of Christ's presence through a theory of transubstantiation impossible.[24]

19. WA 23:160/161.18–162/163.5; *LW* 37:74–75.
20. WA 23:166/167.28–204/205.31; *LW* 37:78–101; cf. Luther's defense of his translation of the passage, WA 26:354–368.31; *LW* 37:239–46.
21. WA 11:440.34–441.4; *LW* 36:286–87. Cf. Formula of Concord, Solid Declaration VII, *BSELK* 1480/1481.23–31; *BC* 604.
22. *BSELK* 1460/1461.10–14; *BC* 595.
23. *BSELK* 1476/1477.22–37; *BC* 602.
24. *BSELK* 1468/1469.16–25; *BC* 599.

Much has been made of the prepositions that are used to describe the relationship of the elements of bread and wine to Christ's body and blood: "under," "with," or "in." Luther did not group the three together, as later followers did, to cover all cases, but Luther, like the Formula of Concord, regarded all three as simply attempts to "accept the words of Christ in their proper sense" and not as a metaphorical formulation.[25] They served both as an affirmation of Christ's true bodily presence in the elements and a rejection of transubstantiation.[26] They do not explain the mystery of his presence.

In the case of the Lord's Supper, Luther did not often use the term "covenant" (*Bund*), rendering διαθήκη instead as "testament." In 1520 he defined the Supper as a testament that bequeaths "truly a great, eternal, and unspeakable treasure, the forgiveness of sins."[27] Christ is the author of the testament, and believers his heirs. The text of the testament is given in the words of institution, especially, "This is my body, which is given for you. This is my blood, which is poured out for you, a new eternal testament." The seal of the sacrament is "the bread and wine, under which are his true body and blood," "living words and signs which we use from day to day." What constitutes the inheritance is "remission of sins and eternal life." What the testator expects from his heirs is "that we preach his love and grace, hear and meditate upon it, and be moved by it and preserved unto love and hope in him."[28]

Christ's institution gave all twelve disciples both his body and his blood. Luther associated the twelve not with the clergy but with the twelve tribes of Israel and thus with the whole church. Therefore, though at the beginning of his public career, he could argue that the body under the bread alone sufficed since the priest received the blood under the wine in the people's presence,[29] the discomfort he expressed already in 1519 while making that concession turned quickly to harsh critique. Luther came to view the withholding of the wine with Christ's blood as tyranny over Christ's people and contempt for Christ's institution of the sacrament.[30]

Questions regarding Christ's presence in the Lord's Supper intertwined with the proclamation and enacting of communion or fellowship with the Lord. In his first treatises on the Supper, Luther also emphasized the communion of believers with one another that is sustained by their communing

---

25. *BSELK* 1468/1469.20–22; *BC* 599.
26. *BSELK* 1468/1469.20–1470/1471.22; *BC* 599.
27. WA 6:358.15–16; LW 35:85.
28. WA 6:359.15–32; LW 35:87.
29. *The Blessed Sacrament of the Holy and True Body of Christ, and the Brotherhoods*, WA 2:742–58; LW 35:49–73.
30. *Babylonian Captivity of the Church*, WA 6:507.6–33; LW 36:27–28.

together. Medieval practice had focused attention on the individual's merely being present in the vicinity of Christ, who was present on the altar, in order to gain merit in God's sight. While the Wittenberg professor also emphasized the individual benefits that come not through simply being present but, further, through receiving the sacrament in faith, he also viewed the "fellowship of all the saints" and their fellowship with Christ, kindled by the sacrament, as an important result of communing. "Christ and all saints are one spiritual body, just as the inhabitants of a city are one community and body. . . . To receive this sacrament in bread and wine is nothing else than to receive a sure sign of this fellowship and incorporation with Christ and all saints. . . . All sufferings and sins also become common property. Thus, love engenders love in return, and it unites."[31] Those who receive the Lord's Supper are bound together in a community of mutual support in the face of every kind of suffering and sorrow.[32]

In his *Treatise on the New Testament* (1520), Luther stated that the sacrament brings believers together to nourish and strengthen faith as they offer prayer "with one accord." They then distribute alms to the poor, good works that are engendered by God's grace but distinct from the sacrament, which is purely gift; these good works are in no way a human contribution to establishing or sustaining the relationship that God bestows through his Word.[33] This fellowship does not exist only within the local congregation, Luther wrote in 1526, for the whole body of Christians throughout the world are one. This is symbolized by the use of bread as the vehicle of Christ's body. For Luther the sacrament was not only Christ being present with his congregation but also an image of the congregation, picturing the body of the elect as the loaf in which many grains are brought together into one unit or as the wine that has been produced by pressing individual grapes together into one cup.[34] The nature of the Supper as a meal for the community became an argument that Luther used to condemn private Masses.[35] Though this topic recedes in relationship to the issues of Christ's presence and the Supper's power to forgive, it does not disappear completely from Luther's teaching.

Luther opposed limiting the impact of the Lord's Supper to its arousing remembrance of Christ's passion, but he believed that it did recall his suffering, death, and resurrection for the individual: its words are addressed directly to each recipient, in contrast to the sermon that is preached to the

31. WA 2:743.7–744.7; LW 35:51–52.
32. WA 2:745.1–18; LW 35:54.
33. WA 6:364.32–365.5; LW 36:93–94.
34. WA 19:509.29–512.21; LW 36:352–53.
35. *The Private Mass* (1533), WA 38:199.14–37; LW 38:152.

entire congregation. This commemoration "proclaims Christ's death" and thus delivers his promise.[36] In the Lord's Supper, believers encounter "the true God, who gives and does not receive, who helps and does not let himself be helped, who teaches and rules and does not let himself be taught or ruled. In short, he does and gives everything . . . freely out of pure grace, without merit, for the unworthy and undeserving, yes, for the damned and lost."[37] Remembering could not help but move a person to trust in the great promise of the gifts of Christ. This aspect of Luther's pastoral concern for the comfort of the believer reflects his conviction that those who are fully justified by God's Word, at the same time as they continue to perceive the presence of sin in their lives (*simul justus et peccator*), need throughout their whole lives to be practicing repentance and receiving forgiveness and the assurance of Christ's gift of life. They need to know that "when God forgives, he forgives everything completely and leaves nothing unforgiven. When I am free of sin, I am also free of death, devil, and hell; I am a child of God, a lord of heaven and earth."[38]

Philip Melanchthon shared Luther's belief that Christ was truly present in the sacrament but became ever more reluctant to define this presence with precise terms. This prompted deviations from Luther's teaching and isolated a group of Melanchthon's followers from the majority of the Wittenberg circle through controversies in the 1560s and 1570s. Some followers of Melanchthon—such as authors of the Formula of Concord: Martin Chemnitz, David Chytraeus, and Nikolaus Selnecker—believed that Melanchthon had shared Luther's view of Christ's sacramental presence quite completely. Others recognized some differences that they believed were not substantial. Still others moved toward a spiritualizing position that facilitated their transition to a view that was very close to Calvin's. In their own age they were labeled "crypto-Calvinist" but probably are more accurately called "crypto-Philippist" because they believed they were representing the position of the older Melanchthon, although they tried to conceal their spiritualizing teaching.[39] These conflicts and others with those committed

---

36. WA 19:504.20–505.16; LW 36:348–49.

37. *Admonition concerning the Sacrament* (1530), WA 30.2:603.12–17; LW 38:107.

38. WA 19:506.16–25; LW 36:349–50.

39. Johannes Hund, *Das Wort ward Fleisch: Eine systematisch-theologische Untersuchung zur Debatte um die Wittenberger Christologie und Abendmahlslehre in den Jahren 1567 bis 1574* (Göttingen: Vandenhoeck & Ruprecht, 2006); Irene Dingel, "The Creation of Theological Profiles: The Understanding of the Lord's Supper in Melanchthon and the Formula of Concord," in *Philip Melanchthon: Theologian in Classroom, Confession, and Controversy*, by Irene Dingel et al. (Göttingen: Vandenhoeck & Ruprecht, 2012), 263–81.

openly to Reformed confessions[40] led the authors of the Formula of Concord to treat the Lord's Supper in detail. They reaffirmed Luther's positions and incorporated the Wittenberg Concord, which Melanchthon had written in 1536 to reconcile Martin Bucer of Strasbourg and Luther, into the Formula of Concord. This statement rejected transubstantiation and a spatial enclosure of Christ's body and blood in the elements, but it affirmed "that through the sacramental union the bread is the body of Christ." It limited the presence of Christ's body and blood to the use of the sacrament within the congregational liturgy. It further confessed that the sacrament's "power does not rest upon the worthiness or unworthiness of the minister who distributes the sacrament, nor upon the worthiness or unworthiness of the one who receives it because, as Saint Paul says, even the unworthy receive the sacrament." The Formula continues with the words of the Smalcald Articles of 1537: "The bread and the wine in the Supper are the true body and blood of Christ, which are not only offered to and received by upright Christians but also by evil ones."[41]

What Does the Lord's Supper Do?

The benefits of the Lord's Supper are proclaimed in "the words, 'given for you' and 'shed for you for the forgiveness of sins' [which] show us that forgiveness of sin, life, and salvation are given to us in the sacrament through these words, because where there is forgiveness of sin, there is also life and salvation,"[42] Luther wrote in his Small Catechism.

Luther viewed the Lord's Supper as Christ's testament, his promise, "indeed, much more: the bestowal of grace and the forgiveness of sin, that is the true gospel."[43] This definition of the sacrament as primarily a word of promise that elicits and strengthens faith undermined the popular medieval

40. Cf. Irene Dingel, "Heinrich Bullinger und das Luthertum im Deutschen Reich," in *Heinrich Bullinger: Life—Thought—Influence*, ed. Emidio Campi and Peter Opitz (Zurich: Theologischer Verlag, 2007), 2:755–77; Dingel, "Calvinism at the Borders of the Empire: Johannes Wigand and the Lutheran Reaction to Calvinism," in *John Calvin, Myth and Reality: Images and Impact of Geneva's Reformer*, ed. Amy Nelson Burnett (Eugene, OR: Cascade, 2011), 139–61; Dingel, "Calvin in the Context of Lutheran Consolidation," *Reformation & Renaissance Review* 12 (2010): 155–87; Dingel, "Pia et fidelis admonitio—Eine Werbung für Einheit von Luthertum und europäischem Calvinismus," in *Calvinismus in den Auseinandersetzungen des frühen konfessionellen Zeitalters*, ed. Herman J. Selderhuis et al. (Göttingen: Vandenhoeck & Ruprecht, 2013), 50–65; Dingel, "Die lutherische Kritik am Heidelberger Katechismus," in *Profil und Wirkung des Heidelberger Katechismus*, ed. Christoph Strohm and Jan Stievermann (Gütersloh: Gütersloher Verlagshaus, 2015), 226–41.

41. *BSELK* 1460/1461.19–1462/1463.32; *BC* 595–96.

42. *BSELK* 888/889.27–890/891.2; *BC* 362.

43. *WA* 26:468.32–34; *LW* 37:325.

view, according to which the priest's consecration of the elements was considered an act that brought benefits, including the forgiveness of actual sins, to those who were attending the Mass, regardless of their faith. Though not shared by all late medieval theologians, this view, along with the impression that the sacrament delivered grace to those who simply came to Mass apart from faith, attracted critique from all Protestant Reformers and from some in the Roman Catholic camp as well.

In 1527 Luther observed, "Irenaeus and the ancient fathers pointed out the benefit that our body is fed with Christ's body in order that our faith and hope may abide and that our body also may live eternally from the same eternal food of Christ's body which it consumes bodily. . . . For Christ surely will make even our body everlasting, alive, blessed, and glorious." Furthermore, the words that God gives in the Supper's promise are also the gospel, which brings salvation to those who believe.[44]

The Lord's Supper took on special importance for Luther as he recognized the daily attacks of Satan. "There are so many hindrances and attacks of the devil and the world that we often grow weary and faint and at times even stumble. Therefore, the Lord's Supper is given as a daily pasture and fodder so that our faith may be refreshed and strengthened and that it may not succumb in the struggle but become stronger and stronger."[45] In 1530 he presented the benefits of receiving the Supper with another metaphor, placing it squarely in the middle of the believer's daily battle with Satan.

> The sacrament is indeed not a sign of his wrath. . . . Rather, it is a sign of his sublimest love and fathomless mercy. How can he demonstrate sublime love and deeper mercy than that he should therein truly give us his own body and blood as food? This is not only a gracious sign but is also supposed to be a food by which all of us who are in his army and engaged in combat should be refreshed and strengthened. It is in reality the pay and provisions with which he remunerates and feeds his army and soldiers until they finally win the victory and carry the day along with him. Oh, it is good coinage, costly red gold and pure white silver, elegant, attractive bread and good, sweet wine! And all this is provided in abundance and richly so that it is very delightful to be part of this military expedition.[46]

As early as 1520 Luther argued that to regard the Lord's Supper as a sacrifice by which the priest repeats the sacrifice of Golgotha—according to some in

---

44. WA 23:254/255.14–258/259.6; *LW* 37:132–34.
45. *BSELK* 1138/1139.23–31; *BC* 469.
46. WA 30/2:621.27–38; *LW* 38:131–32.

order to win release from the guilt of actual sins (since Christ had won release from the guilt of original sin on the cross)—discards "the gospel, Christ, the comfort it gives, and every grace of God." He sharply distinguished the sacrament from the liturgical prayer and praise surrounding it, which is indeed the human response—but no human contribution winning merit!—to God's gift of life and salvation in the Supper.[47] In 1530 he wrote against those who regard the Mass not "as a sacrifice of thanksgiving but as a sacrifice of works, in which they do not thank God for his grace but obtain merits for themselves and others, and first and foremost, secure grace."[48] To this piety, Luther consistently responded, "Christ has sacrificed himself once (Heb. 7:27; 9:25–26); henceforth he does not want to be sacrificed by anyone else. He wishes for us to remember his sacrifice." Regarding the Mass as a repetition of the sacrifice on the cross fulfills the prophecy of Hebrews 6:6, "They crucify on their own account God's Son afresh and hold him up to contempt."[49] Instead, Luther wanted believers to be "reminded of such favor and grace that your faith and love are stimulated, renewed, and strengthened, so that you might not reach the point of forgetting or despising your dear Savior and his bitter suffering and the great, manifold, eternal misery and death out of which he rescued you."[50]

How Is That Possible?

"Eating and drinking certainly do not do it, but rather the words that are recorded: 'given for you' and 'shed for you for the forgiveness of sins.' These words, when accompanied by the physical eating and drinking, are the essential thing in the sacrament, and whoever believes these very words has what they declare and state, namely, 'forgiveness of sins.'"[51] As in baptism, the Word does its work, in this case by marshaling the elements of bread conveying Christ's body and wine conveying his blood to deliver the forgiveness of sins. For Luther, the elements enhance the communication of God's mercy, but it is clearly God's Word that serves as his instrument to reassert the repentant sinner's identity as child of God.

In 1520 Luther had anticipated his explanation to those who would later be learning the catechism: he linked the promise given in the Supper inextricably with faith.

---

47. WA 6:367.13–370.11; LW 35:97–101. Cf. his similar argument in *Babylonian Captivity*, WA 6:522.30–526.33; LW 36:50–57.
48. WA 30/2:610.32–35; LW 38:117.
49. *On the Misuse of the Mass*, WA 8:493.16–37; LW 36:147.
50. WA 30/2:616.36–617.5; LW 38:125–26.
51. BSELK 890/891.4–8; BC 363.

These two, promise and faith, must necessarily go together. For without the promise there is nothing to be believed, while without faith, the promise is useless since it is put in place and completed through faith. . . . Without this faith, whatever else is brought to it by way of prayers, preparations, works, signs, or gestures incite impiety rather than exercise piety. . . . The whole power of the mass rests in Christ's words, in which he testifies that forgiveness of sins is bestowed on all who believe that his body is given and his blood poured out for them. This is why nothing is more important for those who go to hear mass than to ponder these words diligently and in total faith.[52]

Against medieval eucharistic practice, Luther protested,

We must be particularly careful to put aside whatever has been added to [the sacrament's] simple institution by human zeal and devotion, such as vestments, ornaments, chants, prayers, organs, candles, and the whole external pageantry. We must turn our eyes and hearts simply to Christ's institution and it alone, and concentrate on nothing but Christ's very words, by which he instituted the sacrament. . . . For in that word, and it alone, reside the power, nature, and whole substance of the [celebration of the Supper].[53]

Faith arises from the nature of the words of institution as a promise, for God's promises have the power to create trust. God's promises found throughout the Old Testament of a deliverer from all evils are confirmed in the testament that Christ bestowed through his death. By its very nature, a promise

is not to be gained with any works, or powers, or merits of one's own, but by faith alone. Where there is the Word of the promising God, there must necessarily be the faith of the accepting human being. Thus, it is clear that the beginning of our salvation is a faith which clings to the Word of the promising God, who without any effort on our part, in free and unmerited mercy, takes the initiative and offers us the word of his promise. . . . First, there is God's Word. After it follows faith; after faith, love; for love does every good work, for it does no wrong, indeed, it is the fulfilling of the law [Rom. 13:10].[54]

What Is Necessary for Proper Reception and Use of the Lord's Supper?

"Fasting and bodily preparation are in fact a fine external discipline, but a person who has faith in these words, 'given for you' and 'shed for you for the forgiveness of sins,' is really worthy and well prepared. However, a person

52. WA 6:517.8–38; LW 36:42–43.
53. WA 6:512.26–35; LW 36:36.
54. WA 6:514.12–21; LW 36:39.

who does not believe these words or doubts them is unworthy and unprepared, because the words, 'for you,' require truly believing hearts."[55] "Because this treasure is fully offered in the words, it can be grasped and appropriated only by the heart. Such a gift and eternal treasure cannot be seized with the hand. . . . This is done by the faith of the heart that discerns and desires such a treasure."[56] The Formula of Concord reaffirmed Luther's pastoral approach to use of the sacrament by accenting that trust in Christ's words alone makes one worthy to receive the sacrament.[57]

Luther conceded that he himself sometimes did not feel worthy of the gifts God gives in the Lord's Supper. He had to remind himself that God commands his people to come to find comfort in receiving Christ and his promise that he died "for you." Even those who did not feel the need should come to the Supper, because the Word of God tells them of their need and because the evidence of Satan's murderous deception lies on every side.[58]

In 1524 Luther cast his trust in the sacramental promise of the Lord's Supper into verse:

> Jesus Christ, he is our Savior,
> Who turned away from us God's wrath
> Through his bitterest agony;
> He rescued us from pangs of hell.
>> So that we forget this never,
>> He gave his flesh for us to eat
>> Well hidden in this bit of bread
>> And gave to drink his blood in wine.
> Give praise to God, the Father, then
> Who sought to feed you bountifully
> And for your sins and misdeeds many
> His Son surrendered into death.
>> Shy not away but trust completely
>> That this food is for the ailing
>> Whose sins weigh down their failing hearts
>> And quiver ever more from fear.
> He himself says, "Come, poor people,
> Let me pour on you my mercy.
> Physicians need not see the healthy,
> But with them only wastes his skill.

55. *BSELK* 890/891.10–14; *BC* 363.
56. *BSELK* 1142.22–29; *BC* 470.
57. *BSELK* 1482/1483.29–1484/1485.19; *BC* 605–6.
58. *BSELK* 1148/1149.5–1154/1155.32; *BC* 472–75.

> If you trust this promise truly
> And confess him with your mouth
> You are well prepared to savor
> This food that wakes your tired soul."[59]

This trust in Christ's promise framed and determined Luther's use of the Lord's Supper and shapes Lutherans' use of the Lord's Supper today as well.

The Lord's Supper in the Reformed Tradition

The Lord's Supper constitutes the most famous point of division between the Lutheran and the Reformed churches. While the point of the Eucharist obviously cannot be isolated from other issues such as Christology and hermeneutics, it was the cause of the infamous conflict between Luther and Zwingli, which then ensured the fundamental divide within magisterial Protestantism.

To begin with, we might summarize the disagreement as being over this fundamental question: Is the whole Christ, divine and human, contained in, with, and under the elements of bread and wine in the Lord's Supper? And do unbelievers actually eat the body and drink the blood of Christ, only to their damnation, not salvation? The Lutherans affirm this; the Reformed deny this.

Nevertheless, within the bounds of the Reformed churches, there was a further division, though not so acrimonious, between those who tended to follow Calvin on the Lord's Supper and those who leaned toward Zurich. Zurich theologians sought to articulate a fundamentally symbolic/memorial view of the Supper. Calvin and the Genevans offered a view that pushed beyond mere memorialism and stressed the reality of feeding on Christ's flesh for the Christian life. It is this latter view that I shall articulate in this chapter.[60]

The Lord's Supper: A Matter of Importance

Students from Evangelical backgrounds often find the concern for the Lord's Supper exhibited by the Reformers, and especially the division between Lutheran and Reformed, to be confusing, at best a vestige of how the priorities of medieval Catholicism continued to shape sixteenth-century thought. Nevertheless, those who hold to the confessional statements of the Reformers know that the matter is one of important theological and pastoral concern.

59. WA 35:500–501 (author's trans.); cf. *LW* 53:205–51.
60. The Swiss, including Geneva and Zurich, reached an agreement on the Lord's Supper in 1549, the so-called Consensus Tigurinus, which rejected Roman Catholic and Lutheran views and left open the questions that divided Geneva and Zurich.

The Anglican Book of Common Prayer, perhaps the single greatest liturgical achievement of Reformed theology, contains a beautiful communion service that places the Lord's Supper in the context of the proclaimed Word and at the heart of the church's communal life.[61] The whole of the Christian life is enacted in the liturgy, with the importance of the Supper clear throughout, as in this beautiful passage from the 1662 edition, the so-called Prayer of Humble Access:

> We do not presume to come to this thy Table, O merciful Lord, trusting in our own righteousness, but in thy manifold and great mercies. We are not worthy so much as to gather up the crumbs under thy Table. But thou art the same Lord, whose property is always to have mercy. Grant us therefore, gracious Lord, so to eat the flesh of thy dear Son Jesus Christ, and to drink his blood, that our sinful bodies may be made clean by his body, and our souls washed through his most precious blood, and that we may evermore dwell in him, and he in us. Amen.[62]

That is more than mere symbolism. The act of Holy Communion assumed here, in a prayer shot through with biblical allusions, involves humility, faith, the being and nature of God, his work in Christ, forgiveness, union with Christ, and the potent impact of partaking of the elements.

For Calvin, the Supper was central to his practical ecclesiastical policy. It was his refusal to distribute the Supper to those he regarded as acting in a sinful manner that led to his expulsion from Geneva in 1538. That is important, for if the Supper was of no account, then the withholding of the same would mean nothing. For Calvin, however, the ability to stop someone from partaking of the elements was vital to church discipline and was a significant sanction, because the Supper did give something that the Word alone did not. To phrase that more accurately, the Supper gave the same Christ but in a significantly different way. It made a difference because it was not just a symbol but, to use Reformed terminology, also a means of grace.

Thus, when Calvin returned in 1541, he wanted to have the Supper administered weekly for pastoral reasons, both the upbuilding of the saints and the discipline of the backslidden. That the council refused to implement this policy and held instead to a practice of four times a year had everything to

---

61. The Book of Common Prayer, the work of Archbishop Thomas Cranmer, was first published in the reign of Edward VI and underwent numerous editions thereafter. The various modern editions tend to be very close to the 1662 edition, published under Charles II. There is a very convenient edition of the major Reformation editions: Brian Cummings, ed., *The Book of Common Prayer: The Texts of 1549, 1559, and 1662* (Oxford: Oxford University Press, 2013).
    62. Cummings, *Book of Common Prayer*, 402.

do with the need for military support from the Bernese and nothing to do with Genevan theology.[63]

Indeed, this emphasis on the Supper was a hallmark of many of the Reformed. For example, Theodore Beza, Calvin's successor in Geneva, wrote extensively on the subject, particularly in controversy with the Lutherans. But this was not simply for polemical reasons of establishing tribal differences. Beza knew that the Lord's Supper was important for the well-being of the church and its members, so it was necessary to oppose wrong teaching as part of a positive exposition of doctrine as a whole. The anti-Lutheran polemic should not therefore be read as intending to downgrade or marginalize the Supper, though that may well have occurred in later Zwinglian-influenced churches. Rather, the debate was between those who knew the Supper to be of vital importance but who disagreed as to precisely how this was the case.[64]

Neither Rome nor Wittenberg

Reformed understandings of the Lord's Supper were developed in polemical counterpoint to both Rome and Wittenberg. In his *Institutes*, Calvin describes the Mass as a "horrid abomination" and sees it as the capstone of the devil's strategy to destroy the church.[65] Similar language can be found in the Reformed confessions. Thus, the Mass is "blasphemous"[66] and an "accursed idolatry."[67]

The reason for this strength of language is the belief that the Mass represents a re-sacrificing of Christ and thus a denial of his once-and-for-all sacrifice on the cross and a surreptitious way of bringing salvation by works into the equation. Such would make the sacrament into something meritorious and also make the direction of action from earth toward heaven, as the human priest offers Christ to God. This would be a basic denial of the gospel.

Calvin therefore assumes the perfect and sufficient sacrifice of Christ on Calvary and sees this as ruling out of bounds the Roman Catholic construction of the Mass. Transubstantiation, of course, is another point repudiated by Protestants, but the fundamental problem is not so much the metaphysics

---

63. In Calvin's day, Geneva was dependent on the city of Berne for protection from the House of Savoy. Because the Bernese celebrated the Lord's Supper four times a year, the Genevans had to do the same—a reminder that religion and its liturgical forms were profoundly political in the sixteenth century.

64. See Theodore Beza, *A Clear and Simple Treatise on the Lord's Supper*, trans. David C. Noe (Grand Rapids: Reformation Heritage Books, 2016). This is Beza's response to the Lutheran theologian Joachim Westphal.

65. Calvin, *Institutes* IV.xviii.1.

66. Scots Confession 22 (Dennison 2:204).

67. Heidelberg Catechism 80 (Dennison 2:788).

of Christ's presence as the sacrificial dimension of the Roman Catholic sacrament.[68]

If the Reformed are not with Rome, however, neither are they with Wittenberg. Indeed, some of most brutal sacramental polemics of the sixteenth century were not between Protestants and Roman Catholics but between Lutherans and Reformed. In large part, this is predicated on the christological points we have discussed elsewhere (see chap. 3). In the *Institutes*, Calvin highlights what he regards as the absurdity of the Lutheran position by arguing that the objective presence of the whole Christ in, with, and under the bread and wine requires a kind of Marcionite Christology whereby Christ's body was a mere phantasm.[69] Similarly, while the Heidelberg Catechism makes no explicit comment on the Lutheran doctrine in its treatment of the Supper, it does spend three earlier questions explicating the significance of Christ's ascension and pointedly emphasizes the union of the two natures and the localized presence of the humanity in heaven.[70] This argument has proved popular with the Reformed. In his *Reformed Dogmatics*, Herman Bavinck argues that the Lutheran position is inconsistent both with Christ's participation in the Last Supper and with his current session at the right hand of the Father.[71]

Thus, as we approach the positive teaching of the Reformed on the Lord's Supper, we should note at the outset that it assumes both a specific soteriology, whereby the sacrifice of Christ on Calvary was unique and unrepeatable, and a specific Christology, whereby Christ's human nature is circumscribed and seated at the right hand of the Father in heaven.

The Foundation: Union with Christ

The foundation of the Reformed understanding of the Lord's Supper is that of the believer's union with Christ. This is expressed beautifully by the Scottish theologian Robert Bruce in the first of a series of sermons that constitute one of the finest expositions of the Supper in Reformed literature: "There is nothing in this world, or out of this world, more to be wished by everyone of you than to be conjoined with Jesus Christ, and once for all made

68. Calvin, *Institutes* IV.xviii.2–3. This is not to say that transubstantiation is a matter of no importance for Calvin; indeed, he sees it as the theological basis for the propitiatory nature of the Mass (*Institutes* IV.xviii.5).

69. Calvin, *Institutes* IV.xvii.17.

70. Heidelberg Catechism 45–48. The Heidelberg Catechism was produced in part to provide an ecumenical consensus between the Reformed and the Philippists in the Palatinate, thereby isolating the Gnesio-Lutherans. This helps to explain the implicit nature of its anti-Lutheran polemic.

71. *RD* 4:568–70.

one with Him, the God of Glory. This heavenly and celestial conjunction is procured and brought about by two special means. It is brought about by means of the Word and preaching of the Gospel, and it is brought about by means of the sacraments and their ministration."[72] This is consistent with Calvin, who sees the sacraments as a testimony to believers that they form one body with Christ.[73] The Lord's Supper, like the Word, helps forge the believer's union with Christ.

For the Reformed, this cannot be detached from the work of the Holy Spirit. As the Spirit works in and through the Word, so he is vital in the sacrament too. Bruce again: "But there is one thing you must always remember: there is no doctrine of the simple Word or of the Sacraments, that is able to move us if Christ takes away his Holy Spirit."[74] The Lord's Supper is therefore a trinitarian action. It cannot be understood in isolation from God's action in Christ and by his Holy Spirit. Indeed, it relies for its efficacy on the union of the believer with Christ by the Holy Spirit. Calvin articulates this memorably in the *Institutes*, where he says that no blessing can come to those who are not first united to Christ and that such union comes about by the Spirit.[75]

We might also add that within Reformed Protestantism this union is first and foremost a function of the Word preached. We hear the Word, we grasp the Word by the Spirit, and we are thereby united to Christ in a manner that gives us all of his benefits.[76]

One of the inferences arising from this is that the Supper does not provide anything that the believer does not, strictly speaking, enjoy already. United to Christ, what more spiritually can we possess? Bavinck is very clear on this point: "Believers already enjoy this communion [with Christ] by faith, and in the Supper they receive no other communion than that which they already enjoy by faith."[77] This is an important point, because it relativizes the Supper. The sacrament has no independent significance. It does not give us a different Christ or offer any benefits we do not already have in him.

As Reformed Protestants, we are relatively comfortable with grasping the Word by faith as the key theological and existential aspect of personal salvation. This is perhaps why we are comparatively less comfortable and sometimes confused by the sacraments. What do they give that the Word does not?

---

72. Robert Bruce, *The Mystery of the Lord's Supper: Sermons by Robert Bruce*, ed. Thomas F. Torrance (Fearn, UK: Christian Focus, 2005), 30.

73. Calvin, *Institutes* IV.xvii.2.

74. Bruce, *Mystery of the Lord's Supper*, 30–31.

75. Calvin, *Institutes* III.i.1.

76. Ibid., III.ii.31.

77. *RD* 4:578.

As noted above, they give nothing more than the Word. Yet Bruce's point, which reflects the Reformed tradition as a whole, is that Word and sacrament are means of union with Christ, and Bruce's language here is powerful and emphatic. How can this be?

We might approach an answer by asking the provocative question often posed to me by students in my classes who are of a more Evangelical persuasion and who are perplexed by the sacramental piety of the Reformers: What do we receive in the Supper that we do not receive by faith? To which, to repeat myself, we should first give the answer "Nothing!" This should not be a surprise in light of the above paragraphs. Yet there is more to it than that.

When faced with this question, what I typically do is highlight to students the fact that states of affairs are communicated, enhanced, and reinforced by actions that, strictly speaking, convey no new information. Just because something conveys nothing new in terms of content does not mean, however, that it conveys nothing of any special significance.

In class, I typically demonstrate this with a thought experiment related to my wife's birthday. It is a fact that I tell her by word of mouth every day of the year that I love her. But on her birthday I give her a present, something material. The giving of the present presupposes my love for her and my marriage to her. It does not alter my love or change that state in any absolute sense. And yet here is the rub: if I were to forget to give her a present, it would immediately make a difference to the relationship (though this is an experiment I have never dared to try, and so I am merely making an informed guess as to consequences at this point). Why is that, if the words and the gift really convey no different information? After all, we might perhaps say that the phrase "I love you" and the birthday gift convey precisely the same reality: that of the loving relationship that exists between the two of us. But the key thing is this: the words and the gift do so in different ways, and both ways are of great importance to the maintenance of a healthy marriage. Telling my wife I love her is vital, as is giving her a birthday gift. We might go further and say that, of the two, the former is more important, as the latter depends for its meaning on my telling my wife that I do love her. But both fulfill important roles in our relationship. The one conveys my love verbally; the other impresses it on her heart by action.

We can now apply this to the relationship of Word and sacrament. While there is a parallel between Word and sacrament in Reformed thinking in that both connect to the believer's union with Christ, the Reformed nevertheless see the Word preached as having priority. This position receives confessional status in the Westminster Catechisms. Thus, in question 89, the Shorter Catechism asks how the Word is made effectual to salvation, and the answer is given, "The Spirit of God maketh the reading, but especially the preaching, of the word, an effectual means of convincing and converting sinners, and of building them up in holiness and comfort, through faith, unto salvation."[78]

The priority of the Word means that, like Luther, the Reformed did not believe that there could be a sacrament correctly administered without the proclamation of the Word. Calvin says that the sacrament consists of the Word and the sign, with the Word being a proclamation that can be clearly understood by the congregation and not some mumbled incantation that might appear to have intrinsic magical power.[79] Instead, the sacrament comes with antecedent promise that it then signifies and seals to the recipient.[80] But the sacrament is still important, because it makes that of which the Word speaks real to us in a different, powerful, supplementary way. It is both a sign of our union with Christ and a seal of the same.

The Lord's Supper as Sign

Basic to all Reformed understandings of the Lord's Supper is the idea that it is a sign. This position is shared by both those of a more Zwinglian and those of a more Calvinistic persuasion.[81] The choice of bread and wine is also not arbitrary but enjoys a connection to what it signifies: the believers' relationship to Christ as articulated through the idea of food and eating. Nevertheless—and here is where the Reformed differ from the Lutherans—the sign and the thing signified are distinct and not so conjoined as to be identified in the manner in which Luther and his followers understand them to be.

This is a point requiring some nuancing, because the Reformed do use the language of conjunction to speak of the relationship between the sign and the thing signified. The Zwinglians are happy with the language of symbolism and memorialism, but the Calvinists want to make the signs into something more than what we might call "bare signs." Rather, they wish to emphasize both the distinction between sign and thing signified at the same time as pressing

---

78. *The Westminster Confession of Faith and Larger and Shorter Catechisms with Proof Texts* (Willow Grove, PA: Orthodox Presbyterian Church, 2005). The Larger Catechism gives a very rich statement on the power of the Word:

> Q. 155. How is the word made effectual to salvation? A. The Spirit of God maketh the reading, but especially the preaching of the word, an effectual means of enlightening, convincing, and humbling sinners; of driving them out of themselves, and drawing them unto Christ; of conforming them to his image, and subduing them to his will; of strengthening them against temptations and corruptions; of building them up in grace, and establishing their hearts in holiness and comfort through faith unto salvation. (Ibid.)

79. Calvin, *Institutes* IV.xiv.4.
80. Ibid., IV.xiv.3.
81. *Consensus Tigurinus* 9.

the closeness of the connection between the two. Thus, Robert Bruce: "The reason why I call them signs is this: I do not call them signs for the reason that men commonly call them signs, because they only signify something, as the bread signifies the Body of Christ, and the wine signifies the Blood of Christ; I do not call them something because they only represent something. I call them signs because they have the Body and Blood of Christ conjoined with them."[82] Perhaps we can help unpack something of what Bruce intends here by drawing analogies with other signs. If I drive to New York, I pass numerous road signs pointing me in the appropriate direction to travel. The signs are not arbitrary. They are connected to New York, because they are governed by the position of New York relative to the spot in which they are placed. The sign and the thing signified are thus connected yet clearly separate.

This is akin to the Zwinglian view of the Lord's Supper, wherein its efficacy lies in its ability to bring to mind the memory of the Lord's death. Thus, in *Fidei Ratio* (1530), chapter 8, Zwingli declares that the realist language of presence in the Supper needs to be understood in terms of the faithful bringing to mind and thanking God for the saving acts of Christ.[83] Sign and thing signified are tied together—the Word of Christ so connects them in the words of institution—but the connection is not particularly close.

Yet, to return to the travel analogy, on the same trip I could also communicate with my wife on the phone or on Skype in the evenings. I am physically absent from her at such times. What I hear and what I see is not my wife: it is an electronic reproduction of her voice, or colors on a screen. These are, of course, determined by her speech and her appearance, but they are mediated via a computer. She is not really present with me in the room. The sign is still separable from what it signifies, but there is an intimate connection between the two that makes her more present to me than a simple arrow pointing me in the direction of where she is located.

---

82. Robert Bruce, *Mystery of the Lord's Supper: Sermons by Robert Bruce*, ed. Thomas F. Torrance (Fearn, UK: Christian Focus), 35.

83. *Fidei Ratio* was Zwingli's own attempt to make a theological contribution to the Diet of Augsburg, where Melanchthon presented the Augsburg Confession. Cf. the First Helvetic Confession 23:

> And this sacred food we use often for this reason, because through the remembrance of it, we behold with the eye of faith the death and blood of the crucified one. We remember our salvation, not without a taste of the heavenly life, and a true sense of life eternal. Reflecting with inexpressible sweetness, we are refreshed by this spiritual, living, and eternal nourishment. And with indescribable words of joy, we exult exceedingly on account of the life which we have found. Wholly and with all our strength, we pour out thanksgiving for such a wonderful benefit of Christ toward us. (Dennison 1:350)

While all analogies are limited, this seems to bring out something of that for which Reformed theology strives in its sacramental theology. The sign and the thing signified are separate but are also intimately related. Bruce is excellent on this point. First, he says, Christ is present by his Spirit in the believer through the believer's union with Christ. Second, Christ is conjoined with the sign by the Word.[84] Bruce also uses terminology common in Reformed theology for the Lord's Supper, that it is a "visible word."[85] This he elaborates by pointing to the analogy between what physical eating and nourishment do for the body and what feeding on Christ by faith does for the soul. The bread and the wine are a dramatic representation of the reality of our feeding by faith. To emphasize this, he also points to the simultaneity of these two things.[86] Francis Turretin makes a similar claim, referring to this union of sign and thing signified as a moral and relative union. It is not physical or localized but is nonetheless real, because the two things—the spiritual feeding on Christ and the physical partaking of the bread and the wine—are inextricably connected.[87] This, of course, raises the contested issue of what manner of eating the Supper involves, a point on which Reformed and Lutheran disagree. We shall return to discuss this shortly, after adding one further element: the Lord's Supper as seal.

84. Bruce, *Mystery of the Lord's Supper*, 44–48. Cf. the elaborate analogies that Ursinus finds between physical eating and spiritual eating:

> The correspondence, or analogy which there is between the bread and the body of Christ consists in these things: 1. As bread and wine support this temporal life, so the body and blood of Christ are the true meat and drink by which our souls are fed unto eternal life. 2. As bread and wine are received with the mouth, so the body and blood of Christ are received by faith which is the mouth of the soul. 3. As bread is not taken into the system whole, but is eaten, being broken; so the body of Christ is received, being sacrificed and broken upon the cross. 4. As bread and wine do not profit those who eat and drink them without any appetite or desire, and as it is necessary for us to come to the table hungry and thirsty; so the body and blood of Christ profit us nothing unless we come to his table hungering and thirsting after righteousness. 5. As out of many grains one meal is ground and one bread is baked, and as out of many berries pressed together one wine floweth; so we, being many, are, by the use of these signs, made one body, and grow up into one body with Christ, and among ourselves. (Zacharias Ursinus, *The Commentary of Dr. Zacharias Ursinus on the Heidelberg Catechism*, trans. G. W. Willard [Cincinnati: Elm Street, 1888], 416)

85. "The Sacrament is nothing else but a visible Word. Why do I call it a visible Word? Because it conveys the signification of it by the eye to the mind" (Bruce, *Mystery of the Lord's Supper*, 47). Cf. ibid., 30: "The Word leads us to Christ by the ear; the Sacraments lead us to Christ by the eye."

86. Bruce, *Mystery of the Lord's Supper*, 47–48.

87. "Still this union [of sign and thing signified] is so moral and relative as to be also in its own sense real in the legitimate use; not indeed by a contiguity of the sign and thing signified, but with respect to the communicant, who is made a partaker of both at the same time" (Turretin, *Institutes* XIX.iv.4).

The Lord's Supper as Seal

For Calvin and the Reformed who follow him, the sacramental signs are also to be understood as seals. This is the language used in the Reformed confessional tradition. It helps to highlight both the kindness of God in giving the Lord's Supper and the level of power that the sacrament possesses and that mere memorialism misses.[88] The bread and the wine are not merely aids to our memories but also dramatically impress on our hearts the reality of Christ's work and our saving union with him. Indeed, this kindness of God in giving the Lord's Supper as a seal to nurture our faith is a standard part of Reformed theology. Calvin explicitly connects this to human frailty and thus to his idea of God as loving Father always accommodating himself to our weaknesses and sluggishness.[89] Speaking of the Supper in similar terms, Bruce says: "The main lesson to be learned from this, as far as I can see, is the lesson of the kindness and goodness of the ever-living God who has invented so many wonderful modes of conjunction, all in order that we might be conjoined to Him, and that this great and mystical conjunction between the God of glory and us may be increased."[90] This is important language because it speaks of the existential impact of the Lord's Supper on recipients. Memorialism at its crudest simply reduces the sacrament to a memory prompt, something that helps the participants reflect on Christ's death. It offers a quiet moment in the gathered worship service for the congregation to reflect silently on what Christ has done for them. But the language of seal goes beyond this. It connotes something more profound and connects to what we noted above about the believer's already-existing union with Christ. It impresses on our hearts and minds the reality of what we are in Christ at this moment.

This notion of the seal thus also ties in closely with the idea that the Word is fundamental to the reality of a sacrament.[91] It gives a special imprimatur to the gospel promise. That promise is a verbal declaration, but the sacrament of the Lord's Supper is like a seal on an official document such as a diploma. The seal has no intrinsic merit by itself but, when set on a document, gives the document an official validity. Only when the seal is there does the paper to

---

88. E.g., Consensus Tigurinus VII; Heidelberg Catechism 66; Larger Catechism 162; Belgic Confession XXXIII. While the Anglican Thirty-Nine Articles do not use the language of seal, article XXV speaks of the sacraments as "sure witnesses, and effectual signs of grace, and God's good will towards us, by which He doth work invisibly in us, and doth not only quicken, but also strengthen and confirm, our faith in Him" (Dennison 2:762).

89. Calvin, *Institutes* IV.xiv.3.

90. Bruce, *Mystery of the Lord's Supper*, 49.

91. Calvin, *Institutes* IV.xiv.3.

which it is appended have true official status.[92] The sacrament is thus a seal, a means of grace, bringing to us the promise of Christ in a manner that truly reinforces the power of the gospel. It thus has important pastoral implications.

What the Lord's Supper does is strengthen what already exists. Bavinck expresses it this way: "The communion with Christ, which is strengthened in the Supper, is nothing other than that which is brought about by the Word as a means of grace. The sacrament does not add any grace to that which is offered in the Word. It only strengthens and confirms that which has been received by faith from the Word."[93] In short, what the Word brings about— union with Christ—is reinforced, strengthened, and made more existentially real and certain by participation in the Lord's Supper because the Lord's Supper is a seal of what is already true. To return to an earlier point, the Lord's Supper presses the same Christ and the same salvation on the believer but in a different way. And the difference is significant, just as the difference between a verbal declaration of love and a gift or a wedding ring is also significant.

The Nature of Sacramental Eating

The differences between Lutheran and Reformed on the Lord's Supper are manifold, but in the end they all tend to focus on the question of the nature of the feeding that takes place in the sacrament. For the Lutherans, the presence of the body and blood of Christ is not dependent on the faith of the recipient but on the Word of God. The actual body and blood of Jesus Christ are mysteriously consumed in, with, and under the elements of bread and wine. Indeed, they have an objective presence, which means that the unbeliever, too, eats of the actual body and blood, but only to condemnation, not salvation.[94]

For the Reformed, however, the eating is not objective and localized in the manner of the Lutherans but depends, as we noted above, on the prior spiritual union of the believer with Christ and on the relative but real connection of the elements to what they signify. This leads the Reformed to eschew the literal interpretation of the words of institution held by Luther. "This is my body" is understood in terms of representation, not literal predication. In

---

92. Ibid., IV.xiv.5.

93. *RD* 4:577.

94. Book of Concord VII.2. See the comment of Robert Kolb, *The Christian Faith: A Lutheran Exposition* (St. Louis: Concordia, 1993), 233: "We define the real presence by confessing that his presence depends on the Word of the Lord, not on the faith of the person who receives the Supper. Even unbelievers receive Christ's body and blood when they partake of the Supper even though they do not receive its benefits apart from faith. We call that reception by the ungodly or unworthy. The presence of Christ's body and blood does not depend on us. It depends on God's Word."

commenting on these words in his *Harmony of the Gospels*, Calvin states that the words are being used with reference to a sacrament and are thus to be understood metonymically as tying the sign to the thing signified.[95]

"Feeding on Christ" is an idea that is important to Calvin. In his commentary on John 6:35, he observes that feeding on Christ is the effect and fruit of faith.[96] Then, in a remarkable passage in the *Institutes*, he describes the believer's eucharistic feeding as follows:

> But if we are carried to heaven with our eyes and minds, that we may there behold Christ in the glory of his kingdom, as the symbols invite us to him in his integrity, so, under the symbol of bread, we must feed on his body, and, under the symbol of wine, drink separately of his blood, and thereby have the full enjoyment of him. For though he withdrew his flesh from us, and with his body ascended to heaven, he, however, sits at the right hand of the Father; that is, he reigns in power and majesty, and the glory of the Father. This kingdom is not limited by any intervals of space, nor circumscribed by any dimensions. Christ can exert his energy wherever he pleases, in earth and heaven, can manifest his presence by the exercise of his power, can always be present with his people, breathing into them his own life, can live in them, sustain, confirm, and invigorate them, and preserve them safe, just as if he were with them in the body; in fine, can feed them with his own body, communion with which he transfuses into them. After this manner, the body and blood of Christ are exhibited to us in the sacrament.[97]

On one level, we might describe this as a remarkable and poetic flight of theological imagination. But what Calvin is trying to do is give expression to the reality both of the believer's spiritual union with Christ and the significance of this for the sacramental eating.

Calvin is thus presupposing both the localization of Christ's body in heaven and the reality of the believer's feeding on him. Because we are united to him by the Spirit, we feed on him in his Word and in the sacrament of the Lord's Supper. We feed on the same Christ but in two different ways. The sacrament thus nourishes our faith. It is not simply a memorial but something that helps strengthen us for our daily Christian walk.[98]

---

95. Calvin, *Harmony of the Gospels*, trans. William Pringle, 3 vols. (Edinburgh: Calvin Translation Society, 1845), 3:206–7.

96. Calvin, *Commentary on John*, trans. William Pringle, 2 vols. (Edinburgh: Calvin Translation Society, 1847), 1:250.

97. Calvin, *Institutes* IV.xvii.18.

98. "Consider the end for which this Sacrament was appointed. Is it not to lead us to Christ, is it not to nourish our faith in Christ, is it not to nourish us in a constant persuasion of the Lord's mercy in Christ?" (Bruce, *Mystery of the Lord's Supper*, 143).

The question for the Reformed therefore becomes: how is the—for want of a better term—spatial problem overcome? The Reformed are comfortable using the language of "real presence," but how is this presence to be understood in light of Christ's current location? Calvin's answer—which is representative of the Reformed position—should be obvious by now. It is that the spatial problem is overcome through the work of the Holy Spirit. Luther solved this by bringing the whole Christ down into the bread and the wine, and Zwingli in his more radical moments solved it by in effect denying that the presence of Christ was significant for an understanding of the Lord's Supper, but Calvin solves it by carrying the believer from the table to Christ at the right hand of the Father. The key, of course, is the Holy Spirit, by whom Christ, though in heaven, is yet intimately united with his people on earth. There is here a close analogy with Christ's presence in the Word preached: as the Word is received by faith, so the whole Christ is received by the believer, but in a spiritual and not a physically circumscribed form. We might perhaps say that, as we grasp the Word by faith, we are lifted to heaven and united with Christ. The same is true in the Supper.[99]

This leads inevitably to the question of who should take the Lord's Supper. The Reformed are clear on this: only the faithful. The Heidelberg Catechism (question 81) summarizes typical Reformed teaching by saying that the Supper is for all who are truly sorrowful for their sins, trusting in Christ for salvation, and earnestly seeking to strengthen their faith and live more godly lives. Strictly speaking, unbelievers who take the Supper receive nothing. They do not feed on the body of Christ even to their condemnation, because Christ is not objectively present in the elements and they are not united to him in order to feed on him spiritually. They do, however, eat and drink judgment and condemnation to themselves, because they are profaning the table of the Lord.[100]

In the Reformed tradition, this concern to keep the Supper for believers only was, as noted above, a key factor in the struggles in Calvin's Geneva. It also manifested itself in the practice of "fencing the table," whereby, as part of the liturgical action of the communion service, the minister would warn the congregation about the danger of taking the Supper unworthily. Most ministers would acknowledge that the delivery of such a message is an art form whereby an attempt is made to strike a balance between frightening away

---

99. See the comment of Bavinck (*RD* 4:577): "Christ is truly and essentially present with his divine and human nature in the Supper, only in no way other than he is present in the gospel. Christ is no more enclosed physically in bread and wine than he is in the Word proclaimed, but those who believingly accept the sign also, according to the divine ordinance, receive true communion with the whole Christ."

100. Ursinus, *Commentary*, 426–27.

those who might be struggling with their faith and who would benefit from the grace offered through the Supper and those who need to be rebuked and challenged about the sincerity of their Christian profession.[101]

This leads to one final point: for the Reformed, the Lord's Supper also has a horizontal dimension. Zwingli tended to emphasize the horizontal at the expense of the vertical. He was particularly attracted to the meaning of the Latin word *sacramentum* as a military oath by which soldiers pledged themselves to each other.[102] As we have seen, Calvin and the Reformed regard the Lord's Supper as having a much richer significance than this, and yet we should not neglect the horizontal dimension. In the words of the Belgic Confession XXV, "We are moved by the use of this holy sacrament to a fervent love towards God and our neighbor."[103] The Supper thus does have a horizontal significance: it binds believers together and encourages them in love for their neighbors. It is a vital part of the pastoral ministry, which enables the people of God to pursue their calling as salt and light in this world.

Conclusion

The Lord's Supper is the most obvious point of division between Lutheran and Reformed, in part because of its role in the history of the 1520s leading up to the decisive break at Marburg in 1529. While the division rests on significant differences in Christology, it manifests itself in major differences over what the Lord's Supper means. For the Reformed, there is no localized presence of the whole Christ in, with, and under the elements of bread and wine. Yet they also avoid the idea that the Supper is a mere memorial or purely symbolic. Attached to the Word, Christ is really present in the Supper;

101. The Larger Catechism expresses it thus: "Q. 173. May any who profess the faith, and desire to come to the Lord's supper, be kept from it? A. Such as are found to be ignorant or scandalous, notwithstanding their profession of the faith, and desire to come to the Lord's supper, may and ought to be kept from that sacrament, by the power which Christ hath left in his church, until they receive instruction, and manifest their reformation" (*Westminster Confession of Faith* [OPC ed., 2005]).

102. *Commentary on True and False Religion*, in *The Latin Works of Huldreich Zwingli* (Philadelphia: Heidelberg, 1929), 3:180.

103. Dennison 2:447. Cf. J. van Genderen and W. H. Velema, *Concise Reformed Dogmatics* (Phillipsburg, NJ: P&R, 2008), 806. The liturgy of my (Carl's) own denomination, the Orthodox Presbyterian Church, attempts to capture this in its explanation of the meaning of the sacrament:

> The Supper is also a bond and pledge of the communion that believers have with him and with each other as members of his body. As Scripture says, "For we being many are one bread, and one body: for we are all partakers of that one bread" (1 Cor. 10:17). The Supper anticipates the consummation of the ages, when Christ returns to gather all his redeemed people at the glorious wedding feast of the Lamb. (III.C.2; http://www.opc.org/BCO/DPW.html#Chapter_III)

believers really do feed on him by faith, but in a spiritual manner, rooted in their Spirit-wrought union with Christ.

For this reason, there is a sense in which the confessionally Reformed and the Lutherans share common ground. Over against Protestant Evangelicals who tend to downplay or even ignore the Lord's Supper, they understand its importance theologically, pastorally, and historically. That is not to say that the differences are not important: the communication of attributes and the objectivity of Christ's presence are not incidentals of minor significance. However, both sides understand that Scripture clearly teaches the importance of the Lord's Supper and that the church must witness to this fact in its doctrine and life. To relativize this matter would be to relativize the Word of Christ himself.

8

Worship

In the contemporary church, there are perhaps few topics that generate more heat and less light than that of worship. Seeker-sensitive services compete with traditional liturgies; praise bands vie with choirs; advocates of choruses clash with proponents of hymns and psalms. Many Christians are familiar with some, maybe all, of these scenarios. Sadly, what is striking is how nontheological much of this is, seeming often to be merely a question of differences of taste dressed up with a thin veneer of theology.

Worship—what Christians offer to their God in response to his grace in Jesus Christ—is inevitably theological and should be deeply so. This is where a return to the roots of both the Lutheran and Reformed traditions can be helpful, for the Reformers and their immediate successors were not interested in debates about taste or aesthetics for the sake of it. They were concerned that the worship their churches offered to God be appropriate to who God was (and still is) and what he had done for them (and continues to do for us). This was something with which they wrestled long and hard. Thus, their understanding of worship was profoundly theological and deeply rooted in their reflection on God's revelation of himself in Scripture and in the person and work of the Lord Jesus Christ. Differences certainly existed, and continue to exist, between the Lutheran and Reformed traditions on this matter, but reflection on the views of both communions can only benefit us in the present for the simple reason that both communions asked serious questions and gave serious answers. By learning about our respective pasts, we can therefore better equip ourselves for worship in the present.

Worship in the Lutheran Tradition

Martin Luther's redefinition of what it means to be Christian made waves throughout the life of the church. No longer did the believer's actions, above all in sacred or religious activities fulfilling ritual prescriptions, hold the key to the relationship between the sinner and God. Instead, that key lay in God's address to sinners, with his call for repentance and his gift of the forgiveness of sins, life, and salvation that his Word effects through the creation of trust in Christ and his saving work. God's address to his people invited and expected response, Luther insisted. The Sunday liturgy remained a focal point of Christian life but no longer because attendance at Mass gained favor and help from God. It served instead as the chief instance of the conversation God conducts with his people and the model for the life of meditation and prayer that was to constitute the whole week for believers.

Not Merit but Hearing and Praise

Philip Melanchthon made clear in the Augsburg Confession that the Wittenberg theologians appreciated ritual's potential contribution to the expression of Christian unity and to its use in conveying the biblical message, but he sharply repudiated any association of human performance of religious or sacred activities with meriting God's grace.[1]

> Concerning church regulations made by human beings, it is taught that those that may be performed without sin and that serve to maintain peace and good order in the church, such as specific celebrations, festivals, etc. are to be kept. However, people are also instructed not to burden consciences with them as if such things were necessary for salvation. Moreover, it is taught that all rules and traditions made by human beings for the purpose of appeasing God and of earning grace are contrary to the gospel and the teaching concerning faith in Christ. That is why monastic vows and other traditions concerning distinctions of foods, days and the like, through which people imagine they can earn grace and make satisfaction for sin, are good for nothing and contrary to the gospel.[2]

The Wittenberg reformers took for granted that communal gathering to hear God's Word and to give him praise was written into the very way the Creator had constituted his human creatures. Luther did not believe that

---

1. Vilmos Vajta, *Luther on Worship* (Philadelphia: Muhlenberg, 1958); Joseph Herl, *Worship Wars in Early Lutheranism: Choir, Congregation, and Three Centuries of Conflict* (Oxford: Oxford University Press, 2004), 3–22.
2. Augsburg Confession XV, German, *BSELK* 108.7–110.7; *BC* 48.

the commandment to worship on the *seventh* day remained valid for New Testament Christians, but its principle, that human beings need a day of rest designed for common listening to God's Word and honoring God, pertained indeed to them. God had given a most reliable expression of his natural law to Israel through Moses, Luther believed, teaching that "the natural laws were never so orderly and well written as by Moses."[3] Therefore, he translated the Old Testament command to "remember the Sabbath day" as the divine decree to "sanctify the holy day." He advocated continuing the Christian traditions of holding the chief worship service of the week on Sundays and conducting other services throughout the week. This commandment was primarily aimed at providing a special time for hearing and learning God's Word and offering praise through singing and praying. Through common hearing of the sermon and praise of God, Christians found strength for their continuing battle against Satan.[4]

God's Word at the Center

Luther expressed his thoughts on the implications of this in preparing "an order for public worship," ruminations that offered something less than a liturgical order, for the town of Leisnig in January 1523. He criticized medieval practice for silencing God's Word by restricting it largely to the reading of lessons and chanting of psalms and other sections of Scripture. He did not comment on the reality that the educational level of often barely literate or even illiterate priests limited the possibilities of good preaching. He further criticized many who could preach for relying on legends of the saints as their subject matter. Finally, he condemned the ritualistic reliance on the performance of liturgy and participation in it as a work meriting grace and salvation.

Although Luther later permitted and encouraged services with a simple form of Scripture readings, prayers, and hymns during the week in villages, in 1523 he prescribed that "a Christian congregation should never gather together without the preaching of God's Word and prayer."[5] He was concerned about the effective listening of the congregation, advising that for daily services "everything be completed in one hour or whatever time seems desirable, for one must not overload souls or weary them, as was the case

3. WA 18:81.19–20; *LW* 40:98; cf. his sermon on the topic from August 27, 1525, which appeared as a separate treatise, *How Christians Should Regard Moses* (1525), WA 26:363–93; *LW* 35:161–74.

4. Large Catechism, Third Commandment ("You are to sanctify the holy day," in Luther's catechetical paraphrase), *BSELK* 958/959.14–966/967.33; *BC* 396–400.

5. WA 12:35.19–21; *LW* 53:11.

until now in monasteries and convents, where they burdened themselves like mules." In these daily services, sermons of "half an hour or so" should suffice, he thought, and be combined with thanks, praise, and prayer to God. He did not suggest a length for Sunday morning sermons, but his own apparently lasted in general no more than thirty minutes.

The pericopal system of prescribed Epistle and Gospel readings for Sundays and festivals continued in use within the Wittenberg circle.[6] Lutherans generally found that these lessons provided a helpful survey of the biblical narrative and its teaching; the annual repetition helped impress on hearers the basics of both the history of God's interaction with his people and his address to them in law and gospel.[7] Luther himself expressed some reservations about the choice of certain lessons and suggested alternatives in some instances.[8]

The fact that "the preaching and teaching of God's Word is the most important part of the divine service"[9] required the reading of lessons and the proclamation in the sermon. That did not, however, diminish the importance of confession and absolution (both private and congregational) and of the sacraments of baptism and the Lord's Supper, which embodied the promise of the gospel. Particularly in an oral, largely illiterate society they were vital presentations of the cross and resurrection for integrating Christ's saving work into the consciousness of the members of the congregation.[10]

Above all, Luther believed that the conveying of the call for repentance and the proclamation of forgiveness through Christ's saving work governed liturgical decisions. "Let everything be done so that the Word may have free course instead of the prattling and rattling that has been the rule up to now. We can get along without everything except the Word. Again, we profit by nothing as much as by the Word. For the whole Scripture shows that the Word should have free course among Christians." In his visit to Mary and Martha, Jesus demonstrated that "the one thing needful" is listening to God's Word.[11] Thus, Luther emphasized the usefulness of the "catechism" as the orienting program of public worship. "Catechism" referred to the core of the biblical message as summarized in the traditional program for basic Christian instruction in the faith: the Ten Commandments as summary of the law, the

6. WA 12:36.11–17; LW 53:12–13.

7. Cf. the judgment given by the editor of the sermons of Paul Eber, a student of Luther and a leading theologian in the period after his death, *Postilla, Das ist, Außlegung der Sonntags vnd fürnembsten Fest Euangelien durch das gantze Jar . . .* , ed. Johannes Cellarius (Frankfurt am Main: Franz Basse, 1578), 1:2a.

8. WA 10/1.2:63.1–8; LW 75:64; WA 32:141.13–21.

9. WA 19:78.26–27; LW 53:68.

10. WA 12:206.15–209.10; LW 53:20–23.

11. WA 12:37.30–35; LW 53:14.

Apostles' Creed as summary of the gospel of God's actions on behalf of his human creatures, and the Lord's Prayer as the foundation of daily living in new obedience. These three core elements of medieval instruction informed Luther's thinking on how the entire service, including the sermon, should function.[12]

This centering of Christian life and worship on the Word of God and its proclamation quickly made an impact on family life, with preparation of children and servants for hearing the sermon as well as instruction in the faith now a part of parental duties.[13] It also brought preaching into other public rites where it had seldom or never played a role in medieval ritual. Wedding sermons became a standard part of the nuptial ceremony.[14] Earlier, burials affected by Wittenberg reform had discarded medieval characteristics, including the singing of dirges on the way to the cemetery and the focus on Masses to relieve the sufferings of the departed in purgatory. The funeral sermon became central to the funeral liturgy.[15] As Luther wrote in the preface to a hymnal for burials,

> We have removed from our churches and completely abolished the popish abominations, such as vigils, masses for the dead, processions, purgatory and all other hocus-pocus on behalf of the dead, . . . nor do we sing any dirges or doleful songs over our dead and at the grave, but comforting hymns of the forgiveness of sins, of rest, sleep, life, and of the resurrection of departed Christians so that our faith may be strengthened and the people be moved to true devotion. For it is fitting and proper that we should conduct these funerals with proper decorum in order to honor and praise that joyous article of our faith, namely, the resurrection of the dead, and in order to defy death.[16]

12. *German Mass*, WA 19:76.1–22; LW 53:64–65.

13. Throughout the Small Catechism, sections begin with instruction "in a simple way in which the head of a household is to present them" to the children and servants, *BSELK* 862/863.1–892/893.15; *BC* 351–64.

14. Christopher Boyd Brown, "The Reformation of Marriage in Lutheran Wedding Preaching," *Seminary Ridge Review* 15 (2013): 1–25; Erik Margraf, *Die Hochzeitspredigt der frühen Neuzeit* (Munich: Utz, 2007).

15. Eberhard Winkler, *Die Leichenpredigt im deutschen Luthertum bis Spener* (Munich: Kaiser, 1967); Cornelia Niekus Moore, *Patterned Lives: The Lutheran Funeral Biography in Early Modern Germany* (Wiesbaden: Harrasowitz, 2006); Irene Dingel, "'True Faith, Christian Living, and a Blessed Death': Sixteenth Century Funeral Sermons as Evangelical Proclamation," *Lutheran Quarterly* 27 (2013): 399–420.

16. WA 35:478.26–479.2; LW 53:326. Cf. Robert Kolb, "Orders for Burial in the Sixteenth Century Wittenberg Circle," in *Gute Ordnung: Ordnungsmodelle und Ordnungsvorstellungen in der Reformationszeit*, ed. Irene Dingel and Armin Kohnle (Leipzig: Evangelische Verlagsanstalt, 2014), 257–79. Craig Koslofsky contends that Reformation burial practices suppressed a closer feeling of community with the departed, ending the more intimate association of the living and the dead cultivated by medieval piety, but his interpretation is open to doubt. The hope of

Among the topics chosen by Lutheran pastors for their sermons was above all the resurrection of the dead, along with God's providential care for survivors, reminders to hearers to repent before death's visitation, the proper form for expressing the inevitable sadness at the earthly loss of friend or family member, and the life of the deceased as an example of Christian living.[17]

Some elements of Luther's liturgical thinking at that time also fell on infertile soil. He suggested "retaining vestments, altars, and candles until they are used up or we are pleased to make a change" and advocated moving altars away from the wall so that pastors "always face the people as Christ undoubtedly did in the Last Supper."[18] Retention of vestments and altars against the wall has largely lasted in Lutheran churches into the twenty-first century.

Public worship embodied the unity of the congregation and brought its members together in realization of the oneness of Christ's body. That oneness found expression in common prayer and praise and above all in the reception of the Lord's Supper. It should be received, Luther taught, only by those who, even if weak in faith, are not giving public offense in the community: "If the pastor should see a fornicator, adulterer, drunkard, gambler, usurer, slanderer, or anyone else disgraced by a manifest vice, he would absolutely exclude such a person from the Supper—unless he can give good evidence that his life has been changed."[19] Thus, while not demanding private confession before communion, Luther found it useful and not to be despised, as was also true of preparation by fasting and prayer.[20]

The church embraced not only the living but also those who have gone before. In line with his conservative principles regarding public worship, Luther advocated retention of those days on which biblical saints, and a few other heroes of early church history, were commemorated and used as examples; this was in line with Melanchthon's affirmation of the proper use of these saints, among the whole body of Christians, whom he counted all as saints. "The saints are to be remembered so that we may strengthen our faith when we see how they experienced grace and how they were helped by faith. Moreover,

---

resurrection and reunion surely provided a stronger feeling of this sort than had the obligation to finance the saying of Masses for the dead. See Craig Koslofsky, *The Reformation of the Dead: Death and Ritual in Early Modern Germany, 1450–1700* (Basingstoke: Macmillan, 2000), esp. 19–39.

17. Robert Kolb, "'[. . .] da jr nicht trawrig seid wie die anderen, die keine hoffnung haben': Der Gebrauch der Heiligen Schrift in Leichenpredigten der Wittenberger Reformation (1560–1600)," in *Leichenpredigten als Medien der Erinnerungskultur im europäischen Kontext*, ed. Eva-Maria Dickhaut (Stuttgart: Steiner, 2014), 1–25.

18. WA 19:80.26–30; *LW* 53:69.

19. WA 12:216.12–13; *LW* 53:33.

20. WA 12:216.31–37; *LW* 53:34.

it is taught that each person, according to his or her calling, should take the saints' good works as an example. . . . However, it cannot be demonstrated from Scripture that a person should call upon the saints or seek help from them. 'For there is only one single reconciler and mediator set up between God and humanity, Jesus Christ' (1 Tim. 2[:5])."[21]

Luther intended public worship to embrace all in a community, but he also foresaw a time when "serious Christians" would also meet in a house "to pray, read, baptize, receive the sacrament, and do other Christian works."[22] He never proceeded to implement such a practice in a society that remained largely illiterate during his lifetime, but he did recognize the difficulty presented by the mixture of the spiritually indifferent who were required to participate in the late medieval way of organizing society with those who strove to lead a life of faith.

Freedom in Worship

Even if its intensity and extent have been exaggerated, the iconoclasm that had broken out in Wittenberg during Luther's stay in protective custody at the Wartburg in 1521–22 deeply imprinted on his consciousness the need not only for public order but also for the practice of Christian freedom in things not commanded in Scripture.[23] Luther regarded Old Testament ceremonial and political regulations as God's intention for ancient Israel, from which the Lord had freed the church (Col. 2:16–17). Therefore, he advocated a good deal of openness and tolerance in matters of public worship and pious practice so long as Christians subjected themselves to God's Word and expressed the unity of faith. Nonetheless, he also placed this freedom in the context of Christian love. "You are bound to consider the effect of your attitude on others. By faith be free in your conscience toward God, but by love be bound to serve your neighbor's edification" (Rom. 15:2).[24] Therefore, he moved cautiously in introducing new forms for worship.

Later in 1523 his Formula Missae appeared in print with the liturgy still in Latin. This order of service freed the Mass, the liturgy in which the Lord's Supper is offered, from its former ritualistic trappings that claimed to repeat the sacrifice of Christ in its celebration and that offered merit and God's grace

21. Augsburg Confession XXI, German, *BSELK* 128.5–12; *BC* 58. Cf. Robert Kolb, "Festivals of the Saints in the Late Reformation Lutheran Preaching," *The Historian* 53 (1990): 613–26.

22. WA 19:75.3–16; *LW* 53:63–64.

23. Cf. Amy Nelson Burnett, *Karlstadt and the Origins of the Eucharistic Controversy: A Study in the Circulation of Ideas* (Oxford: Oxford University Press, 2011), 15–31.

24. *Christian Exhortation to the Livonians concerning Public Worship and Concord* (1525), WA 18:419.21–25; *LW* 53:48.

for the participants in the service. This Formula retained the basic outline of the medieval service while omitting elements that in Luther's eyes were contrary to Scripture, such as the canon of the Mass, which offered Christ's body and blood to God as a sacrifice in behalf of those in attendance: "Let us repudiate everything that smacks of sacrifice, together with the entire canon, and retain only that which is pure and holy."[25] Throughout his liturgical reforms—in liturgical orders or texts for baptism and confession of sins, in translating and revising the "collect" prayers of the chief service and the chanted portions that came from Scripture (such as Isa. 6, the Sanctus), and the psalm verses used in the entrance hymn (Introit)—Luther retained what he could of the medieval tradition but discarded all that suggested the earning of human merit or other elements of medieval piety and practice that he thought diverted faith from Christ.[26]

Like the Formula, his German Mass of 1526 set forth an order for the chief service of the week, but he insisted that it be used "in Christian liberty as long, when, where, and how you find it practically useful" rather than regarding it as "a rigid law to bind or entangle anyone's conscience." He also urged that churches in each principality or town use the same rites to prevent confusion among those who visited nearby locations.[27] His German Mass of 1526 translated into German hymn forms the traditional parts of the liturgy that were to be retained.[28] However, most churches adopted a translation of the chants and liturgical forms of the Formula Missae of 1523 instead of the German hymns that Luther provided.

Luther's principle of placing decisions regarding liturgical practice and other expressions of piety within the framework of Christian freedom, disciplined by their effectiveness in conveying and supporting the biblical message, led to some differences among Lutherans in the arrangement of the interior of churches, forms of church music, and details of the liturgical outline. Common to all was the centrality of the proclamation of God's Word, its call to repentance, and its bestowal of forgiveness, life, and salvation.

The Visual in Worship

In regard to church architecture, most congregations took over medieval buildings, leaving them much as they were after the removal of altarpieces

---

25. WA 12:211.20–22; LW 53:26; the entire text of the Formula is found in WA 12:205–20; LW 53:19–40.
26. See texts in LW 53.
27. WA 19:72.3–23; LW 53:61–62.
28. WA 19:72–113; LW 53:61–90.

celebrating fictional stories of saints or promoting trust in the saints' ability to exercise superhuman powers rather than pointing the way to Christ. Pulpits were sometimes moved from the side of the congregation to the front of the worship space and were occasionally placed directly over the altar. Altars remained, not as places where sacrifices were made to please God but rather where God presented his gifts, particularly in the Lord's Supper, and received the thanks of his people. Luther's understanding of God's Word regarded Scripture in its entirety as the place where God addresses his people, a place of his presence, and the authoritative expression of his will for believers. Reading Scripture or hearing it through a preacher created an encounter with God.

Indeed, Luther changed the focus of Christian worship from the visual to the oral and aural. That he had, nonetheless, a high appreciation for the visual is apparent in his rich use of word pictures, particularly in his preaching.[29] Luther's colleague Andreas Bodenstein von Karlstadt reacted against the medieval veneration of the saints by rejecting the retention and use of statuary and paintings, particularly in altars, grounding his position on the prohibition of graven images that the Jewish enumeration of the commandments had preserved as the second commandment when the early church incorporated this proscription into the first commandment.[30]

In his dispute with Karlstadt, Luther outlined his understanding of how the spoken or written word relates to and is reinforced by visual images. He wished, too, to destroy "idolatrous images, but images that call to memory and give witness, such as crucifixes and images of saints, are to be tolerated," even as Joshua and Samuel had set up stone memorials commemorating the Lord's interventions on Israel's behalf (Josh. 24:26; 1 Sam. 7:12).[31] "But it is impossible for me to hear and bear in mind [what is read in Scripture] without forming mental images of it in my heart. For whether I want to or not, when I hear of Christ, an image of a man hanging on a cross takes form in my heart, just as the reflection of my face naturally appears in the water when I look into it. If it is not a sin but good to have the image of Christ in my heart, why should it be a sin to have it in my eyes?"[32] In his Prayer Book of 1522 Luther concluded that Bible stories and verses might profitably be painted on the walls of homes, "so that one might have God's words and deeds constantly in view and thus encourage fear and faith toward God." He found no harm in Lucas Cranach's

---

29. See, e.g., Robert Kolb, *Luther and the Stories of God: Biblical Narratives as a Foundation for Christian Living* (Grand Rapids: Baker Academic, 2012), e.g., 61–63, 172–78.

30. *Against the Heavenly Prophets* (1525), WA 18:69.16–70.36; LW 40:86–88.

31. WA 18:74.13–20; LW 40:91.

32. WA 18:83.7–15; LW 40:99–100.

illustrat[ing] the important stories of the entire Bible in their proper order for a small book which might become known as a layman's Bible. Indeed, one cannot bring God's words and deeds too often to the attention of the common people. Even if God's Word is sung and said, preached and proclaimed, written and read, illustrated and pictured, Satan and his cohorts are always strong and alert for ways to obstruct and suppress God's Word. Therefore, our project [Cranach's *Passionale* of 1521] and this cause are not only useful but necessary, indeed, very badly needed.[33]

Luther believed that images of God, particularly of Christ, and those depicting biblical stories did not automatically lead to veneration of the image itself and thus distract from or destroy the faith-filled worship of God. He was convinced that proper illustrations in paintings, woodcuts, and sculpture could indeed aid instruction and devotion. Thus, in the midst of the tensions of 1531, when Emperor Charles had renewed the threat of enforcing the Edict of Worms (1521), which called for eradication of Luther's followers and his execution, he concluded that what was at stake in regard to sculpture and painting was faith, not form.

There would be no harm in carving a statue of wood or stone, but to set it up for worship and to attribute divinity to the wood, stone, or statue is to worship an idol instead of God. . . . The issue is not whether wood is wood or stone is stone, but what significance is attributed to them, that is, how these things are used: whether this wood is God, whether divinity resides in this stone. . . . To base righteousness, worship, confidence in salvation, and the fear of death on such things is to attribute divinity to ceremonies.[34]

On the basis of this principle, noting that some books of the Bible rather generously employed such images, depicting God, angels, human beings, and animals, Luther had proposed,

So now we would kindly beg [Karlstadt and his supporters] to permit us to do what they themselves do. Pictures contained in these books we would paint on walls for the sake of remembrance and better understanding, since they do no more harm on walls than in books. It is to be sure better to paint pictures on walls of how God created the world, how Noah built the ark, and whatever other good stories there may be, than to paint shameless worldly things. Yes, would to God that I could persuade the rich and mighty that they would permit

33. WA 10/2:458.24–459.2; *LW* 43:43.
34. WA 40/1:169.27–170.19; *LW* 26:92.

the whole Bible to be painted on houses, on the inside and outside, so that all can see it. That would be a Christian work.[35]

Thus, illustrations formed an essential part of the design for readers to experience his translation of the Bible.[36] The woodcuts of Lucas Cranach and others provided support for the words of Scripture, the printed catechism, and many other books.[37]

This issue raised discussion in the disputes between Karlstadt and his Wittenberg critics but did not become an issue significant to the division of followers of Calvin and other Reformed theologians from Lutheran theologians until the time of the Heidelberg Catechism (1563) and the Colloquy of Montbéliard (1586).[38] Lutherans continued to use paintings and sculptures in their churches, adapting to the spread of Baroque style with ease in the seventeenth century. Their altars presented most often the resurrection at the very top with the crucifixion or the Lord's Supper as the central depiction in the altar.[39]

Music

Luther enjoyed rich musical gifts, and he believed that Scripture's message could be conveyed effectively not only in sermons but also in hymn texts through which God's people in their own words retold what God says in the Bible. Therefore, Luther himself set a model for the composition and use of hymns that included paraphrases of psalms, including "A Mighty Fortress Is Our God" (Ps. 46) and "Out of the Depths I Cry to You" (Ps. 130). He also

---

35. WA 18:82.23–83.5; LW 40:99. Cf. Mark C. Mattes, *Martin Luther's Theology of Beauty: A Reappraisal* (Grand Rapids: Baker Academic, 2017). I am grateful to Mattes and to Matthew Rosebrock for their insights into Luther and the visual.

36. Cf. Carl C. Christensen, "Luther and the Woodcuts to the 1534 Bible," *Lutheran Quarterly* 19 (2005): 392–93; Peter Martin, *Martin Luther und die Bilder zur Apokalypse: Die Ikonographie der Illustrationen zur Offenbarung des Johannes in der Lutherbibel 1522 bis 1546* (Hamburg: Wittig, 1983); Philipp Schmidt, *Die Illustration der Lutherbibel, 1522–1700* (Basel: Reinhardt, 1962).

37. On the role Cranach and other artists played in constructing the books that spread the Wittenberg message so effectively, see Andrew Pettegree, *Brand Luther: 1517, Printing, and the Making of the Reformation* (New York: Penguin, 2015).

38. Irene Dingel, "'Daß wir Gott in keiner Weise verbilden': Die Bilderfrage zwischen Calvinismus und Luthertum," in *Gott im Wort—Gott im Bild: Bilderlosigkeit als Bedingung des Monotheismus?*, ed. Andreas Wagner et al. (Neukirchen-Vluyn: Neukirchener Verlag, 2005; 2nd ed., 2008), 97–111.

39. Bridget Heal, "The Catholic Eye and the Protestant Ear: The Reformation as a Nonvisual Event?," in *The Myth of the Reformation*, ed. Peter Opitz (Göttingen: Vandenhoeck & Ruprecht, 2013), 321–55; and Heal, *A Magnificent Faith: Art and Identity in Lutheran Germany* (Oxford: Oxford University Press, 2017).

paraphrased the entire metanarrative of the Bible in "Dear Christians, Let Us Now Rejoice" and retold biblical stories in, for example, "From Heaven Above to Earth I Come," "From Heaven the Angel Troop Came Near," and "Christ Jesus Lay in Death's Strong Bands."[40] He retained liturgical chants and sequences that repeated the message of Scripture faithfully but rejected others that did not. Luther highly valued hymns as a means of cultivating trust in Christ and teaching the biblical message. The speed with which congregational singing became predominant in early Lutheran circles should not be overestimated,[41] but the rich legacy of Lutheran hymnody from the pens of authors such as Paul Gerhardt, Philip Nicolai, Johann Heermann, and dozens of others, and of composers such as Michael Praetorius, Johann Crüger, and Heinrich Schütz indeed fulfilled Luther's goal of proclaiming and teaching through song, both in congregational worship and family devotions in the home.

Luther's Devotional Life

Luther modeled a life of prayer for his students. One of his students, Veit Dietrich, recounted that the reformer spent "a minimum of three hours in intense prayer each day," although that prayer was probably combined with his study of the Word. He spoke his prayers softly, as was the monastic custom, even later in life. Dietrich's account stems from the time the two of them spent together at Coburg Castle during the Diet of Augsburg of 1530. Luther fervently sought God's protection and guidance for his colleagues at the diet, who were being called to resist the pressures of their Roman Catholic opponents and confess their faith, holding God to his promises in the psalms that Luther used for his prayers as he called on God to intervene in behalf of the cause of the gospel.[42]

Luther described his practice of praying for his barber, Peter Beskendorf: "When I feel that I have become cold and joyless in prayer because of other tasks or thoughts (for the flesh and the devil always impede and obstruct prayer), I take my little psalter, hurry to my room, or, if the time is right, I go to the church where a congregation is assembled, and as time permits, I say quietly to myself and word-for-word the Ten Commandments, the Creed, and if I have time, some words of Christ or Paul or some psalms." He counseled Beskendorf to pray first thing in the morning and last thing in the evening.[43]

40. Luther's hymns are found in WA 35:411–73; *LW* 53:214–341.
41. Herl, *Worship Wars*, 108–51.
42. June 30, 1530, CR 2:159.
43. WA 38:358.5–359.9; *LW* 43:193.

Luther believed that the entire life of the Christian should be permeated by conversation with God.

In his Small Catechism, he instructed children to pray, confident that "God is truly our Father and we are truly his children, in order that we may ask him boldly and with complete confidence, just as loving children ask their loving father."[44] Thus, they could be absolutely certain that their prayers "are acceptable and heard by our Father in heaven, for he himself commanded us to pray like this and has promised to hear us. 'Amen, amen' means, 'yes, yes, it is going to come about just like this.'"[45] The Large Catechism gave reasons for praying: God has commanded it, God has promised to hear the believer's prayers, and "God takes the initiative and puts into our mouths the very words and approach we are to use. In this way we see that such prayer pleases him and will assuredly be heard."[46]

In introducing his Prayer Book of 1522, Luther wrote, "What is important for a good prayer is not many words . . . but rather turning to God frequently and with heartfelt longing, and doing so without ceasing."[47] The heart must be prepared for prayer. When it is "rightly warmed and inclined," it will avoid rote recitation of formulas (although the Wittenberg Reformer had no objection to using printed prayers, particularly when believers could not muster their own words). As a general rule, though not his only practice, he did "not bind myself to such words or syllables but say my prayers in one fashion today, in another tomorrow, depending on my mood and feeling. I stay, however, as nearly as I can, with the same general thoughts and ideas." If the Holy Spirit guided him to focus on one thing or another and he forgot other concerns, it did not disturb him greatly, Luther wrote.[48]

The Ten Commandments, the Apostles' Creed, and the Lord's Prayer all provided outlines to stimulate prayer, Luther suggested, noting that believers could look to each part of this basic textbook of biblical truth for the "four strands of a wreath" that could be woven together: instruction, which would elicit thanksgiving, then confession of sin, and finally petition for the needs of the person praying or of others.[49] Such prayers combat the evil one, against whom, according to Luther's interpretation, the seventh petition of the Lord's Prayer is directed. This prayer shows "how God wants us to pray to him in regard to everything that attacks even our bodily welfare so that

---

44. *BSELK* 874/875.5–17; *BC* 356.
45. *BSELK* 882/883.3–6; *BC* 358.
46. *BSELK* 1074/1075.3–1078/1079.6; *BC* 442–43.
47. WA 10/2:376.3–5; *LW* 43:12.
48. WA 38:363.2–16; *LW* 43:198.
49. WA 38:364.28–365.4; *LW* 43:200.

we seek and expect help from no one but him. He has placed this petition [deliver us from evil] at the end, for if we are to be protected and delivered from all evil, his name must first be hallowed in us, his kingdom come among us, and his will be done. In the end he will preserve us from sin and disgrace and from everything else that harms or injures us."[50]

Personal and Family Devotion

Luther encouraged family and private meditation and prayer as well as public worship. For those who could read, he advised approaching the Scriptures with his own adaptation of the medieval formula of reading, prayer, and meditation (*lectio, oratio, meditatio*). He transformed it into a practice that presumed the reading of the text and observed that at the same time prayer and meditation on Scripture would be invaded by the concerns of the day and the assaults of one's own desires, the world, and the devil (*oratio, meditatio, tentatio*).[51] His Small Catechism offered a model for such meditation and prayer, for morning, mealtime, and evening. At the beginning and end of the day, the sign of the cross and calling on the name of the Trinity should remind the believer or Christian family of their baptismal identity in Christ, and following a brief prayer, meditation should follow for the illiterate guided by the core of the "catechism," which they had memorized.[52]

Luther's German Mass also contained directions for parental instruction of children in the Christian life, including the hearing of God's Word and prayer. He suggested that parents create in the child's imagination two purses, each with two pockets. From sermons or from teaching of the faith in school, children were to gather Bible verses they had heard and learn them by heart. The purse of faith should have one pocket for verses pertaining to sin and the other pocket for those that speak of Christ's work, including Romans 4:25 and John 1:29. The purse of love should have one pocket for passages fostering love for others and another for encouragement in the face of persecution or misfortune.[53] Evidence is mixed on precisely how quickly and thoroughly parental education of children in the faith spread, but by the seventeenth century a rich tradition of devotional use of Scripture and prayer books in the home had developed within Lutheran communities. Even into the twentieth

50. BSELK 1108/1109.16–22; BC 456.

51. WA 50:659.5–660.30; LW 34:285–86. Cf. Oswald Bayer, *Theology the Lutheran Way*, trans. Jeffrey G. Silcock and Mark C. Mattes (Grand Rapids: Eerdmans, 2007), 33–82; John Kleinig, *Grace upon Grace: Spirituality for Today* (St. Louis: Concordia, 2008), 29–37.

52. BSELK 892/893.13–894/895.3; BC 363–64.

53. WA 19:77.24–78.24; LW 53:66–67.

century, works such as the *Sacred Meditations* of the great dogmatician Johann Gerhard and the *Garden of Paradise* and *Books on True Christianity* by the Lüneburg ecclesiastical superintendent Johann Arndt accompanied the faithful from infancy to grave.[54]

Lutherans have taken forms of worship and the artistic presentation of the biblical narrative and the history of the church very seriously throughout the last half century, leading to "wars" over worship forms. Their development of new forms of expressing the biblical message and the church's reaction to it have generally not departed from article XV of the Augsburg Confession: the various liturgical, artistic, and pious usages and customs that Christians devise for their expression of the faith "may be kept without sin" so long as they "serve to maintain peace and good order in the church."[55] While some adiaphora are truly more significant for the life of the church and play a more critical role in the instruction of Christ's people and the confession of the faith, they remain neutral matters, and believers may exercise Christian freedom in choosing the forms of such practices and implementing their use, for the life of believers always moves from hearing to speaking and singing God's Word and giving him praise.

Worship in the Reformed Tradition

One of the most obvious differences between Lutheran and Reformed churches is the aesthetic. Traditional Lutheran churches often look quite similar to their Roman Catholic counterparts, with stained-glass windows, crucifixes, and pictures of Christ. Reformed churches—at least those that reflect the roots of the tradition in the sixteenth and seventeenth centuries—will usually not have such. This is no accident but is deeply rooted in the different convictions of the Lutherans and the Reformed on the nature of Christian worship. Indeed, it goes to the very heart of how the two communions understood the Reformation. Just as Luther saw it as a great recovery of the gospel, so it is arguable that the Reformed saw it as a mighty struggle to reinstate true worship in the church.[56] Thus, for example, Calvin can summarize the entirety of Christianity as follows, in his tract *On the Necessity of Reforming the*

---

54. Johann Gerhard, *Meditationes sacrae: Das ist Geistreiche Herzquickende und lebendigmachende Betrachtungen . . .* (Magdeburg: Francke, 1607); Johann Arndt, *Vom wahrem Christenthumb, heilsamer Busse, wahrem Glauben, heiligem Leben und Wander der rechten wahren Christen . . .* (Frankfurt am Main: Hoffmann, 1605); Arndt, *Paradiß-Gärtlein, Voller Christlicher Tugenden . . .* (Braunschweig: Duncker, 1612).

55. Augsburg Confession XV, German, *BSELK* 108.7–110.7; *BC* 48.

56. This is a large part of Calvin's concern in his *Reply to Cardinal Sadoleto* (1541).

Church: "If it be inquired, then, by what things chiefly the Christian religion has a standing existence amongst us, and maintains its truth, it will be found that the following two not only occupy the principal place, but comprehend under them all the other parts, and consequently the whole substance of Christianity, viz., a knowledge, *first*, of the mode in which God is duly worshipped; and, *secondly*, of the source from which salvation is to be obtained."[57] The underlying theology of Lutheran and Reformed may have had many points of contact, particularly on issues of salvation and authority, but the differences in confessional self-understanding of what exactly the Reformation was addressing created different sets of priorities and different applications of the Word to the life of the church. The precise nature and forms of worship were particular concerns for the Reformed.

At this point we should also note that, while there is a sense in which the Reformed see the whole of life as worship—Calvin's concept of piety as the true knowledge of God that pervades the believer's entire existence necessarily involves this—they did give special attention to the nature and forms of the gathered worship of the church as a whole. It is this corporate worship to which we will give most attention in this chapter.

The Origins of the Reformed Understanding of Worship

Luther's Reformation was intimately connected to his own existential struggle, but there is no hint of a similar path for Ulrich Zwingli or indeed others on the Reformed side of the Reformation debate.[58] Zwingli's concern seems primarily to have been the reform of society as a whole in accordance with the Word of God. From the inception of the Reformed Reformation, therefore, Scripture had a sweeping regulative function that marked it off from the Lutheran tradition.

When it came to worship, this manifested itself in a number of obvious ways. In essence, the Reformed view of worship was that whatever was not prescribed or positively sanctioned in Scripture was therefore forbidden. Thus, in Zurich a very clear-cut reading of the second commandment on graven images was used to outlaw both sacred representative art in churches (images, stained-glass windows) and even the use of music in worship.[59] The latter

---

57. John Calvin, *Tracts Relating to the Reformation*, trans. Henry Beveridge, 3 vols. (Edinburgh: Calvin Translation Society, 1844), 1:126.

58. This is not, of course, to deny that there may have been such existential struggles. It is merely to note that we are not told of them and that such played little role in the public ministries of the Reformed.

59. See James F. White, *Protestant Worship: Traditions in Transition* (Louisville: Westminster John Knox, 1989), 59–61.

also reflected a fear of musical aesthetics as distracting from true worship, for which we can find an antecedent in Augustine.[60]

The simple aesthetic of worship was also developed in Geneva by Calvin, who had been influenced both by his time in Strasbourg under the influence of Martin Bucer and by his French colleague Guillaume Farel. For Calvin, false worship is both the content and the manifestation of false belief and rebellion against God. Thus, in the Catechism of 1538, he states that all men worship, but wicked men do so falsely, for it is not the true God but one of their own imaginings to whom they pay homage.[61] Indeed, we might say that for Calvin, the Reformation is constituted by reformation of worship, both theology and practice. Thus, in addressing Cardinal Sadoleto, he actually compliments him on identifying worship as the central issue of Christian piety:

> I have also no difficulty in conceding to you, that there is nothing more perilous to our salvation than a preposterous and perverse worship of God. The primary rudiments, by which we are wont to train to piety those whom we wish to gain as disciples to Christ, are these; viz., not to frame any new worship of God for themselves at random, and after their own pleasure, but to know that the only legitimate worship is that which he himself approved from the beginning. For we maintain, what the sacred oracle declared, that obedience is more excellent than any sacrifice (1 Sam. 15:22). In short, we train them, by every means, to be contented with the one rule of worship which they have received from his mouth, and bid adieu to all fictitious worship.[62]

He makes a similar point about the perils of false worship in the prefatory letter to King Francis in the *Institutes*, where he argues that the miracles Rome ascribes to her saints are really designed to draw people away from true worship.[63] Indeed, worship—the true and the false—is a constant theme throughout the *Institutes* such that it is the basic point of distinction between Christians and unbelievers. Then, through the concept of *piety*, so important to Calvin's theology, he makes the point that true knowledge of God is not something we might describe as merely intellectual or abstract but instead something that pervades the whole of life.[64]

---

60. In *Confessions* X.33, Augustine reflects on the seductive nature of music and expresses a liking for the position of Athanasius of Alexandria, who would have the psalms sung in a manner that involved so little modulation of the voice that it was closer to talking than to singing.

61. Dennison 1:409–10.

62. Calvin, *Tracts* 1:34.

63. Calvin, *Institutes*, prefatory letter 3.

64. Ibid., I.ii.1.

This points to a fundamental element of the Reformed theology of worship: because it connects to knowledge of God, it is intimately connected to God's revelation. That, one might comment, does not seem to be a particularly radical point and is something on which all Christians can agree. Do we not all seek to worship God in a manner consistent with who he has revealed himself to be? For the Reformed, however, this takes on a particularly sharp practical form, as noted above in the Zurich context. The knowledge of God regulates not only the meaning of worship in terms of its theological significance but also the liturgical shape and action of worship as actually manifested in the life of the church. For Calvin, the devising of false forms of worship, detached from God's revelation, was the obvious manifestation of the sinful human desire to meet God on our own terms rather than accept his grace.[65] As we saw in the quotation above from his *Reply to Cardinal Sadoleto*, for Calvin it was God's Word that was to regulate the form and content of our worship.

The Importance of John Knox for the Regulative Principle

Perhaps the sharpest expression of the regulative principle is found in the tradition of Scottish Presbyterianism stemming from the life and work of John Knox. Intimately involved in the Reformation in both England and Scotland, Knox was an interesting figure, more of an activist than a theologian and certainly somebody of clear-cut views, which he did not hesitate to press onto others.[66] The fundamental idea that drove him was the sin of idolatry. The Reformation was to be the destruction of false worship and the establishment of the pure. Failure to do so could bring judgment against the nation. In particular, Knox believed that the Roman Catholic Mass lay at the heart of that church's idolatry. This he famously argued by way of two syllogisms:

> All worshipping, honoring, or service invented by the brain of man in the religion of God without his own express commandment is Idolatry. The mass is invented by the brain of man without any commandment of God. Therefore it is idolatry.[67]
>
> All honoring or service of God whereunto is added a wicked opinion is abomination. Unto the mass is added a wicked opinion. Therefore it is abomination.[68]

---

65. Ibid., II.viii.5.

66. For Knox's life, see Jane E. Dawson, *John Knox* (New Haven: Yale University Press, 2015).

67. *A Vindication of the Doctrine That the Sacrifice of the Mass Is Idolatry*, in *The Works of John Knox*, ed. David Laing, 6 vols. (Edinburgh: James Thin, 1895), 3:34. The spelling has been modernized in all quotes from Knox's *Works*.

68. Knox, *Works*, 3:52.

The focus in both syllogisms is the Mass, but the underlying principle and the applications are clearly of much wider import. In effect, the principle rules out of bounds in worship anything that is not specifically required by Scripture and thus sets the Zurich practice on a clear, logical foundation.

A key biblical text for Knox was 1 Samuel 15 (as it was for Calvin in his *Reply to Cardinal Sadoleto*), the account of Saul's battle with the Amalekites. Commanded to destroy everything—men, women, children, beasts of the field—Saul yet spares the king, Agag, and the best of the sheep and the oxen. When Samuel arrives and demands to know why Saul did not carry out the Lord's instructions to the letter, Saul replies that he was saving the best of the livestock to sacrifice to the Lord. This might seem a worthy motive and desire, but as Knox explains, that is not how Samuel saw the matter:

> But Saul, standing in opinion that he had not offended, because he did all of good intent, saith, "I have obeyed the Lord's voice, I have destroyed the sinners of Amalek, I have saved the king only, and the people have reserved certain beasts to be offered unto God." And so defended he his own work to be just and righteous. But thereto answereth Samuel, "Delighteth God in burnt-offerings, and not rather that his voice be obeyed? The sin of witchcraft is not to obey his voice, and to be stubborn is the sin of idolatry." As though Samuel would say, There is nothing that God more requires of man than obedience to his commandment: yea, he prefers obedience to the self-same sacrifice ordained by himself, and no sin is more odious in God's presence than to disobey his voice; for that God esteems so odious that he compares it to the two most abominable sins, incantation and idolatry: so that disobedience to his voice is actual idolatry.
>
> Disobedience to God's voice is, not only when man wickedly doth contrary to the precepts of God, but also when of good zeal, or good intent, as we commonly speak, man doth any thing to the honour or service of God which is not commanded by the express word of God, as in this plainly may be espied. For Saul transgressed not wickedly in murder, adultery, or like external sins, but had saved an aged and impotent king, which thing who would not call a good deed of mercy? And he had permitted the people, as is said, to save certain beasts to be offered unto the Lord; thinking that therewith God would be content and appeased, because he and the people did it of good intent. But both these Samuel called idolatry; first, because they were done without any commandment; and, secondly, because in doing thereof he thought himself not to have offended.
>
> And that is the chief idolatry where we defend our own inventions to be righteous in the sight of God, because we think them good, laudable, and pleasant. We may not think ourselves so free and wise that we may do unto God, and unto his honour what we think expedient; no, the contrary is commanded by God, saying, "Unto my word shall ye add nothing, nothing shall ye diminish therefrom, that ye might observe the precepts of your Lord God:" which words

are not to be understood of the decalogue and moral law only, but of statutes, rites, and ceremonies; for God requires equal obedience to all his laws.[69]

The point is simple: the motivation for an act of worship, no matter how sincere and well-intentioned, does not sanctify the action if the action itself is not explicitly commanded by God himself. The consequences for Saul could scarcely have been more dramatic: the loss of his kingdom to David. The lasting lesson is that, when it comes to worship, both form and content are of vital importance, with form as much a matter of fidelity to the teaching of Scripture as content is.[70]

Undergirding this notion, of course, are two basic ideas. First, there is the holiness of God and the sinfulness of human beings. God is holy and therefore can only be worshiped in a manner consistent with that holiness; human beings are sinful and constantly liable to invent their own wicked ways of worshiping God. Second, as a result, God's revelation in Scripture is to be the norming norm of worship as it is of doctrine.[71]

For Knox, this concern for the regulation of the outward form of worship by Scripture shaped his entire career, especially in his reaction against the background of Roman Catholic practices. One of the most notable moments came in 1552 when the Second Book of Common Prayer was about to be issued in England under Edward VI. Knox discovered that kneeling was still to be required as the posture for taking the Lord's Supper. Knox objected, because he considered kneeling to imply worship of the bread and the wine and thus transubstantiation. He therefore protested in a sermon before the king. After a certain amount of political wrangling, the prayer book (which had already been printed) was released with a note pasted inside, the so-called Black Rubric, making clear that kneeling did not imply worship of the eucharistic elements.[72]

The Book of Common Prayer was a masterpiece not only of liturgy but also of liturgical politics. Faced with having to press the Reformation forward

---

69. Ibid., 3:36–38.

70. In the last ten years in the United States, the adjective *Reformed* has come to be used by many churches that merely hold to what we might characterize as Calvinistic views of divine sovereignty, without consideration of worship practices. But in fact *Reformed* is historically a much broader term, also connoting particular forms of church life. Thus, matters such as the nature and content of worship are also important to what it means to be Reformed. Adherence in some shape or form to the regulative principle is nonnegotiable if one is to claim the name.

71. Cf. the comment of Calvin, "It is abomination in the sight of God to frame to him a worship which he does not require, or to embrace one devised by man without the sanction of his word." *Antidote to the Articles Agreed Upon by the Faculty of Sacred Theology of Paris*, in *Tracts*, 1:115.

72. See the narrative in Diarmaid MacCulloch, *Thomas Cranmer* (New Haven: Yale University Press, 1996), 525–33.

through an unsympathetic and broadly Catholic Parliament, Thomas Cranmer negotiated Protestant theology through more traditional aesthetics. As the prayer book became the means for subsequent Protestant monarchs to impose their authority on the religion of England, it also became a bone of contention with those whose imaginations had been gripped by the more radical and simple models of worship exemplified on the continent. As a result, the English and then the Scottish Reformations were singularly marked by concerns over the practical forms of worship, culminating in the Westminster Assembly of the 1640s, and thus profoundly shaping the Reformed understanding of worship down to the present day.

Nevertheless, the attitude of the Reformed to worship—that it was to be kept simple and regulated by God's Word—was not an Anglo-Scottish distinctive. Thus, for example, the Belgic Confession XXXII declares: "And therefore, we reject all human inventions, and all laws which man would introduce into the worship of God, thereby to bind and compel the conscience in any manner whatever."[73] Noteworthy here is the reference to the binding of the conscience. This is a point that can sometimes be easy to forget in our current context, where the political nature of Western democracy and our understanding of individual rights provide a very different social framework for the church. Debates about worship in the sixteenth and seventeenth centuries were always simultaneously debates about political and ecclesiastical power: the state's power to compel the church to do certain things and the church's power to compel individuals likewise. In an era when church and state were two sides of the same coin, the nature of the relationship of the powers of the two spheres was critical. A clear-cut emphasis on the regulative principle delimited the power of the state with regard to the church's worship and indeed also the power of the church to demand conformity to extraneous rites not built on a scriptural foundation. This is one reason why the Westminster Confession's discussion of worship (chapter 21) follows on immediately from chapter 20, which deals with Christian liberty and freedom of conscience.

It also helps to explain the strong antiliturgical bent of much English and Scottish Reformed practice. Liturgy became so associated with the Book of Common Prayer and with state imposition of the same that it became hard to separate the general principle from the particular local manifestation. Leading English Puritan John Owen was only one of the more influential voices opposed to the idea of liturgy as a whole.[74] Yet this position has ultimately

73. Dennison 2:443–44.
74. See Owen's 1662 tract, "A Discourse concerning Liturgies," in *The Works of John Owen, D.D.*, ed. William H. Goold, 17 vols. (Edinburgh: T&T Clark, 1862), 15:2–56.

not proved dominant. Even the Westminster Assembly, in its Directory of Public Worship, was forced to offer model prayers and patterns for worship, although it eschewed the construction of a formal liturgy.[75] The regulative principle did not in itself require the rejection of all formal liturgy.

In fact, the regulative principle as developed in the Westminster Standards argued that worship consisted of five basic elements. Given the Reformed concern to make sure that nothing is included in public worship that does not have explicit sanction in Scripture, it is not surprising that the components of Reformed worship are relatively simple. Indeed, the Westminster Confession identifies five elements of worship: prayer, reading and hearing of the Word, preaching and hearing of the Word, singing of psalms, and the administration of the sacraments.[76] Underlying these is what is called an ordinary-means-of-grace understanding of the church and its ministry: God's grace is to be found in the Word read and especially the Word preached, in the sacraments, and in prayer.[77]

These are elaborated in the Westminster Assembly's Directory for Public Worship (1645) in a manner that positively states the Reformed position but also contains an underlying anti–Roman Catholic and antiliturgical polemic. The congregation is to gather in an orderly fashion, "not bowing themselves towards one place or other," a clear swipe at the idea of genuflecting toward an altar or facing east.[78] The Word is to be read by those ordained as pastors or teachers, or on occasion those intending to go into the ministry to

75. Of course, all worship services have a liturgy, given that they follow an intentional order (even if a chaotic one) and involve singing of songs that have previously been written and/or chosen, etc.

76. Westminster Confession of Faith 21.3–5. Some Reformed also include giving of tithes and offerings as a part of worship. The Reformed typically distinguish between the elements of worship and the circumstances of the same. While the line between the two can sometimes be a little unclear, essentially the circumstances of worship are things that are theologically indifferent, such as the location and the precise time of Sunday worship. These can vary and yet not impact whether the act under consideration is worship or not. The elements of worship are essential such that, if they are absent, the action is not worship. Having said that, most Reformed Christians do not consider it necessary to have the sacraments administered at every worship service.

77. Westminster Shorter Catechism: Q. 88: "What are the outward and ordinary means whereby Christ communicateth to us the benefits of redemption? A. The outward and ordinary means whereby Christ communicateth to us the benefits of redemption are, his ordinances, especially the Word, sacraments, and prayer; all which are made effectual to the elect for salvation" (*Westminster Confession of Faith* [OPC ed., 2005]). Q. 89 then goes on to emphasize that it is especially the preached Word that is made effectual to salvation.

78. *A Directory for the Publique Worship of God* (London: Company of Stationers, 1645). A modern edition of this work is available: *The Westminster Directory of Public Worship*, ed. Mark Dever and Sinclair B. Ferguson (Fearn, UK: Christian Heritage, 2008). Page references are from the original edition.

test their gifts.[79] The length of the portion of Scripture is left to the wisdom of the minister, but it is recommended that one chapter of each Testament should be read.[80] After the Word is read and a psalm is sung, the minister is to lead the congregation in a prayer designed to encourage repentance and a hunger for grace. Interestingly enough, while the Directory is antiliturgical in its rejection of the set forms in the Book of Common Prayer, it still contains model prayers, presumably on the grounds that clergy need to have some idea of the kind of things that should be said.[81]

The Directory introduces the preaching of the Word with this wonderful statement about its significance and power: "Preaching of the Word, being the power of God unto Salvation and one of the greatest and most excellent Works belonging to the Ministry of the Gospel, should be so performed, that the Workman need not be ashamed, but may save himself, and those that hear him."[82] After the sermon, the minister is to lead in prayer again, and then the congregation should sing a psalm.[83] In fact, the Directory says, "It is the duty of Christians to praise God publiquely by singing of Psalmes together in the Congregation, and also privately in the Family. In singing of Psalms, the voice is to be tunable and gravely ordered: But the chief care must be, to sing with understanding, and with Grace in the heart, making melody unto the Lord."[84] So the psalms are to be a vital part of Reformed public worship and private family worship.

Psalm singing has always been an important part of Reformed worship. In part, this derives from strict application of the regulative principle, whereby it is considered important that even the forms of words used in singing are to be regulated by Scripture. In many modern Reformed churches, however, exclusive use of the psalms has been set aside on the grounds that it is the content, not the form, of what is sung that is the real subject of scriptural regulation. Nevertheless, the beauty of the psalms, the fact that they are part of the Word of God, and the range of emotions to which they give voice continue to make them a staple of Reformed worship.

The Rejection of Images

Much of what has been said so far would also reflect Lutheran views of worship. The basic elements of worship, the importance of the Word preached,

79. Ibid., 6–7.
80. Ibid., 7.
81. Ibid., 8–13.
82. Ibid., 13.
83. Ibid., 18–19.
84. Ibid., 40.

and the roles of prayer, sacraments, and psalms are shared by both magisterial Protestant traditions. Yet there are also significant differences. The regulative principle as understood by the Reformed is one reason why Reformed worship is distinct from that of the Lutherans in a way that is usually obvious as soon as one enters their respective places of worship. Lutheran churches often have an elaborate aesthetic, with stained-glass windows and crucifixes as part of church architecture and decoration. A strict application of the Reformed regulative principle, however, means that images of the divine are illegitimate because of the strictures of the second commandment; therefore, there will be no images of Christ and no crucifixes in church. Take the statement in the Heidelberg Catechism regarding the second commandment. In questions 94 and 95, the catechism makes the unexceptionable claim that idolatry is forbidden. Then, in questions 96 to 98, it applies the second commandment to mean that no images may be used in worship, and no images of God may be made at all. Question 98 is especially interesting and forthright: "Q. 98. But may not pictures be tolerated in churches as books for the people? A. No, for we should not be wiser than God, who will not have His people taught by dumb idols (Jer. 10:8; Hab. 2:18–19), but by the lively preaching of His Word (2 Pet. 1:19; 2 Tim. 3:16–17)."[85] The cultural background to this question is obvious. In an era of high illiteracy, the question of how people who cannot read might come to know the Bible is a pressing one. Pictures might seem one obvious answer, for they tell stories in a way that is accessible to those who cannot read. Yet the catechism (in line with general Reformed teaching) rejects this as a matter of principle.

Clearly, a wealth of theology is assumed in this statement: God is present by his Word and not by images. That is significant. In medieval Catholicism, the Mass was the place where heaven touched earth; for the Reformers, God made his presence felt primarily through the preacher proclaiming his Word. Moreover, as we explain in chapter 2, the third use of the law means that the Decalogue applies today under the new covenant on this point as it did for the Jews under the Mosaic dispensation. The standard Reformed view is that the incarnation does not change the meaning and scope of the prohibition on images. Each of these points is somewhat controversial in the wider Christian world, and even among the Reformed the question of the impact of the incarnation on images is a matter of constant discussion, but it is clear that these basic principles are assumed by the Heidelberg Catechism and are thus representative of the overwhelming consensus of the Reformed church.

85. Dennison 2:792.

In the context of this book, such an understanding of images also represents a major difference from the Lutherans. On the whole, the Reformed preoccupation with idolatry as a central category to describe contemporary problems was not shared by Lutherans, and this difference was reflected directly in the respective aesthetics of the Reformation. For the Reformed, the famous painting of Luther preaching in his pulpit and pointing with his finger to a crucifix would have been an abomination, a clear breach of the commandment against image making. For the Lutherans, however, it was a perfect representation both of the task of preaching—to point people to the crucified Christ—and of the theology of the cross. The latter emphasized the weakness of God revealed in Christ, of God's revelation under contraries. Representational art played a significant role in this.[86]

Yet if images were forbidden, this did not mean that worship could not be beautiful in its simplicity. Liturgies were a common feature of Reformation-era Reformed life, with those of Calvin and Knox being obvious examples. Cranmer's Book of Common Prayer is perhaps the most famous. Although it retained certain elements of Roman Catholic ceremonial, such as kneeling at communion (as noted above), its theology was firmly Protestant and its eucharistic understanding Reformed, not Lutheran. Any reader of the work will be struck by the lyrical elegance of the prose, consistently peppered with biblical allusions and connected at many points to previous liturgical works so as to make it catholic in the best sense.[87]

Owen and the Heavenly Sanctuary

The regulative principle was not merely what we might regard as a biblicist idea, however, one simply applying the brute force of the Bible to church practice in order to abolish all outward beauty in worship. In the hands of John Owen, for example, it was coordinated with a rich understanding of Christology and was given a clear theological basis in the person and work of Christ. To state the obvious, Reformed theologians like Owen, in common with their Lutheran and Roman Catholic counterparts, regarded Christ as the fulfillment of the Old Testament sacrifices and temple worship. The most obvious result of this was that the temple no longer existed. Owen and

---

86. One famous example would be Lucas Cranach the Elder's painting of Luther's preaching in his triptych in the Church of St. Mary in Wittenberg. Luther stands in the pulpit, pointing with his finger to Jesus as he hangs on the cross. The point is clear: preaching is directing people to the crucified God. Lutherans had no hesitation in using representative art in such a theological fashion. No equivalent picture of Calvin exists!

87. An excellent introduction to the origins and subsequent history of the Book of Common Prayer is Alan Jacobs, *The Book of Common Prayer* (Princeton: Princeton University Press, 2013).

many other Reformed theologians saw this fulfillment of the temple in Christ as significant for the nature of Christian worship in abolishing not only the sacrifices but all the ceremonial elements attached to them.

In fact the earthly sanctuary merely prefigured the heavenly one to come, and so sanctuary worship is now transferred to heaven. It was this that Owen saw as significant for worship here on earth. At the most basic level, the heavenly temple is the primary location of Christian worship. By faith, Christians here on earth partake of this heavenly worship and indeed have some insight into its beauty. In a memorable passage, worth quoting at length, Owen declares:

> Believers at present have, by faith, an admission into communion with this church above, in all its divine worship. For we "are come unto mount Zion, and unto the city of the living God, the heavenly Jerusalem, and to an innumerable company of angels, to the general assembly and church of the first-born, which are written in heaven, and to God the Judge of all, and to the spirits of just men made perfect, and to Jesus the mediator of the new covenant, and to the blood of sprinkling, that speaketh better things than that of Abel," Heb. 12:22–24. . . . O that my soul might abide and abound in this exercise of faith!—that I might yet enjoy a clearer prospect of this glory, and inspection into the beauty and order of this blessed assembly! How inconceivable is the representation that God here makes of the glory of his wisdom, love, grace, goodness, and mercy, in Christ! How excellent is the manifestation of the glory and honour of Christ in his person and offices!—the glory given him by the Father! How little a portion do we know, or can have experience in, of the refreshing, satiating communications of divine love and goodness, unto all the members of this assembly; or of that unchangeable delight in beholding the glory of Christ, and of God in him,—of that ardency of affections wherewith they cleave unto him, and continual exultation of spirit, whereby they triumph in the praises of God, that are in all the members of it! To enter into this assembly by faith,—to join with it in the assignation of praises unto "him that sitteth on the throne, and to the Lamb for evermore,"—to labour after a frame of heart in holy affections and spiritual delight in some correspondency with that which is in the saints above,—is the duty, and ought to be the design, of the church of believers here below. So much as we are furthered and assisted herein by our present ordinances, so much benefit and advantage have we by them, and no more.[88]

The first thing to note about this passage is its connection to the Protestant notion of salvation. It is grounded in faith, not sight. Worship is, we might say, a little taste of heaven on earth, not in the sense of pulling it down to this

88. *Works*, 1:254–55.

earthly sphere but in terms of being in heaven through faith. Thus, there is an obvious theological connection with the Reformed view of the Lord's Supper: in the Supper, the mind is raised by the Spirit to feed on Christ in heaven. The Holy Spirit negates the significance of geographical placement. Both the doctrine of justification by faith and the notion of the believer's union with Christ are clearly determinative of what Owen understands worship to be theologically. We are intimately connected to Christ in the here and now by Spirit-wrought faith.

What is perhaps most noteworthy, however, is Owen's reference to the beauty of heavenly worship. This is a term he uses again and again throughout his writings with reference to the heavenly sanctuary and that he connects, as here, to the worship of the earthly assemblies of the church. Thus, it is clear that the notion of beauty is important for Christian worship, but it is beauty located in the ongoing work of Christ in the heavenly sanctuary. The result of this is that earthly worship is to be aesthetically simple, for elaborate aesthetics are both a distraction from contemplating the beauty that is in heaven and a retrograde step with the appearance at least of moving back to Old Testament principles of approach to God. To emphasize earthly ceremonial is a zero-sum game, requiring a de-emphasis on the heavenly reality of the sanctuary and of Christ's person and ongoing work as located there.

It might be argued that the Reformed position as articulated by John Owen has a certain Platonic or even ascetic quality in its downplaying of the importance of aesthetics here on earth on the grounds that they are positively harmful to worship. That criticism has some legitimacy. Certainly, the Reformed faith produced no sacred music to rival the Renaissance polyphony of Palestrina or Tallis, nor the Lutheran Masses of Bach. As to representational artwork in sacred context, that was more or less forbidden. And that pinches. Believers are embodied beings who are destined for a new heaven and a new earth, and it may well be that Owen and those who follow him posit too sharp a break between the church on earth and the church in heaven. Nevertheless, there is a sense in which beauty is in the eye of the beholder. The Reformed worship service with its simple aesthetics focused on the basic elements of prayer, preaching, singing, and sacraments has an austere beauty of its own, as anyone who has ever attended, for example, a traditional service of worship in a Presbyterian congregation on Scotland's Outer Hebrides will affirm. The unadorned human voice and the air of tranquil and reverent piety possess their own peculiar and often powerful beauty. Simplicity has its own aesthetic and can indeed have its own unadorned beauty. Owen would say that where Christian worship is concerned, this is because the hearts of those present have been raised by faith to heavenly portals, and thus heaven in a sense touches earth.

Conclusion

Much more could be said about Reformed worship. Given the role of infant baptism and the understanding of covenant children, the issues of catechizing and of family worship are also important. A positive commitment to Sabbatarianism or worship on the Lord's Day and the rejection of the traditional liturgical calendar are also important hallmarks at least of the Presbyterian tradition.[89] But the central point of the Reformed understanding of worship has been stated above: worship is to be regulated both in content and, as much as possible, in form by the Word of God. This leads to a simple aesthetic and to what is commonly called an ordinary-means-of-grace ministry, focused on Word and sacrament. Simple and plain it may well be; but when the Word is accompanied by God's Spirit, it needs no further outward adornment to be powerful unto salvation.

89. See *Directory*, 40.

Conclusion

At the end of this volume, we repeat our hope that readers will have gained a better understanding of their own traditions—whether Reformed, Lutheran, or other—as they examined our essays. We hope that they have gained a more precise grasp of what another or two other confessions of the Christian faith have expressed as they have presented the biblical message in their own times and places. The mighty Savior of whom Carl spoke in the introduction to this volume has expressed his will that his people be one and that they be one in their confession of him and his gift of new life. We intend this volume to be a stimulus for personal growth in the faith and for the exchange of insights into Holy Scripture among those who come from differing confessions of the Christian faith.

This volume challenges its readers to revisit settled solutions to questions raised by our reading of the biblical text or by our immersion in our traditions of reading Scripture and applying it to our lives and the lives of others. We hope that we have helped to set aside misimpressions based on any number of factors. Some within each tradition have represented their own heritage within cultural settings that made it difficult to represent them fairly. From selective exposure to faith, some have gained images of the other confession that do not represent the whole of what that confession has tried to say in its biblical witness. These and other stumbling blocks have made it difficult to talk with others about our own expression of our faith in Christ and theirs. We hope that our essays will kindle open and frank discussions among like-minded Christians within their own churches and with other brothers and sisters in Christ from other families in the faith.

Groups of pastors, students, and laity may find that the volume offers the opportunity to come together with longtime friends or with strangers in our vicinities to discover common ground and to explore serious differences. Every such group will find its own approaches to our essays, but we offer the following questions as discussion starters.

1. What are the specific points of similarity and of difference in regard to each topic between the Reformed and Lutheran traditions?
2. How did confessors of the faith in each tradition find their positions in Scripture and use their interpretations of the biblical text to confess and explain biblical teaching for their own situations?
3. How did historical context influence the formulation of public doctrine on specific points of teaching and proclamation? How is the twenty-first-century context similar to and different from the earlier historical contexts?
4. How did theological and philosophical presuppositions shape the formulation of public teaching in each tradition? How do we evaluate those presuppositions today?
5. How do issues of the application of the biblical message to fellow believers and their spiritual well-being and of spiritual care for them shape our understanding and presentation of God's Word today?
6. What differences will deeper acquaintance with my own and other confessions of Christ's message for his people make in my evangelistic outreach and witness of my faith? In my teaching of the faith in congregation and family circle? In my preaching and pastoral care?

With these and other questions that readers frame for themselves, we pray that healthy and fruitful exchange of convictions, perspectives, and insights may enliven the faithful following of our Lord Jesus Christ in our day.

Scripture Index

Name Index

Subject Index

Abraham 6–7, 9, 47, 60–61, 155, 156, 163, 167, 171, 173
allegory 15, 25
Anabaptists 147, 150, 157, 161–63, 170, 171
analogy of faith 4, 8, 25–28
anhypostatic/enhypostatic 47–48
Anselm and atonement theory 64, 74–75, 82, 120
anthropology, theological
  Adam and Christ 82
  and God's law 39–50
  and the Holy Spirit 56, 118–19, 127–29, 133–45, 151–52. *See also* reason; sin; will, bound and free
  and language 16
  medieval 2–4
antinomianism 132, 140–41, 145
Apocrypha 10
Apollinaris/Apollinarianism 60, 75
Apology of the Augsburg Confession 42, 97, 130, 135
Arminianism 82–83, 104
assurance of salvation
  based on election 98–100, 102, 104, 107–8, 114–15
  based on means of grace 151, 160–61, 180
  based on promise of Christ 13, 95, 118, 136, 167–68, 170–71, 185
  and prayer 219
atonement 33–34, 64–65, 74–75, 82–85, 95, 119–23, 134, 152–53
  limited/effectual 83–84, 104
  universal 83, 108

Augsburg Confession xi, 97, 103n52, 129, 130, 134, 139, 198, 208, 213, 221
Augsburg Confession *variata* 134n62

baptism 35, 38, 45, 95, 120–21, 125, 126, 130, 147–74, 176, 177, 188, 210, 213, 214, 220, 234
Belgic Confession xii, 47, 76, 103, 200, 204, 227
Bible. *See* Scripture

callings/vocations 39, 128–29, 213
canon of Scripture 10–11, 21, 24
catechesis/catechetical tradition 26, 28, 33, 43, 80, 158, 210–11, 217, 220, 234
celestial flesh of Christ 67
Chalcedon, Council of (451) 59–60, 66, 71, 75–76, 181
Christ, person of 59–86, 204–5. *See also* natures of Christ; personal union of Christ's natures
  location of human body 28–28, 179–81, 203
  Osiander's view of 130–31
Christ, work of. *See* atonement; justification
church
  and analogy of faith 26–28
  Christ's rule of 84–85, 206
  doctrine of 8, 117, 157, 180
  history of 133
  membership in 163–67, 171–74
  proclamation of God's Word in 8, 17–24, 30, 208, 212–13, 221–22, 228, 232–33
  role of love in 53–54
circumcision 156, 163–64, 170–73

Made in the USA
Middletown, DE
15 January 2024

47842489R00163